Praise for *Be the Ultimate Assistant*

"The essential reference guide to the art of managing the details of today's high profile and powerful lifestyles. It doesn't matter if you work for a movie star, middle manager or corporate chairman, this book helps you to achieve an über-competence that can be used from the boardroom to your living room."

Karen E. Klose, *Personal Assistant to Richard Gere*

"An invaluable text on partnership and communication helping me to prioritize my own personal and professional needs and those of my assistant."

Gabrielle Berberich, *Film Director/Producer*

"The advice doesn't only apply to celebrity assistants, but anyone working with a person whose time is in demand and who has a great deal of pressure. This book will end up dog-eared and covered in post-it notes in a very short space of time."

C.A. Taylor, *Celebrity Assistant, London, U.K.*

"A great accomplishment! Bonnie fully describes the often misunderstood role and day-to-day experience of a celebrity assistant which most definitely translates to the world of all administrative professionals."

Hope Rippere, *former CEO Communications Manager, Hewlett-Packard Company*

"Five stars for this double delightful team of Bonnie Low-Kramen and Olympia Dukakis who prove a celebrity tell-all can be fun but never mean. You don't have to be a star or an assistant to get an enormous kick out of this revealing and charming book!"

Laura Cunningham, *Writer, New York*

"The book is on my desk now and I too am a celebrity assistant. It's a fast read but also a reference book you keep near you. The challenge of pleasing your employer all day, every day is not limited to this profession. As such, I would recommend this book for anyone, in any profession, as well for those who ponder supporting those whose life is in the fast lane."

Claudia Allon, *Personal Assistant to Barry Slotnick*

"The ultimate text for our profession. Written with extraordinary intelligence, priceless advice and plenty of humor; I only wish I had a copy when I first started in the business! I especially applaud the concept of assistants sharing information within our group, we can only benefit from helping one another. Bonnie deserves a standing ovation and a heartfelt 'thank you' from assistants everywhere."

Harriette Holmes, *Executive/Artistic Asst. to Michael Wilson,*
Hartford Stage, Connecticut

"I could not put it down. Her advice was very helpful to me in my work with the Chief Medical Officer of a health system. The book was the perfect way to adjust my attitude and renew my passion for my work."

Kalynn Pempek, *Executive Assistant, Wisconsin*

"This book is one-of-a-kind. There is simply nothing else like it out there about our work. What a great help it is for all of us, especially the new generation of PAs."

Susan McTigue, *Assistant to Ellen Burstyn*

"The paradox is that the book is both an instruction manual and a page turner. As a former New York assistant, I discovered that the author has undeniable expertise demonstrated with a refreshing collaborative approach."

Vickie S. Evans, *C.E.O., The Red Cape Company, Texas*

"A treasure! As a result of taking Bonnie's class, I was placed with a celebrity and have used her book as my key reference text in doing my job. Whoever you assist, do yourself a favor and buy this book."

Brian Pardus, *Former Assistant to David Barton, New York*

"I want to make a career change and am thinking about being a personal assistant. This book is inspiring, energizing and supportive. I recommend it to anyone who wants to do a great job for someone else while feeling empowered and good about themselves."

Dan Sinisi, *Aspiring Assistant, Pennsylvania*

"Superb job! Most self-help, how-to books are usually pretty boring. Not so of this book!"

Anne(Nancy) Hansell, *CPS, Senior Administrative Specialist, Wyeth Pharmaceuticals, Pennsylvania*

Be the Ultimate Assistant

Bonnie Low-Kramen

Be the Ultimate Assistant

A celebrity assistant's secrets
to working with <u>any</u>
high-powered employer

BONNIE LOW-KRAMEN

Assistant to Olympia Dukakis

2012 Edition
Edited by Laura Schreiner

Excerpt with permission from *Psychology Today* Magazine, Copyright © 1995
To order this book: www.BonnieLowKramen.com

Cover Design by RJ Communications

U.S. Copyright Registration #TX 6-084-373

Be the Ultimate Assistant
A celebrity assistant's secrets to working with <u>any</u> high-powered employer
ISBN# 978-0-9763268-1-6

NK Publications
P.O. Box 1735
Radio City Station
New York, NY 10101
www.nkpublications.com

DEDICATION

To Robert, my soulmate.

To Adam, my motivation, my inspiration, my compass.

To Ruth and Sol "Bill" Low, my parents, who believed
I could do anything I put my mind to.

To all my friends and colleagues at
New York Celebrity Assistants, who so generously
shared their experiences with me.

To professional assistants worldwide.

And to Olympia and Louis –
I am forever grateful for the boundary-less opportunity
to work, dream, play, and learn fully.

"Unless you try to do something beyond what you have already mastered, you will never grow."
Ronald E. Osborn, Author

Webster's Dictionary Definition
ASSISTANT

Noun: A person who helps, aids, abets, does for, enables, accompanies, attends, escorts, cooperates, comforts, and supports another person

CONTENTS

FOREWORD
by Olympia Dukakis

S ince 1986, Bonnie Low-Kramen and I have worked together
– each of us learning from the other, each of us challenging
the other, defining and re-defining ourselves and our relationship,
which over the years has changed and evolved – a vital dynamic in
all successful employer/assistant relationships.

Bonnie was like a daughter to my mother, an aunt to my
children, a sister to me.

I suspect that professional and deeply personal lines must cross
if you are together for more than two decades as Bonnie and I
have been, sharing highs and lows, many new experiences, not to

mention an office and three telephone lines.

What I am most aware of is that because of who Bonnie is and the work she performs so well, I found a freedom for myself that is crucial. I am free to name what is important to me and how I want to do things because of Bonnie's ability to be conciliatory in discussions and negotiations. I am free from those activities that blur my focus and drain my energy. I am free to make my work my priority.

Bonnie makes herself responsible for everything – she can be depended upon, trusted to follow through always! I do not stand watch. Bonnie holds the fort. And all this in addition to the talents and skills necessary to run an office, to keep the finances clear and solid, and my schedule intact.

How many people after a session with Bonnie have said to me, "*I want a Bonnie in my life. How do I get one?*" We earned this relationship through trial and error, and of course, most importantly, through respect, honesty and trust. I have always been struck by the seriousness with which she takes her work, her profession, her career choice.

I am so proud that Bonnie is a founding member and former president of New York Celebrity Assistants, that she lectures, that she has written this book. She has never seen a window she would not open or a corner she would not turn.

She is, in fact, the "ultimate assistant." If that is what you aspire to, read this book carefully.

Olympia Dukakis

Words I try to live by. B L-K

"Make each day your masterpiece."
John Wooden, highly regarded
and inspirational former
UCLA Basketball Coach, author

INTRODUCTION

I love being an assistant. In fact, I strive to be an "ultimate" assistant, someone who seeks excellence and improvement – not just on some days, but every day. I don't always succeed, but this is what I try to do. If you are reading this book, you may also be so inclined. Ultimate assistants are like that, and I am privileged to know quite a few.

The talented, smart, and savvy women and men who do this work go by many titles: *Celebrity Assistants, Personal Assistants, Professional Assistants, Executive Aides, Executive Assistants, Executaries, Administrative Assistants, Administrative Aides,* and *Secretaries.* No matter what your title is, I have the deepest respect, regard, and admiration for the important work you do.

Our jobs often defy "descriptions" because the scope is so vast. The ironic result of this is that our value and influence is frequently underestimated precisely because there is confusion about what we do *exactly.* The nature of our work is to be behind the scenes, compounded by the fact that, in general, assistants downplay their power and accomplishments by being modest about them. It makes sense then, that there is a lack of current and accurate information reflecting who we really are and what we do. So, with Olympia's support, I finally decided to try to be a part of the solution by writing a book.

I wrote this book for three reasons. The first is that our work is frequently misunderstood and has been subject to warped misconceptions by the media. The second is that there were too few resources for assistants, and certainly not only those who work for celebrities. Third, there is a tremendous curiosity about the work. I decided that I was in a unique position to set the record straight and tell it the way it really is to those who actually want to know the truth of it.

You are reading the 2012 edition of this book, the first of which was published in 2004. Since then, I've given more than fifty presentations to administrative professionals around the country, in England and in Canada. What an enlightening experience to have met so many of my colleagues, the majority of whom are women. We talked. I listened and learned. These meetings inspired this latest edition and a new chapter, "Gender in the Workplace," (Chapter 14.)

At these presentations, I am always moved and impressed by assistants who have been working for twenty-plus years. They are in the room seeking information, still curious to find ways to do their work better, to be the ultimate. Life-long learning is an embraced concept. These conferences and meetings serve to validate, educate and celebrate the members of our profession. They are empowering and inspiring, and I encourage you to make it your business to join professional associations to access these meetings.

The dizzying proliferation of technology – wireless tablet computers, smartphones, and social networking – is continuing to shape the ever-evolving role of the assistant, strongly impacting the ways we communicate professionally and personally. Our employers depend on us to stay current on the security and confidentiality concerns which have emerged as a result of these technologies. The job description of an assistant is morphing yet again.

I have learned a great deal in my twenty-five years as the personal assistant to Olympia Dukakis – lessons I sincerely hope will translate to your work as a professional assistant and that you can pass on to your colleagues. I believe the free-flowing sharing of information is the most powerful and positive way to support and strengthen our profession. I am clearer than ever that while differences in our work exist, the areas of commonality far outnumber them. We care about the same things and do whatever it takes to get our jobs done.

Whether you are an assistant, want to be an assistant, or are just curious about the profession – I hope you enjoy the book, pick up a tip or two, and continue to love whatever it is that you aspire to do.

Bonnie Low-Kramen

PREFACE

*H*aphazard, serendipitous, and anonymous.

The path to getting to work as the assistant to a celebrity feels precisely this way, even in this, the age of the all-powerful Web. It is a responsible, demanding job requiring intelligence, skills and flexibility; yet, until recently, there have been precious few resources for us. Professionals in any other career you can name have all kinds of resources: professional associations, books, classes, even annual conventions. I am happy to report that these are now available and happening for professional assistants.

I became a co-founder of New York Celebrity Assistants (NYCA) in 1996, and now the time has come for me to write a book about my profession. I intend for this book to be one full of real information, a book which can be a valuable resource for anyone interested in being a professional assistant – no matter which type of high-powered person employs you.

Every celebrity assistant's path to his or her job is unique. Here's mine. My career as a celebrity assistant to married actors Olympia Dukakis and Louis Zorich was not planned. In fact, nothing about my career was planned. The only thing I knew for sure after graduating from Rutgers University in 1979 with a degree in "English with a Theatre Arts Option" was that I was determined to make a living in show business.

I began in the expected place – as an aspiring, non-union actress.

My mother, of course, fretted over my choices. *"Don't you think you should study something a little more sensible to fall back on?"* No way. I was hooked. Starred as Mame in my high school senior play. There was no turning back.

Because my ex-husband was a restaurant manager in a suburb of Chicago, that's where I began – freezing my butt off chasing non-Equity auditions in downtown Chicago. It was a dismal experience. I was so nervous before auditions that I physically shook and spent hours in the bathroom doing all the things that one does in a bathroom – including checking my hair and make-up, and examining my body twenty-two times. So much waiting – then the rejections and disappointments. I lasted three months.

One fateful day I got so frustrated because it took me more than an hour to go around one city block in the snow as I searched for a parking space in order to make it to my open-call audition. As I sat at a red light one half hour after my appointment time, I realized that I couldn't do this anymore – try to be an actress, that is. I just didn't want it enough. I turned around and headed back to the suburbs.

I drove straight to where my career in show business truly began. St. Charles, Illinois, at the Pheasant Run Dinner Theatre. As I drove, I determined I would go there and apply for any job they had open – I didn't care what. It turned out they needed a waitress and the job was mine. I was a terrible waitress. I hated it and it showed. I got next to no tips and was near despair. I lasted two nights. The good news was that they also had an opening in the box office. I grabbed it. This was more like it.

I made $4.25/hr. to start and was thrilled to get it. Working in that box office turned out to be the perfect first job. Like so many theatres, the box office was the hub of activity. Everyone passed through there – actors, directors, designers, audience members, etc. I came to know them all and learned how everyone fit together. I worked for a wonderfully strong and brainy woman named Gilda Moss (picture Anne Bancroft, even the voice), and she showed me that it was okay for a woman to take charge and be in control. In fact, she expected it, and at the age of twenty-one, I needed to hear it. After a few months, I was promoted to box office manager and received a raise to $4.50/hour. What I didn't earn in dollars, I gained in experience. I learned how to deal with all kinds of people. I also learned organization, time management, how to take responsibility, and to own my mistakes.

Thankfully, my experience in auditioning and trying to be an actress did not go to waste. It helped me gain a valuable tool: empathy. From the beginning, I could relate to what the actors were going through: the nerves, the insecurity, the pressure to perform, the rejection – all of it. This feeling about actors has served me all of these years as one of the most vital I possess in my work.

One indelible memory was of the night I arrived back from my Hawaiian honeymoon in May, 1979. The phone was ringing as we walked back into our apartment around 6PM. It was Gilda. She said that the actress who played the drunk hooker (who had no lines) was sick and could I come in and play her part? The show was Neil Simon's *California Suite* and curtain time was 8PM. I dropped my suitcases, kissed my new husband goodbye, and happily drove to the theatre. I was doing what I set out to do – helping to make a show – by doing whatever it took.

My way, my path, my burning desire, was to work in the theatre. I needed to be a part of the process of making a "show." I was not motivated by money or fame – crazy, but true. I was just grateful my husband had a "real" job as a restaurant manager since, admittedly, I was making very little money. My journey led me from Pheasant Run to the Alliance Theatre in Atlanta (Group Sales), to WXLA-TV in Atlanta (Assistant to Producer and Writer), to Texas A&M University in College Station (Program Director), to the Alley Theatre in Houston (Ticket Services Manager), and to the Shubert Organization in New York (Group Sales). I owe a debt of thanks to some incredible teachers at these jobs who taught me the good, the bad, and the ugly parts of the "business" – office politics, the art of delegation, and the game of "good cop/bad cop," to name just a few.

Over the years, I held a number of part-time jobs to help pay the bills. I realize now that the experience of each was invaluable to being an assistant. Some of these jobs included shoe salesperson, fashion show model, proofreader, cosmetics salesperson, office temp, restaurant hostess, and bus driver for Hertz at O'Hare Airport.

Throughout my entire career, I flew by the seat of my pants – I winged it and began to trust my instincts. I didn't have any books to read about running theatres or classes or seminars to take, or even newspaper or magazine articles to read on the subject. This was pre-Internet, so no help there either.

In 1985, I was bored stiff working for the Shubert Organization selling *A Chorus Line* and *Cats* and all their other shows to school groups all over the country. I knew it was a dead-end job, but I didn't know my next move. One day I received a call from a friend I had worked with at the Alley Theatre saying he was coming to New York, so we got together for a drink. When we met at a bar on 42nd St., he brought along another friend, Scott Michaels, who was the Marketing Director for the Whole Theatre in Montclair, New Jersey. Scott talked about needing a Publicity Director and asked if I might consider the job, even though I had never done publicity. This was one of my first of many lessons in the power of "who you know" and exactly how much you can accomplish over a cocktail. A highly respected New York theatre actress, Olympia Dukakis, was the Producing Artistic Director of the theatre. In 1985, Olympia Dukakis was not a household name.

On a snowy January night after work, I took the bus from New York City to Montclair to meet with Olympia Dukakis. Her policy was that no one was hired at the Whole Theatre without meeting her first. I dressed up for the interview and found the modest offices on the second floor of an office building. The first time I set eyes on Olympia, she was sitting on top of the copy machine wearing a t-shirt and baggy mustard-yellow jeans with holes in the knees and no make-up. She gave me a hearty handshake and we talked for about thirty minutes. I loved how direct she was, how strong, how obviously smart, and how beautiful. "Yes," I thought, "I can work with this lady." She said I was hired. I began on Tuesday, January 28, 1986 – the day the Challenger spacecraft exploded. Needless to say, I'll never forget that day. I soon realized I was mighty glad I had already worked for seven years under strong personalities like Gilda and others before getting to "Mount Olympia." I had never met anyone like her and have not since. One of my favorite Olympia stories from the Whole Theatre days was the time in a staff meeting when she didn't think people were really getting her point. I sensed frustration boiling in her. She climbed up on the conference table and started yelling and jumping and repeating what she had just said! I loved it. Some other staffers were shocked and intimidated and yes, even a little afraid of Olympia. Not me. I grew up in a Jewish household full of loud voices and strong feelings. I gained strength and direction from Olympia's passion and understood what mattered to her. We worked well together, and that's how we began – two people committed to finding an audience for the plays she was selecting.

Olympia Dukakis has been one of the most powerful teachers of all in my career, and I dare say, one of the most profound influences in my life. She says, "*We earned each other.*" Yes, we did. I am now one of the people who knows her best, and I am still awestruck by her willingness and passion to go to the wall for the people and things she believes in. Olympia has the courage to say the things that need to be said. I admire her tremendously for this and as a result, value her opinions and honesty. To really understand the kind of person Olympia Dukakis is, I must share the "motorcycle" story which happened several years before I arrived on the scene.

In the early 1980's, Olympia was hired for a play at a suburban New Jersey dinner-theatre located about forty-five minutes from her home. One day she was running late as Louis tried to drive as fast as he could in order for Olympia to arrive for "half-hour" – actors need to check in with the stage manager thirty minutes before curtain time. She had no understudy. When they encountered bumper-to-bumper traffic, Olympia spotted a young man on a motorcycle weaving through traffic. She leapt out of the car and frantically explained to him that she was an actress who was very late for her show, and that "*you will please drive me there – now.*" Done. Olympia knows what it is to "*do whatever it takes*" and after all, the show must go on. It did – twenty minutes late.

When Olympia announced in January, 1987, that she would be leaving town for a month to shoot a movie in Canada, I did my job as PR Director and gathered the facts. "*Who else is in the movie?*" Olympia answered, "*Cher, Vinnie Gardenia, Danny Aiello, and some new guy, Nicolas 'Gage'.*" "Hmm," I said, "*Do you mean Nicolas 'Cage'?? Who is directing?*" Olympia's answer, "*Norman Jewison.*" "*What studio?*" Her answer, "*MGM.*" "*This is huge!*" I thought, and I began to yell. The other staffers gathered around to find out what all the excitement was about. All Olympia seemed to be focused on was that she and I had a lot of work to do before she left town. As you may know, Olympia won the 1988 Academy Award as Best Supporting Actress for that role of Rose Castorini. I am convinced to this day that I knew the significance of *Moonstruck* way before Olympia did. I also hope she gets nominated again because we would do it so much better this time.

While she was away shooting *Moonstruck*, Olympia needed someone she trusted to go to her house, check the answering machine, and deal with the messages. She asked me to do it, and I said yes. She and I spoke by phone every day to keep up with our

PREFACE

theatre work. I remember a two-hour phone meeting one Sunday morning to review the language and "look" for the next season's theatre brochure. It was during this first of many road-trips that I realized we could do truly substantive work long-distance over a phone and by fax. It's a skill we continue today, twenty-five years later.

Although we didn't know it at the time, that was the beginning of my work as a "celebrity assistant," which commenced with the single task of checking an answering machine. We figured out the job description one day at a time, one need at a time. After Olympia won the Oscar, the phone never stopped ringing, and all of our lives changed. In 1990, the Whole Theatre closed due to the severe budget cuts to the arts in New Jersey. On the night the Board voted to close the theatre, I presented Olympia with a typewritten plan outlining how I pictured us working together which included a salary proposal. She called me the next day and said, "*We'll begin on Monday.*" We opened an office out of her home, like so many other celebrities. Neither of us dared to guess or even think about how long our new relationship would last. I needed a job and Olympia needed help. And so we began.

What an enriching and unexpected surprise this relationship has been for both of us. Here's an example of what I mean. Several years into our work together, Olympia and I traveled to Nashville for a speaking engagement and everything had gone smoothly. At the post-speech reception, Olympia was "working" the room by taking photographs and giving autographs. Meanwhile, a man who had his back to me caught my eye.

He looked so familiar. I approached him and saw instantly that he looked just like my father who had died when I was fifteen years old. He had the same body, the same eyeglasses, the same bass voice, and the same name – Bill. I lost it when I heard his name. Bill was one of the organizers of the event and he could not have been sweeter to me when I managed to tell him why I couldn't stop crying. After we returned to the hotel, I told Olympia what had happened because she could tell that I was still shaken by the experience. We spent the rest of the night talking about our fathers and what they meant to us in our lives. It turns out our fathers had a lot in common and so did we.

Back to the state of the profession... The irony is that since the mid 1990's, there has been a marked increase of media interest in the profession of celebrity assisting. Before then, no one seemed to know or care that celebrities employed assistants to keep their lives going or that there was even a name for it. Suddenly, the media began asking questions and people began paying attention. The problem with many of these media articles (some of which I have participated in) is that the profession is often painted in extremes and focus on the dysfunctional as opposed to the healthy. Either we are ditzy groupies dying to bring our employer a cup of tea in an exotic film location, or we are abused slaves getting smacked on the head with a telephone as we toil! Not much middle ground is mentioned, not much of the way it works most of the time. I've complained about the misconceptions long enough.

That's how I got here - and that's the reason for this book.

CHAPTER 1

CELEBRITY ASSISTANTS: AN EVOLVING CAREER

"If Frank leaves me, I'll probably get over it, but if any of the ladies who work with me, if they leave me, I'll kill myself."
—Kathie Lee Gifford,
Entertainment Tonight, January 2001

As you already know from the Preface, one of the main reasons I wanted to write this book is because my profession is frequently misunderstood and often maligned. This book gives me the chance to set the record straight and talk about how things really are. It will also be filled with practical information you'll need to find the right job and perform it well.

Would you know what to do to… (*answers to follow*)

- Get a lost passport replaced overnight?
- Convince airline personnel to hold a plane for your high-powered employer?
- Get the State Police to provide an escort for a celebrity stuck in traffic?
- Locate a make-up man when the only clue you have is that he is "in Miami?"
- Find exactly the right exotic puppy in time for your employer's birthday?

31

- *Passport Replacement?* www.itseasypassport.com 12-hour service. Also, go straight to the Passport Office if you are in a major city and it's not a Sunday!

- *Hold a plane?* A colleague was seated in First Class waiting for her famous singer employer who was horribly late. She received a panicked call from him on her cell phone. The singer personally spoke to the flight attendant and promised concert tickets for all the flight attendants and the pilot. Problem solved.

- *Get the State Police to provide an escort?* I grabbed the blue (government) pages of my phone book, prayed, and dialed. Once I convinced the officer I was not a nut, he helped us. I sent him an autographed photo to thank him.

- *Find the make-up man somewhere in Miami?* Lucky guess! I knew he liked nice hotels so I found him on the second try. Whew.

- *Exotic puppy on the double?* www.cyberpet.com

This is the world of professional celebrity assistants. Pulling off small miracles, last-minute saves, solving the most unusual problems – these are the acts which make being a celebrity assistant unique. The celebrity assistant has been around since celebrities have been around, yet little remains known about the job.

Here's a fast-paced profession which is highly demanding – requiring intelligence, resourcefulness, discretion, initiative, computer skills, and last, but not least, consummate people skills. Oh yes, it's also helpful to be clairvoyant!

Those are just *some* of the qualities needed to be a top-notch celebrity personal assistant. Furthermore, the women and men (mostly women) who do this unique work have to figure it out on their own because unlike most professional assistants, celebrity assistants work primarily alone and there are limited resources available to learn how to do this complicated work.

The past fifteen years have seen tremendous changes in the work of *all* professional assistants, and it is a challenge to keep up and stay current. Think of how our world has changed just with e-mail, the Internet, and cell phones. What is utterly clear to me is that all assistants have much more in common than not. It doesn't really matter who it is that you assist. The skills and personality necessary to be an excellent assistant are *exactly the same.* Our world is about *personalized, customized organization* specific to our employers.

It's a special attitude as well. I work *with* married actors Olympia Dukakis and Louis Zorich, as opposed to *for* them. They are my celebrity employers, not my "bosses." If I had my way, I would retire the word "boss" from all verbal and written communications because the connotation is too negative, archaic, and inaccurate. My preference is to use the words "manager," "supervisor," or "employer" to identify our partners in work. (More about this in Chapter 14.)

In our high-tech, fast-paced world, it's not enough for celebrities to have only trusted family members or friends watching over their business affairs. Enter highly skilled, professional assistants for whom this is their profession, their career. The media views it as a fairly new profession, and it's getting increased attention due in large part to society's fascination with the lives of high-powered people and celebrities. Nonetheless, it is a profession in and of itself. Celebrity assisting has become a specialized branch of "executive assistants." People from other fields, such as being a publicist, restaurant manager, or concierge can certainly break in to the profession; but being a celebrity assistant requires a certain skill-set some of which is innate, but most of which is learned.

One of my goals for this book is to provide you with a true sense of what the life of a celebrity personal assistant is all about, and offer some tools and ideas about how to pursue the work if you choose to do so. I suspect that by the time you finish this book, some of you will know that being a celebrity assistant is definitely not the work for you. There will be others of you who will be absolutely certain that you want to pursue this work because it is compatible with your personality and work style.

I'll not only share my own personal experiences, but because of my involvement with New York Celebrity Assistants (NYCA) and speaking at conferences for executive assistants across the country, I am fortunate to know dozens of assistants and will share some of their stories as well. Of course, I won't be able to name names in some stories, but sharing this information is my way of giving you a more complete picture of the work. I hope that these stories are directly applicable, meaningful, and helpful to your work as an assistant.

Why is there even a need for celebrity assistants? Why does the profession exist at all? This is the part the media gets wrong all the time. We are often referred to as "the ultimate luxury," a frivolous indulgence, or even a status symbol. The media attempts to sensationalize the work of celebrity assistants by focusing on abuses and lawsuits that take place. I can tell you without a doubt, this is not the case with most celebrities. It is quite the contrary – we are an absolute necessity and while there might be some sensational moments, the work itself is just that – *work*.

Think of the kinds of people who have personal assistants – famous and not-so-famous wealthy people who are very good at what they do. They demand the same excellence and perfection in the other areas of their lives. The life of a busy celebrity is simply at a different pace from other people in "regular" professions. The celebrities I personally know of, including Olympia Dukakis, have lives filled with travel and major demands on their time for everything from costume fittings, make-up tests, photo shoots, dialect coaching, rehearsals, meetings on current projects, meetings on future projects, doctors' appointments, press interviews, physical training sessions, etc.

Work activities usually happen in condensed periods of time. For example, a lead actor in a feature film can be gone on location up to three months working five and sometimes six days a week, for sometimes twelve hours a day. A lead actor in a TV movie will be gone four to six weeks working at least five days a week, for twelve or more hours a day. That pace requires tremendous focus and total concentration. A professional athlete has an even more grueling travel schedule. Most people in other professions do not live like this – they don't leave home for months at a time. Take a moment to think about what it would take for you to leave home for three months.

Celebrities' lives can be extremely hectic just dealing with their careers. When you add in the ordinary realities of everyday life like buying groceries and spending time with family and friends, for example, it can be overwhelming. Assistants bring order to the chaos by handling the endless details that would eat up a great deal of time that celebrities need to spend doing whatever it is that makes them celebrities in the first place. In Olympia's case, she might need to spend her time memorizing her lines for the next day rather than checking to see if the car is arranged or where she will meet the make-up artist. Her body and voice are her instruments; they are all she has when she works, so she needs to maintain them carefully. I book yoga classes, vocal lessons, chiropractor, massages, hair and nail appointments, etc. – all these things that support her work. *They are important uses of her time.*

Calling in "sick" on a movie set is not an option; productions can get shut down if a key actor can't work. This is another example of how the life and the work of a celebrity, in this case an actress, is different and more pressured than other professions. Allow me to stress that employers need to be able to spend time doing the things that *only* they can do. They also must make sure they get enough physical rest to do their work. Celebrity assistants do everything else. These things apply to any busy celebrity – male or female, in all areas of celebrity – movie star, TV personality, musician, philanthropist, Wall Street mogul, soap opera star, supermodel, or rock star.

Another thing that makes this work unique is that most of the assistants I know say that their work is 50% personal, 50% business, on average. This is certainly true for me, though on any given day, that percentage can get skewed in a huge way. For me, some days are completely focused on business – paying bills, scheduling, creating reports, and handling fan mail. Other days are all personal – running errands, shopping, planning an upcoming party, etc. Most days are a combination of both. This fluctuation is another major reason why this work is hard to get a handle on for people outside the profession. It is all about needs – the needs of celebrity employers will be varied at any given time, and this is precisely why they need us.

Another little-known fact about this "personal" work is that assistants can find themselves doing varying amounts of work for their employers' families – spouses, ex-spouses, children, siblings, etc. This situation arises for a variety of reasons, but often occurs when employers travel a great deal. As the boundaries blur, balancing the demands of all these individuals can present unique challenges for assistants. Furthermore, this expectation is rarely discussed during the interview. Experienced assistants know to ask these kinds of questions in order to best prepare for the job.

It's interesting to note that it is not only assistants to celebrities who are challenged by additional personal requests by their employers. Corporate assistants have also reported that this is happening more and more, and they are not sure how to respond when the business/personal boundaries become fuzzy from time to time. Flex-time and "virtual" offices where assistants and employers are working from home are contributing to this. Creative problem-solving is needed. I encourage all assistants to think of their job descriptions as not set in stone, but rather as a work-in-progress, requiring an open and ongoing dialogue with their employers in order to adapt and respond to changes as new needs arise.

Professional assistants today are on-call 24/7 and have their cell phones on at all times. They have computers with high-speed access both at the office and at home; and when employers are computer literate, they communicate with their assistants via smartphones, text messaging, e-mail, instant messaging, telephone, fax, or all of these! Assistants take their laptops on vacation in order to not be overwhelmed by hundreds of e-mails when they return to work. All the people in the celebrities' lives have their assistants' contact information, and it's okay with everyone involved to use these numbers at whatever time of day they have a need. As technology changes and the world moves even faster, the need for computer literate, well-educated, well-spoken, and super-savvy assistants increases every day.

*"Life is to be lived.
If you have to support yourself, you had better find
some way that is going to be interesting.
And you don't do that by sitting around."*
Katharine Hepburn

*"The Duchess' mother, who I was very close to,
tragically died in a car crash in Argentina. I had
to fly down to help organize her funeral. Helping
to organize a funeral service, write a eulogy, and
negotiate an estate succession are not the every day
duties on most assistants' 'to do' lists."*
John O'Sullivan
10-year assistant to Sarah Ferguson,
Duchess of York

CHAPTER 2

WHAT IT TAKES:
QUALITIES AND SKILLS
NEEDED FOR THE WORK

*W*hen I am asked to describe what I do in a sentence, I say that I work to eliminate chaos and thereby, I provide Olympia Dukakis and Louis Zorich with peace of mind. That's a tall order – giving other people peace of mind about their lives – but that's my job. They get to relax about the details of their lives. They know that when they are away on a job – out of the state or out of the country – if they don't hear from me, everything is fine.

Louis Zorich comments: *"I feel tremendous relief and comfort just knowing that our assistant, Bonnie, has handled all the details to things. She does the worrying! For example, I know that the car will arrive on time and that the tickets will be at the box office when I ask for them. I am free to relax and enjoy myself, which has become even more important as I've gotten older."*

Everyone of importance in their lives has my home phone number and knows to call me if they need Olympia or Louis – this includes their children, relatives, close friends, agents, and colleagues. I don't get called at home a lot – maybe once or twice every weekend, and sometimes not at all. We have mutual respect. If we call one another on off hours, we know it's important. That is not the case with all celebrity employers and their assistants, though.

I bring order to a jumble of information which I do on auto-pilot. It's administrative triage. To be successful at this work, you need to be the kind of person who enjoys making sense out of *non*-sense. Do I make mistakes? Absolutely. Do I admit them? You bet, and I take immediate responsibility. That helps build trust. In all these years, it would be ridiculous (and totally untrue!) to say that I haven't blown it from time to time. Fortunately, I discovered Olympia's attitude about mistakes early on. They are going to happen – but let's learn from them and only permit them to occur – *once*.

Here's one story. Olympia was doing five different speeches over nine days in five different cities, and I was not going to be with her on the tour. Olympia gives several different kinds of speeches, depending on the audience. She has the Acting Speech, the Ethnic Speech, the Women's Speech, the Taking Charge of Your Health Speech – well, you get it. It was my job to send her off with not only all the travel details and contact information for each city, but also the correct speeches for each audience.

You guessed it. One night, she started delivering the Acting Speech but the group was there to hear the Women's Speech. Thankfully, Olympia realized it ten minutes into the speech, switched gears and it all worked out. Pulling this off was a testament to how extremely bright and intuitive Olympia Dukakis is.

When we spoke the following morning, there was no yelling. She wasn't happy about the mistake, but all Olympia wanted to make sure of was that the remainder of the speeches were correct. I will never forget that horrible feeling in the pit of my stomach when I learned what happened. I have definitely made mistakes since then about other things, but she has never again delivered another wrong speech.

I have heard stories of complete silliness, though, a certain amount of which a celebrity assistant just needs to tolerate. I ask you, what business doesn't have some ridiculousness? The assistant to a well-known actor told me about the time the actor called her from London at 4AM New York-time to complain that his bathroom was running out of toilet paper and could she handle this? If this kind of thing happens over and over again, you have some choices. Try to train your employer diplomatically, deal with it, or quit. The skill here is dealing with it so you can get to an acceptable comfort level, and not suffer with ulcers from the anxiety.

Being an assistant to a celebrity is a do-whatever-it-takes profession, and a positive attitude helps a great deal. An example – I expect to work longer hours during the days and the night before Olympia leaves on a big trip. There's always packing and tying up loose ends, both personally and professionally. On one of these nights, I felt happy because it looked like we were going to finish around 9PM. Then, Olympia walked into our office with a distressed look on her face. The passenger elevator was broken, and she was worried that she wouldn't be able to get down to the street level in the morning when she was scheduled to leave for the airport. We are on the sixth floor, so we needed a Plan B – fast.

Our only option was the freight elevator, which is the only other elevator, except that we don't have a key for it or know how to operate it. So at 9PM, I was calling the building manager to find out who had a key. Then, I was instructed over the phone how to work this old-fashioned elevator (think 1950's Doris Day movie) by a person with a very strong accent who I could barely understand. My next task was to teach Olympia's husband Louis how to operate the freight elevator in case the passenger elevator was not repaired by the morning. By 10PM the lesson was done, although by morning, the passenger elevator was repaired. Plan B was not needed, but I wasn't leaving that night until we had one. It's just one of the many kinds of last-minute problems that need the quick thinking – and quicker action – of the professional assistant.

What follows is a chart listing the qualities and skills desirable for being a professional assistant. Some qualities are innate, as in you are born with them or not. Other skills can be learned, such as computer literacy. The third column includes qualities which will not help you as an assistant.

Only you know how many of the desirable qualities and skills you possess. I can tell you that the more you have, the easier your work will be as a professional assistant.

DESIRABLE INNATE QUALITIES	LEARNED SKILLS	UNDESIRABLE QUALITIES
Organized	Computer Literacy	Disorganized
Respectful	Internet	Control Freak
Creative problem solver	Written communication	Star-struck
Resourceful	Verbal communication	Moody
Responsible	Telephone etiquette	Needy for constant
Professional	Prioritizing	feedback
Detail-oriented	Anticipate problems	Needy for constant
Empathic	Networking	attention
Great memory	Technology – cell phone,	Gossipy
Think on your feet	scanner, computers,	Immature
Sense of humor	hand-held devices,	Insecure
Even-tempered	fax machine	Defensive
Self-motivated	Public Speaking (Chap. 4)	Easily flustered
Positive attitude	Event Planning (Chap 5)	Lazy
Flexible	First-aid, CPR,	
Sensitive to other people	Heimlich Maneuver	
Able to multi-task		
Take initiative		
Protective and nurturing		
Sublimate ego		

I often refer to the following tips as "tricks of the trade." Here's more about what I mean...

- ***Great Organizational Skills*** – Vital and arguably the single most important skill you must possess. Whether you are a list-maker or have an eletronic calendar or date book, it is imperative that you design a way to organize another person's life in a customized way. Usually this means that your own life is very organized, too, but this is not always the case. The system you develop is specific to your employer. For example, your employer might prefer to receive the daily schedule via e-mail and another's preference might be to see it on a 5x7 card. This work is extremely detail-oriented, so being organized cannot be overemphasized. You are the person people depend on to get it right. The best assistants enjoy getting it right and being the one with the answers which need to be easily accessible.

- *Respectful* – This is a vital quality that is a given for ultimate assistants. Showing respect tells the recipient that they are important and of value. Conversely, people remember when they are disrespected and it negatively impacts future interactions.

- *Creative problem solver / resourceful* – As in using contacts and connections. An assistant with this quality will hear a problem and automatically come up with one or two possible solutions without being asked. Example: If your employer is doing business in London and wants to send flowers to a client there, how do you decide from whom to order them when your contacts are in your home city? One idea is to call the concierge at any of the four or five star hotels in London and ask advice. Even though your employer is not a guest at the hotel, the concierge will usually be happy to help.

- *Responsible* – To a fault. Every detail is taken care of. When something goes wrong, you fix it without blame and then plan ahead by saying to yourself, "What can I do so this doesn't happen again?"

- ***Professional*** – Professionalism means that you keep the big picture in view at all times and your actions are to be viewed as such. Professionalism is demonstrated by how you speak, write, dress, and behave. Staying professional in the midst of a crisis or stressful situation is the test of an excellent assistant.
- ***Detail-oriented*** – A detail-oriented assistant delights in understanding the nuances between "Dove Gray" and "Battleship Gray" and enjoys spending time hunting down that rare first-edition book and the best coconut cream pie in San Francisco. Example – Before your employer leaves town, make sure ATM cards and phone calling cards are all working. Better to solve any problems *before* your employer gets on the plane. Another example – I was going to Punta Cana in the Dominican Republic on vacation, and I hurriedly booked the flight. The week before the trip, I was reviewing the travel plans and realized I had booked the flight into the wrong airport on the island! The airports were an eight hour drive apart. Fortunately, I found this out before getting on the plane, but it was an expensive lesson to learn.
  Along those same lines – Be sure to get specific about whether your employer's engagement is in Kansas City, *Kansas* or Kansas City, *Missouri*. Also, double-check that your employer's passport is current and that the last name on airline tickets matches the passport name *exactly*. Finally, did you know that many countries will deny entrance even if your passport expires six months from the date you travel? South Africa and Russia are two of them. Check and double-check!
- ***Great memory*** – For details, faces, names, phone numbers, e-mail addresses. I have about two hundred phone numbers in my head. This is a real time saver, especially

when we are in a limo, on the road, or just in a hurry.

- ***Ability to think on your feet and react quickly and calmly to most situations*** – This is an important one. My colleagues call these "save the day" stories; I think of them as pulling off small miracles. A major league baseball player's assistant told me she convinced a conductor to hold a train from leaving until her employer was on board. No easy task and totally against the rules, but she saved the day. I have two favorite "miracle" experiences. I referred to this first story earlier. Olympia was stuck in gridlock traffic on the NJ Turnpike, so she was going to be late for a speech sixty miles away. When Olympia called me from the car, I heard the driver say, "*The only way you'll make it is with a police escort.*" Olympia paused and asked, "*Well Bon, want to give that a try?*" I tried not to panic and said, "*Why not?*" I have not met an assistant yet who cannot relate to that awful feeling in the pit of your stomach that comes from being asked to do something that you are not at all sure you can do. I grabbed the blue pages of my phone book, took a deep breath, and called the State Police. After convincing the officer that I was not a crazy person, he then agreed to arrange giving her limo an escort. She was still late, but the audience gave her a standing ovation for her effort to get there. Years later, Olympia admitted to me that she was amazed I was able to pull that one off. Me too! The second story also involves the police. It was the Saturday night before Olympia was flying to London for the British premiere of the film "*Steel Magnolias.*" Her flight was in twelve hours. We had all forgotten to get her clothes out of the cleaners, and of course, her London clothes were in there. I called the local police who located the owner of the cleaners; they got him to open the store at 9PM, and we retrieved the clothes. Big relief.

What would *you* do?

- **_Sense of humor_** – I can't think of any job where this doesn't come in handy. It's just as important to know when to turn it off and be low-key.
- **_Even-tempered_** – Don't get flustered or lose your cool. *You* are the "go-to" person in a crisis.
- **_Self-motivated_** – You like working alone and are very effective with minimal supervision. You can be very focused, even when there is chaos going on around you. You can concentrate on what needs to be done.
- **_Positive attitude_** – You never say "no" when you can figure out how to say "yes." You exhaust every option first. Olympia knows that if I tell her something can't happen, it's truly because it can't happen. Then I offer alternative options.
- **_Ability to put people at ease around your employer_** – Some people are nervous and star-struck and generally behave strangely with famous people. You work to diffuse any discomfort for your employer.
- **_Flexible_** – You don't mind that your schedule for the day gets moved around on a regular basis. When I walk into work each day, my attitude is, "Okay, what's changed today? What project is in, which is out? Will I actually do what I thought I was going to do today?" The ultimate assistant will make it all work despite the changes. I heard an expression recently: "The happiest person is one who enjoys the scenery on the detour."
- **_Sensitive to other people_** – You "tune in" to voices over the phone and to the body language of people. For example, as you feel more confident, you will be able to say, "I think you'd better call back so-and-so now. She sounded a bit frantic." It builds trust if you are able to do this and it turns out that you were right.

- **_Ability to multi-task_** – You understand that twelve different balls are up in the air and are at various stages of progress. You can easily do several things at once – talk on the phone, motion someone into a meeting, and check your e-mail. A note of caution though: Don't type while talking on the phone. There are times when giving your undivided attention is called for. Be sensitive to that. Another hint is to always bring something to do while you wait on lines: read scripts, faxes, catalogues, mail, whatever.
- **_Taking initiative_** – See a problem and act or ask if it is okay that you act. Early on in our work together, I once went a little too far. I tried to take initiative on something for which Olympia did not really want help. She finally kidded me by saying, "_You know, Bonnie, I've been putting on my 'snowsuit' by myself for a long time now._" We laughed, and I got the message.
- **_Protective and nurturing_** – You watch your employer's back in every way and see him or her through any rough patches.
  And last, but certainly not least…
- **_The ability to sublimate your ego_** – You are not the celebrity, therefore, you can't behave like one. You are there to support your employer, not to dress better or stand out more. You genuinely and sincerely enjoy being behind the scenes and supporting your employer to do his or her work.

Since organization is the number one, most important quality you need to succeed as an assistant, here are some specific examples of being organized.

When Olympia is driving somewhere, I get the exact directions from Point A to Point B and discuss them with her the day before the trip. Did you know that some addresses in New York City don't necessarily jibe with where the front door is located? I call ahead to find out where she will actually enter the building. I cannot stress enough the importance of these small details.

If we are getting furniture delivered, it is up to me to schedule the use of the freight elevator. I'll move around any other appointments that might interfere, such as the cleaning service. Nobody tells me to do these things. I do them because they make sense and allow the household to run smoothly.

I take my "book" with me everywhere. It contains Olympia's schedule with all key contact information. It's our bible. I even take it on vacation with me – just in case – and yes, I've used it.

Reconfirm all appointments a day or two ahead, preferably with a real, live human being. There are few things worse than having your employer show up at a meeting when the other person is a no-show. This happens more than you can imagine, given our dependence on voice messages and e-mail. While these are wonderful time-saving devices, not everyone is scrupulous in checking messages, machines can malfunction, and e-mail can get trapped in cyberspace.

Make sure your office is well supplied. Have extra print cartridges on hand so your work doesn't stop if the cartridge goes dry. You don't want to be sent into chaos by having to go to the office supply store right when you are on deadline with a project. There will never be a good time for the cartridge to go dry. Stock copy paper, batteries, light bulbs, business stationery, etc. You are the "Office Manager" too, if you run a one-person office. Of course, this is usually not too difficult since as a group, assistants love office supplies. Don't ask an assistant *if* he or she has a pen, just ask about the color you want.

Keep lists! I have paper and pens handy at all times, even next to my bed and in the car. Lists of phone calls to make, things to do, items to order, etc. Assistants need to receive and hold a lot of information, and often get it fast and furious. The only way I know of to make everything happen is to write it all down when the issue is mentioned, on paper or electronically – even if you are not going to deal with it right away. It is impossible to "just remember" everything that needs to be done. Put these lists in places where you can check them daily in order to update your overall schedule. Discuss priorities with your employer so that he or she can be involved in deciding how you are spending your time. I have often said to Olympia, *"You've told me you want Items 1, 2 and 3 done ASAP. I feel I can get two of them done today and the third tomorrow. Which two do you prefer?"* This lets her know I am aware of her priorities, but it also lets her know that I am being realistic about what is possible to accomplish so she is not disappointed.

Here are important learned or acquired skills for a professional assistant:

- *__Computer Hardware & Software__* – Knowing the difference between a PC and a Mac is the tip of the iceberg known as computer literacy. Microsoft Office is the standard office software. Knowledge of Microsoft Word for word processing, Excel for spreadsheets, PowerPoint for presentations, and Outlook for your calendars and e-mail is key. Great keyboarding (typing) skill is critical to your work getting done on time. Computer skills can also add substantial dollars to your salary.
  Not all celebrities are computer savvy, nor do all require that their assistants be; but more and more, computer skills are essential. The ability to do research and get quick answers via the Internet is a real plus. Olympia, for example, has very little interest in using a computer, but she expects me to stay up to speed.
- *__Internet__* – The Web has become vital in everyday work – shopping, research, travel, etc. It is *the* invaluable and

essential tool in the work of a professional assistant.

- *Superior communication skills* – The ability to speak and write to all kinds of people to get what you want – from celebrities to CEO's to house staff to agents to the porter in the building. Bonus skill – speaking one or more foreign language.

- *Great phone skills* – Manners (see Chapter 6), etiquette, discretion, how to say "no" nicely. The assistant is usually the one to have to say "no" because celebrities receive so many requests for their time. One of my favorite lines is, "You can't blame people for trying." I try to let them down easy.

- *Ability to instantly prioritize and then re-prioritize as the situation changes* – Example: If we have a morning of furniture shopping planned but I come in and the apartment has no heat, I size up the situation, deal with it, and maybe shopping gets moved to another day. Waiting for the plumber becomes the top priority for the day.

- *Ability to anticipate potential problems* – Emphasis on "anticipate." For example, I know that Olympia likes a strong reading light; so when we were packing her up for the beach house, I made sure to include some 200 watt bulbs. I anticipated that the rental house wouldn't have those on hand. Another example: I check the weather report for each city she is traveling to in order to pack the proper clothes; otherwise, I will get a phone call asking that I overnight the right ones. You can save yourself a lot of time and aggravation by anticipating your employer's needs, asking questions, and practicing putting yourself in his or her place.

- *Networking* – Know that every person you meet is potentially helpful to you in one way or another. Manage your contacts religiously. Don't burn bridges unless absolutely necessary. It's a good idea to build a relationship with the local notary and the county clerk in charge of jury duty. You will more than likely need favors from these people someday.

- *Technology Management* – Computer, cell phone, smartphone, pager, fax machine, scanner, webcam – knowing how to use and fix them, teaching your employer about them, and keeping supplies for them at the ready. Know where the instruction manuals and warranties are kept. The better you can be at this, the more efficient you will be and the more smoothly your office will run.

- *First-Aid, CPR, Heimlich Maneuver* – These desirable skills are taught through the American Red Cross and add to an assistant's overall knowledge-base, confidence and marketability.

Here's something else that is rarely talked about when it comes to gadgets. Gadgets cause stress and anxiety. Yes, they help us do our work better. *Eventually.* There is a learning curve that comes with getting to know each one, and that means time and mental energy. You may also be expected to teach others what you learn, which can add stress. Valuable and concentrated time is needed to learn new computers and software, etc., and the impact of this should not be underestimated.

In light of these preferred qualities and skills, here are some qualities that will *not* serve you in your work. Being controlling, star-struck, moody, needy for constant feedback and attention, easily flustered, gossipy, insecure, and defensive. Hopefully, these words are self-explanatory and don't apply to you!

A final story for this chapter is about the quality of empathy, which according to Olympia, is one of the most important things I offer as her assistant. The summer of 2003 took Olympia and me on a ten-city, twenty-day book tour to promote Olympia's memoir *Ask*

Me Again Tomorrow. We were on airplanes and in different hotels every two or three days as we moved from city to city. The schedule was full and while very fun, it was also very tiring. Toward the end of the tour, Olympia walked into my hotel room one afternoon, and she found me wandering aimlessly because I was so exhausted and overwhelmed! She started laughing and proclaimed, *"See?! Now you really understand what it's like! Now you get why I lose and forget things when I'm on the road. I'm so happy."* She was right. I didn't really understand it until then, and it is now one of Olympia's favorite stories about our work together.

> *"People do not understand that our jobs can entail being an organizer, travel agent, property manager, publicist, chief-of-staff, errand runner, personal shopper, event planner, driver, and therapist. This is why it drives me crazy when I hear 'just an assistant' or when people speak as if an assistant's position is menial. Sure, there have been assistants who were in the news for doing their jobs poorly to the point of being sued or arrested; but for the majority of us who take these jobs seriously, we maintain every effort to do it well."*
>
> S. Lynn Matsumoto, 5-year assistant
> to actress Edie Falco

CHAPTER 3

JOB DESCRIPTION: THE SKY'S THE LIMIT

*M*y mother has been asked for years by her friends, "*What exactly does Bonnie do?*" Her answer has become very simple – "*Everything.*"

I'll share with you how my work has evolved over the years because my job description has expanded incredibly in that time. It certainly didn't start out that complicated. Most celebrity assistants don't stay in their jobs this long. Most work an average of one to five years before moving on to another assistant position or related career. Also, all celebrity assistants don't perform exactly the same job functions, but what I will describe will be an overview of the possibilities.

Most celebrities have at least one assistant. Some have more than one. Here's how it works. There is a number one assistant, the person who bears the main responsibility to assist the employer. He or she delegates tasks to the numbers two and three assistants. In the case of some movie actors, they have an "office" assistant and another "location" assistant who travels with the actor to wherever the film is shooting.

When I first started, my main responsibility was being the keeper of Olympia's master schedule, which meant everyone (except her family, but sometimes even them) needed to go through me to schedule time with Olympia. I was also her publicist, therefore, I handled all the media requests. I fielded her calls and dealt with her mail and correspondence including fan mail. Lastly, I handled all travel arrangements. That was pretty much it at first. Time was very precious, so Olympia and I would meet face to face or talk by phone for a few minutes each day to catch each other up. Of course, I still do all of these things and other than being a publicist, these are the everyday kinds of things you could expect to be asked to do.

The first week we had an office in Olympia's home (this was after I had been working with her for four years at the Whole Theatre), I told her we couldn't function without a fax machine, a typewriter and a computer. She agreed and handed me a credit card saying essentially to make it happen and just try to get good prices. I did. After a year of things going pretty smoothly, I began to pay all the bills, create financial reports on Excel for the accountant, handle the medical insurance paperwork, read and give opinions on scripts, and travel with Olympia when she made appearances around the country.

A few years later, in addition to all of the above, the "personal life" responsibilities became a more integral part of my job. We took a field trip to the island of St. Maarten where Olympia bought two vacation homes. I typed term papers for her son. I served as party planner for numerous parties including her son's wedding. I helped buy and sell four homes here and abroad, including the apartment in Manhattan, which is the home office. It was my job to coordinate the renovation of the apartment and manage the move, which pretty much took me the whole six months that Olympia spent in England doing a play. My job included going to appliance stores to take Polaroid photos of refrigerators and stoves and overnighting them to Olympia for approval. Modern technology makes these tasks so much easier now.

One of most important "personal" responsibilities I had was to help select the nursing home for Olympia's mother, Alexandra, and handle the small mountain of paperwork involved with that. When Olympia was shooting a movie out of the country, I received a call from the nursing home telling me that Alexandra's false teeth were missing. That's a big problem for anyone, but especially for a ninety-year-old woman. I decided to go there and take a look for myself since I had come to know her habits. I found her teeth in the pocket of her bathrobe, and I also found a few other things under the mattress. Everyone involved was relieved, and I only told Olympia about it after the problem was solved. Assistants do *whatever it takes.*

Now all of these things are part of my job. When most people hear this diverse job description, they seem overwhelmed. It may be daunting to some, but it suits me and is business as usual for assistants.

My colleagues gave me examples from their job descriptions which range from the no-skill-required to "I'm sure glad I have a college degree" level of responsibility and everything in between. Assistants have fed the homeless with Mother Teresa, filmed the birth of their employer's baby, coordinated the shipping and taxidermy of a deceased giraffe, flown on Air Force One, and given CPR to a dog. They manage multiple houses and work with curators on installing art collections. They take pets to the vet and out for their walks, and they pick up kids from school. They order prescriptions, submit the health insurance papers, arrange for cars to be serviced, turn over summer clothes to winter clothes, change light bulbs, and interview prospective nannies, housekeepers, and personal chefs. I think one of my colleagues summed it up best when she said that one minute you might be meeting Michael Douglas, and the next, you might be cleaning up a broken jar of pickles.

I love that Olympia and Louis put up very few obstacles to my learning process. In fact, they want me to do as much as I can handle. My opinion is welcomed, trusted, and valued. The job is never dull.

Happily, no two days are *ever* the same.

What this job can also be, at times, is stressful. We take this work seriously and thus, all of us need our own strategies for stress management. The stress often comes from being uncertain about how to approach an issue. I have come to affectionately call this uncertainty my "puddles of discomfort." Some puddles are deeper than others, some I've been sitting in longer than others, but I always have a few going at a time.

Sometimes on a day when my head is spinning, I just leave the office and take a walk around the block. I get some fresh air and some perspective at the same time. It helps me, and I feel better. I also run, take guitar lessons, and go to the beach. I remind myself that this is not brain surgery, and Olympia reminds me that nobody is going to "theatre jail." My colleagues take yoga classes, jog, meditate, go to therapy, volunteer for charities, attend the theatre, and get massages. One has a sailboat and another bought a vacation home in Italy. Whatever your solution, it is important to have a plan to manage the inevitable and unavoidable stress.

One of the things assistants often find challenging is to have a personal life because of the demanding job description. As a result, most celebrity assistants are single. I have one child, as do many of my colleagues. Very few have more than one child. I know of two who do, but their children are adults.

What if you work for an extremely wealthy person (*Forbes* calls them "high net-worth individuals") whose name is *not* instantly recognizable? Or the employer who is intensely private and does not want his or her assistant to use the name to get things done? The assistant to his billionaire employer comments, "*The doors don't open as easily or as quickly.*" How do the assistants to these people arrange the best seats to the hottest Broadway show or a prime table at Nobu for Saturday night or arrange for their employers to be one of the first to buy that limited edition car without getting a migraine? The answer is a combination of connections, charm, and often money in the form of heavy tipping. Personal relationships and connections are extremely important to cultivate especially for the assistant to a not-well-known "celebrity."

An example: The assistant to a Fortune 500 couple needed to arrange for a very intricate cake to be made and there was only one New York City baker they wanted for the job. Unfortunately, the baker extraordinaire was going to be away on vacation during the week the cake was needed. Charm and persuasion was not going to work. Finally, the assistant said, "*I will pay you double the amount. Name your price.*" The baker agreed to come back for one day from his vacation to make the cake for this regular client. The assistant not only paid double, but included an additional $200 in cash as added appreciation. It is the smart employer who gives the assistant discretion and latitude in these matters. Another example from the same assistant – "*Want to receive excellent service without uttering a word? Pull up to a store in your employer's super-luxury car driven by his chauffeur and make sure the staff sees you. Works every time.*"

Another colleague also works for a billionaire employer. He advises, "*Maintain a number of resources for when money and charm cannot obtain the desired result. These include an event ticket broker, a personal concierge service, and a members-only travel agency. These sources are not found in the Yellow Pages; they usually only take clients through referral or paid membership. They can be expensive but worth every penny when you have exhausted all other means of obtaining tickets to a sold-out event or getting seats on a booked flight. Also, don't forget about the extensive services that come with the American Express Platinum and Black cards.*"

It is not uncommon for people of high wealth to own multiple homes in the United States and abroad, one or more private planes, and many businesses. In addition, it follows that they employ large staffs, and renovation projects seem to always be in progress. And because money is not an issue, life is in constant flux and changes are the norm. The assistant is often needed to travel to the different homes to organize various projects. With the help of many others, including the household/estate manager, butler, and housekeepers, it takes an extraordinarily organized assistant to manage all of this activity.

One closing note about the job description no matter who you work for. An assistant might work alone in a home office, but he or she does not work *alone*. Every great assistant has an A-team of pros to call upon for various needs who will definitely be remembered at holiday time – housekeeper, pharmacist, travel agent, florist, caterer, plumber, dentist, ticket agent, manicurist, personal shopper, hair stylist, colorist, trainer, chiropractor, masseuse, concierge, electrician, handyman, cardiologist, limo driver, airport greeter, etc. The best assistants know exactly who to call in order to not only get the job done, but get it done to your employer's exact specifications.

CHAPTER 4

THE ART OF PUBLIC SPEAKING

Statistics show that more people fear public speaking than flying, illness, and even death. Others might not fear it quite that much, but they rank speaking in public far down on their "fun things to do" list. Thus, the reason for this chapter.

Assistants are often called upon to speak to groups of all sizes. You might be asked to sit in on a meeting and speak on behalf of your employer. Your employer might be running late, and you need to "entertain" the guests until his or her arrival. Your employer will be depending on you to be representing him or her in a professional manner.

The first step to improving your public speaking is simply to acknowledge that it is going to happen. That fact alone will help you to mentally prepare. I can tell you that with some effort and practice, you can greatly improve your public speaking, and by doing so, increase your effectiveness in your work and all of your communications.

The Seven Keys to Better Public Speaking

#1 _Attitude._ I believe it – attitude is everything. As a speaker, you have something important and valuable to share, and your audience will feel that if you are able to convey a positive attitude.

#2 _Expectations._ Everyone has them. Hopefully, both you and your audience are working from the same set of expectations. When that happens, not only will you be an excellent communicator, but you will be meeting your audience's expectations. Take the time to get very clear on what is expected.

#3 _Know Your Audience._ Understand who they are and why they are there. Put yourself in the audience's place. Relax! The audience is rooting for you and doesn't expect you to be perfect. The audience will win if you focus on your message. You want them to win.

#4 _Know your subject._ Knowing your subject automatically increases your comfort level if you understand what you are talking about inside and out.

#5 _Preparation, Planning & Practice._ Your confidence level increases even further if you take the time to rehearse in front of a mirror or with a friend or a video camera. Just the act of saying and repeating the words helps relieve nervousness.

#6 _Delivery._ Make eye contact, use gestures, vary your speed, volume, and tone of voice, and believe in what you are saying. Your audience will only believe it if you believe it first. Enthusiasm, humor, and sincerity count!

#7 _Logistics._ Look at the space and do a sound-check with the microphone at least an hour _before_ speaking. There's no sense saying a word if the audience can't hear you. Pre-set your pens, notes, water, etc. Dress appropriately and comfortably.

Like most things, the more you speak in public, the easier it gets. Who knows? You might actually learn to like it!

Olympia is very fond of this Chinese proverb which is carved in a marble plaque on her desk.

That the birds of worry and care
fly above your head,
this you cannot change,
but that they build nests in your hair,
this you can prevent.

*"When Ellen Burstyn was getting ready to celebrate
her 60th birthday, we planned a wonderful party at
her home for all of her dearest friends, old, new, a
few famous, but most not. Workers restoring her 19th
century home mingled with producers and actors and
family.*

We gave a party and everybody came!

*When it was time to cut the birthday cake and serve
dessert, we were wall-to-wall people, all happy,
well-fed and having a glorious time.*

*I was wearing many hats as personal assistant, guest,
hostess, photographer, overseer of the kitchen, and
whatever else needed attention.*

*As Ellen caught my eye, I turned to see her with
several cake-filled plates lined up her arm, merrily
serving birthday cake to her guests.*

*I complimented her on her ability to balance the
plates so well.*

She wryly responded, 'I wasn't always an actress!'"

Susan McTigue, 19-year assistant
to Ellen Burstyn

Chapter 5

EVENT PLANNING

*M*ost assistants will, at some point, be involved with planning events for their employers. I want to begin by saying how much fun planning events can be. It's a lot like putting on a show which is probably why I like it so much. Of course, there are the sad events to plan, such as funerals, but more about that later in the chapter.

Over the years, I have planned many events. On the professional side – countless meetings, press conferences, lunches, photo shoots, and benefits. On the personal side – Olympia and Louis' son's wedding, Louis' seventieth birthday party and their fortieth wedding anniversary party, to name just a few.

In this chapter, I will share with you what I know about creating events – what works, what doesn't work, some things to think about, and ultimately, how to make you and your employer look very, very good.

What every one of the events I've planned has in common is this – collaboration. Every event requires the coming together of concept and execution; and <u>you</u> are the person standing in the middle in charge of all this activity, orchestrating the pieces coming together.

Let's be clear about something right away. Assistants are expected to pull off a great event while simultaneously doing all of their other work. Planning an event usually does not mean their other responsibilities go away. It becomes a time-management issue, so our organizational abilities need to shift into the highest gear.

MAKE IT PERSONAL

In our high-speed world, it's become very special to get together, to have what some call "face time." It is rarer to have the opportunity to be together in a room for any extended period of time, face-to-face, looking into each other's eyes, shaking each other's hands, making a connection. Perhaps your office is similar to mine in that my phone does not ring as much as it used to because of e-mail. Even speaking on the phone has become more special, to not be thrown directly into voicemail has become worthy of noting. We say, "*Oh, how great that I actually got you!*" instead of having our machines talk to each other. So planning any event – a lunch, an awards ceremony, a wedding – has *increased* significance because we are all communicating electronically and impersonally most of the time.

Here's a lesson I learned from the film world, but I apply it all of the time. It can be called "It's All in the Details." The personal touch works. Oftentimes, the marketing budget for a film which promotes that film to the world is larger than what it cost to make the film in the first place. "*My Big Fat Greek Wedding*" is a good example of this. The film cost $3 million dollars to make, the marketing budget was $19 million dollars, and it grossed $240 million dollars! Why do they do that? The studio enlists the stars of the movie to do interviews and go on talk shows to promote the film. The thinking is: treat the star very special – five star hotel, favorite flowers in the hotel room, reservations at the latest "in" spot, hotel signing privileges, chauffeured limo, hair and make-up artists, and massages upon arrival. What the studio gets in return is a happy, appreciated star who will sell the movie in a very positive way, and that *sells tickets*. This attention to detail pays off in big ways, and that's why studios do it.

Any event *you* are planning has an element of "selling tickets." Figure out what you and your employer are trying to accomplish and work backwards. If, for example, you have a guest of honor and your mission is to have him or her feel like a celebrity or buy more of your product or motivate him or her to use your services, here are a few suggestions. Find out your honoree's favorite flowers or colors and have the table arrangements made from them. Ask your honoree's assistant about his or her favorite music, food, dessert, or restaurant. What is equally important to find out is what he or she might be allergic to or if there is a food aversion. You will need to know if someone smokes or does not drink alcohol. I was involved with an event where a key person had a phobia about tall buildings. He refused to use an elevator and would not go above the third floor in any building. That's an important detail! Use your colleagues to understand what is important to your honoree. If part of your job is to give this person the perfect gift at your event, your honoree's assistant is invaluable for this task. Use their advice, brainstorm, and network with your colleagues about unique and unusual gifts.

High-powered professionals receive a lot of gifts that they really don't need or want. Do you keep a gift drawer or gift cabinet for the rejects in order to re-gift? Wouldn't it be great to give a gift that someone truly and sincerely appreciates? You are going to be spending money anyway, so you might as well spend it on something that is going to make an impression. Olympia appreciates when it is obvious that someone took the time to understand what she likes, and most of the time that means the gift-giver has called me first for suggestions. What are their hobbies or areas of great interest? Who is a favorite author or musician? Are they fascinated by the latest electronic gadget? Find out and it will be worth the effort.

Thinking "outside the box" and being a creative problem solver has never been so easy. The Internet is a great source of information and ideas – use Google.com to research your honoree, and you might find a great clue there from an interview he or she might have given or an article that was written about him or her. You will make serious points for doing your homework and striving for the personal touch.

One example of this is from a wedding shower which took place at a hotel restaurant. The waitresses and bartenders were all given custom t-shirts to wear for the event. Each was printed with funny and sweet messages. One had a heart with the bride and groom's names inside. Another said, "Just you wait, Sally!" with cartoons of the bride and groom. These shirts helped contribute to the playful and fun atmosphere of the event.

Here's an example from my life. (I like to think I practice what I preach.) In planning my son Adam's Bar Mitzvah, I struggled to figure out something unique to do at the event that he would remember years after it was over. Then it came to me. I would sing a song to him, a song that had meaning to us both. I sang "*The Secret of Life*" by James Taylor. In addition to the song's message of "enjoying the passage of time," Adam witnessed his mother facing her anxiety about singing in public. Adam and his friends still remember his Bar Mitzvah as a very special day, in part, because of that personal touch.

THE PLAN

Here's a scenario. Your employer has asked you to arrange an important dinner on a given date. Hear her out at this meeting and take notes. Your employer will tell you the things about the event that are of utmost importance, whether it is the special occasion itself, the attendees, the venue, or that the dinner must happen no later than X date. She is leaving the rest up to you. First, you must choose a date and clear it with everyone. Hopefully, that process won't be agony, but be prepared to change the date if a key person can't make it. In order for you to safely move on to the other details, and if there is time, send out a "Save the Date" e-mail. In addition to securing the date on everyone's calendar, this communication also can set the tone for your event. Keep your employer informed as to your progress in writing via e-mail or however you communicate with one another. Copy her on everything that goes out.

My strategy with Olympia is that once we have the event "concept" meeting, the goal is to protect her from the minutia as much as possible. For example, we sit down and she tells me we want to do a cast and crew party prior to the first performance of a play, we are going to have it at her apartment, and that one of the cast members is going to be doing all the cooking. I need to coordinate with him to arrange food delivery and any other things we need. With the meeting over, the ball is now in my court to make it all happen. Only you will know how involved your employer wants to be with the details and decision-making. For example, will it matter to her what color napkins and plates are used? If so, you must involve her with the choices. If not, then make the best decision and cross it off your ever-present "to do" list.

Next, how do you decide on the place if you have not been told where to have your event? If someone comes up with the bright idea of going out for a sunset cruise, you must be sure none of your guests hates boats or gets seasick. But besides that, it's a great idea! If you plan events regularly, read entertainment and food websites, and dining guides in magazines and newspapers. There you will learn about the new, trendy, "in" restaurants and hotels that are looking for new business. The most important thing you can do is confer with your colleagues, your fellow assistants, to see if they have any great recommendations. Once you have targeted a venue, arrange a visit so you can have a face-to-face meeting with the sales manager. This meeting enables you to see and feel the space and decide together the things that can be done to make your event special. There is no substitute for first-hand knowledge of the space and people involved. Make it your business to know.

Expect to be given a budget and requested to save money wherever possible. Restaurants and hotels need business. Work with the catering director and ask directly what can be done to save money. Some ways to economize include changing the day of the week for your event or eliminating or changing a menu item. You might limit the premium liquors at the bar and/or the number of hours for the event. You can also offer to allow the venue to distribute business cards or brochures, but be sure to check this with your employer first. All of these factors affect the bottom-line price. Remember, *everything is negotiable.*

Different caterers have varying areas of expertise and specialty. You and your colleagues should share information about someone who does truly fabulous sushi or someone else who does extraordinary desserts. I suggest keeping a running file by category. Caterers also differ in terms of the kinds of services they provide. Some only provide food and others can supply waiters, bartenders, dishes, glassware, etc.

I cannot overemphasize the importance of making a personal contact. People do things for people, not companies. A manager will go above and beyond for *you*, and by extension, for your employer and your company. These personal contacts can pay off in huge ways, especially if you become a frequent client or give referrals.

EVENT DETAILS

If your event is very large and complex, you and your employer might want to consider using a professional party planner. They charge by the hour and can be invaluable when it comes to areas where you need extra help. Custom invitations, unique centerpieces, or entertainment are some examples of this.

The following is a list of possible factors for your event. Whichever ones apply must be included in your overall master schedule and "to do" lists.

- Formal invitations
- RSVP list
- Place cards/reserved seating vs. general/open seating
- Gifts for attendees
- Centerpieces/room decorations
- Entertainment
- Audio/visual equipment (microphone, podium, lighting, etc.)
- Transportation (limo, bus, van)

An important note about musical entertainment – live music, a DJ, whatever. Be sensitive to the volume of the music and the selection of songs. This detail can make or break your event. Sometimes guests who cannot have a conversation over the music simply choose to leave early. Remember, you are in control and can request that the volume be turned down or adjusted for the comfort and enjoyment of your guests.

If you have an out-of-town guest staying at a hotel or even in the home, a very nice welcoming touch is to pre-arrange delivery of flowers and a tray of snacks and beverages which will be waiting upon their arrival in the room. Do your homework about their general likes and dislikes For example, do not leave wine for someone who does not drink.

LONG-DISTANCE EVENT PLANNING

If you are asked to organize an event that is not in your city, don't panic. Depending on the event's size and importance, a site visit by you and/or your employer might be in order to complete planning details, and an on-site point-person must be chosen. Fortunately, most venues have websites and offer "virtual tours." They are no substitute for actually being there, but they help a great deal. The key to long-distance events is great communication with your contact at the venue.

AN INSIDE TIP: AIRPORT GREETERS

Let's say you have one or more guests flying in for your event who require special attention, but you don't have the time or ability to go to the airport yourself to personally greet them. The airlines all have a handful of what they call "Special Services" people who greet celebrities, VIP's, and bereaved families; but you cannot always count on them because they don't have that many on staff. But there is also a "greeter service," people to whom you pay a fee to meet and greet your special guest at the airport – *guaranteed*. Simply put, these professionals are your surrogates at the airport, only they are often better because they know all the airline personnel, and can eliminate standing in lines, and provide access to VIP lounges. Their job is to make movement through the airport as seamless as possible. The greeters will also meet an arriving plane and escort your guests to their next flight or waiting limo.

For example, the greeter can meet a limo curbside, greet your VIP, handle the luggage and ticketing, eliminate lines, and then personally escort this person to the VIP lounge. The greeter stays with your VIP until the plane is called for boarding. This service at Newark Airport costs approximately $100 per arrival or departure. Olympia and most every celebrity I know of swears by this service. Trust me, airport greeters are worth every penny.

I can offer two recommendations from first-hand knowledge.

LJR Associates is based in Los Angeles, but has reps at most major U.S. airports. Contact: Linda Rippel (310) 406-2279 LJRLA@ aol.com

Diamond Air is based in London, but it employs greeters all over the U.S. and U.K. Contact: Christina Lawford (011) 44-208 897-9183 cl@diamond-air.co.uk.

SECURITY & PRESS

Many of the people you deal with are high profile, and that means at some point in planning your event, you probably will be dealing with issues of security and the press. Sometimes a high-profile person will travel with his or her own security detail. It will be important for you to understand the needs of the security team up front so you can build that into your planning.

If obtaining security personnel becomes your task, the first thing you should do is speak with representatives from the location of your event. Chances are they can provide security for an extra fee. The advantage there is they know the space extremely well. You may choose to bring in an outside company, but if you do that, you also need to let everyone involved with the event know what is happening. In the aftermath of 9/11, access to buildings in New York City sometimes requires photo identification, so be sure to find out all of this ahead of time in order for your guests to be fully informed about what they need.

When confidentiality is an issue, the sales team of the venue needs to know who you are trying to protect and the importance of not revealing the name of this individual to the public or paparazzi. Sometimes celebrities use aliases (false names) at hotels in order to protect their privacy. I recall one particular occasion doing that for Olympia. Unfortunately, I neglected to tell Louis about it; so when he tried reaching her at the hotel, they would not send his call through because he did not know we had decided to use the alias. Another valuable lesson learned.

If the press is interested in whomever you have at your event, plan ahead of time regarding what will happen when and time that into your realistic schedule for the event. When members of the press are present, it is your job to organize it so that the interviews and/or photos happen when you and your employer want them to happen, not the other way around. Ideally, you and the press rep will collaborate to work out a mutually agreeable plan.

Have you noticed that some people have a "thing" about getting their picture taken? Your guests need to know ahead of time if there are going to be cameras present and if they are expected to be photographed or interviewed. That might mean, for example, your employer needs professional hair and make-up appointments the morning of your event which need to be built in to the overall schedule.

FUNERALS

The need for the personal touch is never greater than for a funeral. Funerals are an example of an event where an objective, clear-thinking assistant is worth his or her weight in gold. When strong emotional feelings are running high in a crisis such as this, it will be the assistant who is calmly asking the right questions and filling in the blanks with the funeral director. *What funeral home has been chosen? Is everyone clear on the schedule of when things are happening? Who is speaking or singing in honor of the deceased? Do the mourners have written directions to the cemetery and the services? Is there enough food for everyone? Hotel rooms and cars for the out-of-towners? Have the music and flowers been handled? Have payments been arranged?* Once these and many other questions have been answered, the assistant begins sensitively solving the problems and paying close attention to personal details.

The assistant may also be responsible for gathering legal documents such as wills, cemetery plot contracts, estate plans, house deeds, etc.

IN CONCLUSION

Here's the good news. You don't have to be an expert event planner to have an amazing event. *Your* job, though, is to ask the right questions, to know what issues are important related to the event, and to know who to go to for great solutions. The "givens" in event planning are that you, the assistant, need to understand the priorities and parameters, never let them out of your sight, and know that *everything* related to the event becomes your problem to solve.

Once your event is over, I hope you get to enjoy that wonderful, satisfied feeling that comes with doing a great job...right before your employer starts talking about how you are going to top it next time! Good luck!

"Manners are more important than laws.
Manners are what vex or soothe, corrupt or purify,
exalt or debase, barbarize or refine us,
by a constant, steady, uniform, insensible operation,
like that of the air we breathe in."
    Edmund Burke, Philosopher

"There is no accomplishment so easy to acquire
as politeness, and none more profitable."
    George Bernard Shaw, Playwright

CHAPTER 6

GOOD MANNERS MATTER

*W*hen I think back to my childhood, I clearly recall the lessons from my mother. I remember her insistence on good manners and on being polite. I was always asked, *"Did you say 'please' and 'thank you'?"* and *"Did you send a thank you note?"*

You know what? Mom was right – manners and being kind matter. A lot. The best assistants know that to have good manners is not old-fashioned at all. Quite the contrary. It is the cornerstone of great working relationships which are all based on respect, honesty, and trust.

We live in an extremely fast-paced, high-tech world. We communicate via e-mail, text messages, and voice mail much of the time. Our world has become increasingly impersonal and assistants need to fight the impulse to get sucked in. One of the bi-products of functioning in this environment is that it is very easy to skip over feelings. It may sound a little crazy, but it takes work and close attention to interact *personally* with people. Sometimes the extra five minutes you spend chatting with someone on the phone makes all the difference. It is good manners, and it is worth it. It also happens to be good business.

In our work as assistants, it is vitally important to exhibit good manners, and a big part of that is to be aware of the personal side of people's lives. To remember birthdays, anniversaries, the holidays, new babies, opening nights, new homes, and on and on.

It is the assistants' job to always, always (did I say always?) say "thank you" – on behalf of themselves and often more importantly, their employers.

A surprising statistic is that the sending of holiday greeting cards is down by a staggering sixty-five percent in the United States. The top reason why is not cost but *lack of time*. People reported they didn't have time to send out holiday cards. This is a depressing idea to me that people are not making time to tell the most important people in their lives that they are remembered, cared about, and loved.

When someone goes out of his or her way for you and your employer, it is imperative to acknowledge the gesture, even if it was for something small. Shooting off a quick e-mail takes very little time, but it is important. Do you have to? Of course not. Should you? Yes, because it helps build strong relationships and personal connections. There are dozens of people with whom I communicate almost exclusively through e-mail, and this is how we get to "know" each other. Don't underestimate the power of the written word.

A word about e-mail. E-mail is a powerful communication tool. My experience is that I often get a faster response from e-mail than I do from a phone call. Also, because the communication is in writing, the information is frequently more trustworthy than verbal communication. Conversely, anyone who uses e-mail a great deal understands that e-mail can often be inadequate, and the reader can sometimes misinterpret what you intended to say. Most everyone knows not to use all capital letters because it comes across as screaming. Hard feelings can result from a simple typo or even from the bold, red font that you selected without thinking much about it. That knowledge requires us all to be extra careful in being clear about what we are trying to communicate.

Depending on the kindness, you have many choices. You can send a hand-written personal note, a typed note, flowers, or a warm e-mail. You can make a sincere phone call or bake a cake. But *do something*. Immediately. Don't wait to express appreciation. Timing is important. Acting right away sends the important message that you and your employer care and are thoughtful. Your employer is busy or quite possibly out of town, so he or she depends on you to handle this personal touch. These guidelines are equally true about expressing apologies for something that has gone wrong, even if it was out of your control. Nothing diffuses hurt feelings, anger, or disappointment better than a sincerely expressed *"I'm sorry."*

What's the pay-off? People saying to your employer, *"Where did you find your assistant? She/he is amazing. So friendly, kind, efficient, helpful (choose one!)."*

People wanting to go out of their way for you is another pay-off. Take the time to resist shortcuts and do strive for the personal touch. It might mean the difference between someone going the extra mile for you in the future or just saying, *"Sorry, can't help you."*

Real life example:

One of my colleagues, Janice Naehu, applied for a position with an A-list film writer/director. Janice told me she had a lot of competition, many of whom were more qualified than she, but that she and the director had a great interview and "clicked."

She was offered the job the next week. Years later her employer revealed that Janice was the only candidate to write a thank-you note. He said that it showed class and made a big difference in his decision to hire her.

Other important ways to show good manners and achieve stronger interpersonal relationships:

- Imagine yourself in your employer's shoes and understand that your actions reflect on him or her. It's called empathy.
- Return phone calls in a timely fashion – the day the call

comes in or on the next business day.

- Follow-up even if you have no news. Call to say, *"I just wanted you to know that I haven't forgotten about (fill in the blank) and will let you know as soon as I hear something."* I have found that people appreciate this consideration very much.
- Be sincerely polite in all of your communications, verbal and written – no exceptions.
- Keep your word. Always do what you say you are going to do.
- Give people your undivided attention. This means not answering e-mail while speaking on the phone to someone. (Can't you tell when someone is doing that?)
- Hold doors open for others.
- If someone looks lost, ask if you can help.
- Dress appropriately for all occasions.
- Offer a compliment to break the ice and make sure it is sincere.
- Go out of your way to help someone who has rarely helped you. The results are sometimes very interesting. Consider it a sociology experiment.
- Don't interrupt unless absolutely necessary. The message sent is, "whatever you are saying is not as important or as interesting as what I am about to say." In other words, be an active listener.
- Be diligent about the correct spelling and pronunciation of peoples' names.
- In general, be thoughtful, respectful, and kind. It doesn't cost one cent and you will (usually) get back what you give out. Life is too short to keep score.

Know this – As a professional assistant, your behavior is noted. Your employer will hear when people feel great about you, and conversely, they will hear if somehow you have not responded in a preferred way. Always err on the side of being polite or helpful. It's not only about good manners – it's about decency, kindness, and showing that you care about other people.

I have a colleague who says that the world would be a much better place to live if everyone were kinder with one another, more polite. This might seem simplistic at first, but I actually think there is something to it.

You do not want a reputation as a gossip or someone who loves dishing the dirt. This behavior will backfire. All it takes is one e-mail landing in the wrong Inbox.

One last lesson from Mom. If you can't say anything nice, don't say anything at all. Thanks, Mom. But sometimes we can't resist being like Olympia's character, Clairee, in the film *"Steel Magnolias"* who said, *"If you have nothing nice to say, come sit by me!"*

"I like the diversity and the freedom this job offers. I've worked from a regular office set-up, from Richard's house, from my house, on location, etc. New York, Los Angeles, London, Rio de Janiero, St. Maarten, Vancouver, and French Guiana... Things don't stay the same; change is always happening in one way or another."

Audrey Bamber, 22-year assistant
to Richard Dreyfuss

CHAPTER 7

THE WHERE OF IT: WORK ENVIRONMENTS

*C*elebrity assistants sometimes do their work in unusual places – limousines, hotel elevators, airplanes, movie sets, restrooms, and beauty salons (talking possible only when the blow dryer is off), to name a few. This aspect of my work is another reason being a celebrity assistant is considered so unique. Where would you be most comfortable working?

1. Employer's Home Office

For example, I work out of Olympia's home office, which is literally a room in her apartment. As everyone knows, not many jobs are like this. I usually keep normal hours – 10AM-6PM – but there are times when I can be there until late at night if we are on deadline or if Olympia is leaving for a trip. A couple of times it made sense for me to sleep at her home since we were leaving together on a trip early the next morning. Another time, a big snowstorm was predicted for the next day and we had a lot of work to do, so I stayed over. I am fine with that. It doesn't happen often and I can usually prepare for it.

Some assistants live in their employer's homes or guesthouses. This kind of arrangement is more common in Los Angeles. As you can imagine, when you are in someone's home, it can be difficult to separate business from personal issues, to keep boundaries clear.

The home office definitely has its challenges, but many celebrity assistants work this way. I recall a morning when Olympia's mother Alexandra told me she was sick, and it meant knocking and entering Olympia's bedroom to awaken her to tell her about her mother's illness. Olympia was glad I woke her up, but it made me uncomfortable nonetheless. Because I work in Olympia's home, I try to be intensely sensitive to her privacy. She comes to me in our office when she is ready to work.

I don't disturb her unless I know she needs to get somewhere or a call comes in that I know she will want to take.

When you are working for celebrities in their homes, be sure to ask these kinds of questions about how they want to be dealt with in their personal space. They will welcome your concern because it shows you are trying to be considerate of what they feel is important.

2. Assistant's Home Office

Some assistants work out of their own homes and go to wherever the celebrity is on any given day. This arrangement is often part-time and requires excellent communication between the assistant and celebrity. Most assistants have full office set-ups at home and with their laptops and cell phones, can work anywhere.

3. Office Separate from Home

This environment is an office that is outside and apart from the celebrity's home. One example of a set-up like this is a Broadway star whose home was in the penthouse of an apartment building, and the "office" was in an apartment on a separate floor in the same building. Another example is an actress whose home is on the Upper East Side and the office is in a building a few blocks away. The actress and assistant don't see each other very much – they talk on the phone a great deal, use e-mail, and have a driver who shuttles papers back and forth as needed. A best-selling author who lives in Florida comes to New York one or two times a month. His assistant runs his office in New York, so they see each other when he comes to town or when the assistant travels to Florida. This infrequent kind of contact and communication is not unusual; it just happens to be one of the aspects of our work that is not common knowledge.

In whichever environment you work, an assistant needs to be self-motivated because there may be times when you are working alone and don't see your employer for weeks at a time. This is certainly the case with me. A few years ago Olympia was in London for six months, the longest amount of time she was ever away. We communicated primarily by fax because of the six-hour time difference.

The other extreme can also be true. An assistant might work in the same room with other assistants or at a network with a lot of people and noise and activity around and several people looking over his or her shoulder. One assistant I know considered quitting because one of her co-workers started smoking and her employer permitted it. They came up with a compromise. Only you know what environment would make you happiest and the most comfortable.

4. On-Location Office

Some assistants travel with their celebrity employers to film locations. Agents can build in travel expenses, housing, and even a small supplemental salary for the assistant into an actor's contract. The assistants find themselves living in hotels, getting a per diem allowance for food, and spending many days on location using cell phones to make things happen. This is a unique way to live – it can be glamorous and fun, but it also means tremendously long hours and very hard work, depending on the demands of the employers.

It is a challenge in this situation to eat, sleep, or exercise regularly. The assistants who do this kind of work are usually not married. They truly enjoy going from place to place, meeting new people all the time, and learning new cities – fast!

In my case, Olympia prefers to have me back at the office, "holding down the fort" while she is away doing a play or movie. I work on future projects, take care of repairs on the apartment, and catch up on organizing and paperwork. I am always busy. Any film has a lot of staff and Olympia finds that they can do the things she needs while away.

My first time on a movie set was in 1991 when Olympia shot a film in Australia called "*Over the Hill.*" She gave me one of her contract's plane tickets as a gift. (Sometimes actors will get two or more plane tickets in their contracts.) It was great fun, and I also ended up having renewed respect for actors. One day, the call time was 4:30AM for hair and make-up, the scene was on the beach at sunrise, and the caravan of four-wheel drive vehicles had to make it down the beach before high tide to get the scene shot. A crew person got bitten by a jellyfish, which caused the production to lose time; a Jeep almost tipped over trying to get down the beach, where driving on sand is worse than driving on snow; and the mechanical dolphin didn't work on cue. It was sheer madness! But this is how it often goes. Great adventure but crazy-making because so many things were not in anyone's control.

I had some personal fun over there, too. The production lent me a car which I used to explore the gorgeous Noosa Heads coast. A big part of the adventure was driving on the left side of the road for the first time. Going on location can be a blast, but it is a given to expect the unexpected and for everything to take longer than you think.

5. Studio or Network Office

This working environment is in an office at a movie studio or television network. For example, every talk show host from Jay Leno to Oprah Winfrey has at least one assistant. The show pays the salary and the office is wherever the show is taped. Therefore, the assistant is officially an employee of the network, not the celebrity. Sometimes the celebrity contributes additional monies towards the assistant's salary in order to keep him or her happy because the network rarely pays very well.

These are the five different kinds of environments celebrity assistants work in. When you interview for a position, this is a key question to ask.

"I'm always surprised at the number of people who ask intruding questions and actually expect an answer! They may not realize that we are extremely loyal, and keeping our employer's private matters private is one of the most important elements of our job."

Mary Jordan, 10-year assistant to
Best-Selling Author James Patterson

CHAPTER 8

S. C. E. P.

* SECURITY   * CONFIDENTIALITY
* ETHICS   * PRINCIPLES

*T*he relationship between the assistant and celebrity employer is an extremely close one, made even closer if you work in his or her home. There is a need for tremendous trust, and it is critical never to betray that trust. I know assistants who have been contacted and offered money by the tabloids for gossip about their employers. I have never personally been approached. There is an increasingly voracious hunger in our country for "dishing the dirt" on celebrities, and sometimes big money is paid in exchange for information and photographs.

In a sentence, you won't last very long as a celebrity assistant if you participate in unethical behavior, and you could also be sued and prosecuted. Your reputation is everything, and the word gets around, trust me.

At New York Celebrity Assistants (NYCA), we care a great deal about confidentiality. Every prospective member must sign a contract of non-disclosure when attending meetings. Information shared at meetings among celebrity assistants stays in the room; it goes no further. Members discuss issues and topics relevant to our work such as unique gift-giving, celebrity security, and publicity issues. We are striving for excellence in our profession, and the confidentiality of it matters a lot. As an assistant, your employer may ask you to sign a similar document saying you will not grant interviews about him or her for your term of employment and sometimes beyond.

The world knows to get close to the assistant is to get close to the celebrity. So it is often a difficult part of the job of an assistant to not reveal what you know. You must be good at politely *not* giving out information. An example – a talk show hostess was newly pregnant and the rumor mill got started at the production office, but she did not want to reveal the news quite yet – her choice. The assistant had to field calls and questions from family, staff, etc., but discreetly not give information – either way. The assistant was asked, "*So is it true? Is she really pregnant?*" The assistant tactfully replied, "*Wouldn't it be great if she was?*" and moved on.

This is a very tough part of the work. To know what to say, when to say it and to whom. This is when celebrity assistants are referred to as "gatekeepers" – you are hired to know who to keep away. When in doubt, I encourage you to ask your employer directly about these issues. I assure you, he or she will give you guidance on how these matters should be handled.

In the aftermath of 9/11, professional assistants nationwide had to become experts on security and disaster management very quickly. We were dealing with anthrax scares causing us to have latex gloves on hand to open mail. We bought heavy plastic sheeting and duct tape to protect our offices from potential chemical attacks. Also purchased were extra water and canned goods in case we were trapped for any length of time.

One of the best pieces of advice we received came from the American Red Cross, and is worth the price of this book. Your key chain should have a small but powerful flashlight hanging from it. Any hardware store stocks this item. More lives could have been saved on 9/11 had more people had flashlights to guide them on their way down the pitch-black stairways. When there is no electricity, this tiny item can help save lives. Today, flashlight apps are available for any mobile device, but the keychain light is great to have as well.

The amount of time and energy given to security issues is completely dependent on who your celebrity employer is and the level of need. Your employer might require one or more bodyguards. His or her home might have an extensive security system which you need to understand and operate. Your work might necessitate creating a list of people whose calls are "always" put through, another list for the "sometimes," and a third list of the "absolutely never." You might have regular meetings with your employer's security detail to create Plans A-F for various scenarios which may or may not occur regarding stalkers, paparazzi, avid fans, etc.

One of my favorite memories is from the late 1980's when we did a benefit at the Whole Theatre where Olympia was the Producing Artistic Director and I was the PR Director. Our guests of honor were Gov. Thomas Kean of New Jersey and Gov. Michael Dukakis of Massachusetts who is Olympia's first cousin. Both men agreed to do a short press conference with Olympia before the benefit, and each arrived with their own Secret Service detail. These security men were enormous, well-armed, and not very friendly looking. When the time came to begin the press conference, everyone looked to *me* to tell them what to do and where to go. No one was making a move unless I said so.

I remember feeling very powerful that night. This is when I learned that no matter what the event is and how much security is present, there is a need for someone to be in charge and know what's going on – and most often, that someone is the assistant.

"I want to be a personal assistant. What salary can I expect? What skills will I need?" Such easy questions to ask, but difficult ones to answer meaningfully.

The simple answer is...it all depends. Have you any relevant experience? Do you have, for example, in-depth knowledge of arranging travel and would that be, at one end of the spectrum, getting the best cut-price airline tickets or, at the other end, organizing a Gulfstream G-5? What will the celebrity need? Someone to ease the pain of day-to-day life, ordering lunch, waiting for the plumber to arrive?

Or, if celebrity life is a couple of notches up from the rest of us— reading film scripts, talking to financial advisers, getting the Modigliani insured, dealing with The White House FBI Security team?

The salary can therefore be entry-level ($35K/year) and it might not have medical benefits. But it could also be into six figures ($120K) with full benefits, bonus and all sorts of attractive perks.

As for the skills...the more the better. MSWord and Excel are more or less mandatory. Common sense - huge. Service mentality – you want to be an assistant. It sounds like such a self-evident statement, but can't be stressed enough. And if you don't have a drop-dead Rolodex, have it as a Life Goal to build one up."

Margaret Kennedy, Recruitment Consultant based in New York

CHAPTER 9

LET'S GET FISCAL: SALARY AND BENEFITS

I speak regularly with many staffing professionals in New York City and around the country because of the workshops I teach for assistants. The recruiters, sometimes referred to as "headhunters," feed me current information on the job market, some of which might be surprising.

Since 9/11 and the economic meltdown of 2008, the job market for celebrity assistants and executive assistants in New York is improving. There are good jobs, but the competition for them is fierce. Recruiters report receiving up to three hundred resumes *per day*. They also continue to say that even though famous people can well afford to pay a personal assistant fairly, some celebrities feel that they shouldn't have to pay the going rate because they are famous. They feel that the assistant should feel fortunate to work for them. Sometimes they want very experienced assistants, but only want to pay entry-level salaries. NYCA and these recruiters are working together to educate and change this mindset. I think we are making progress, especially with the increased demand for more experienced, skilled people.

That said, salary and benefits vary widely depending on your employer, your responsibilities and your experience. In general, if you have very little experience, expect to be offered around $50K/yr. with no benefits. The more responsible the position, the more experience you have, and the more experience your employer desires, expect to hear salaries of $60K and up, which will most often include health benefits. The higher the salary, the more likely the employer will want to have access to you "24/7" – twenty four hours a day, seven days a week. You will carry a cell phone for instant access. Very experienced assistants can expect to be offered $75K to work a ten-hour day and receive full health benefits. Very few individual celebrities will offer health insurance, so you will have to be sure your salary can compensate for that. Celebrities may offer paid vacations but normally want you to schedule them around their schedules. In this profession, you need at least three to four weeks off a year to recharge your batteries and avoid burnout. Negotiate this before your first day on the job.

You will solidify the terms of your deal directly with your employer, one of the recruiters, or the employer's accountant, business manager, or lawyer. Very few assistants I know have been asked to sign contracts of employment due to the mutual desire to terminate or change the arrangement if needed. Many have been asked to sign *Contracts of Non-Disclosure* or *Confidentiality Agreements.* Some celebrities have their own corporations, several assistants, and other employees, in which case you are more likely to receive benefits such as health insurance and a pension plan.

If you are on the verge of being hired, ask these questions up front and be realistic and honest about what you need to make ends meet. If you are the right person to fulfill their needs, they will negotiate. Never accept the first offer and initially ask for more money than you are willing to accept. Remember, the way of the business world is to always negotiate, and I suggest you do the same.

Recruiters report that some employers have reputations for being difficult to work for, and as a result, have a hard time holding on to assistants. New assistants are then offered higher-than-normal salaries, "combat pay," to help compensate for this unfortunate reality and to motivate them to stay.

Consider this. Not every employer is a good business person or a manager of people, and sometimes he or she needs help to improve in this area. It's not logical to think that just because a person is talented in one area, that he or she is proficient in *every* area. Understanding this can be the key to working out a personalized plan for reviews, planning, and salary increases. Know that your celebrity or high-powered employer is probably as uncomfortable about discussing salary and benefits as you are.

I am often asked how to negotiate a raise in salary. This is not easy for anyone I know. Here's a scenario. A newly-famous celebrity needs an assistant *yesterday*. Important things are falling through the cracks, and both the agent and publicist are insisting an assistant be hired. At your interview, you discuss money with the celebrity's business manager, who does not really understand the scope of the work you will be performing. You settle on a starting salary of $60K/year, which is $10K less than you had in mind.

If you really want the job but get the distinct feeling that the money will not come up any higher initially, I suggest that you propose a three month review. Negotiate this point up front. That means in three months time, you will meet again and take another look at the compensation. Your goal will be to make yourself indispensable in that time. Of course, the three month review might turn into a four, five, or even six month review depending on how busy everyone is. Remember that the life of a busy celebrity is different from any other "normal" profession, and it is vital to be professional but not rigid.

I also suggest building in a yearly review so it is automatic and you are not re-inventing the wheel every time. When this time of year comes around, schedule the meeting two to three weeks ahead of time, and accompany the scheduling request with something in writing which reviews the past year's progress, especially noting any additions to your responsibilities. To have this kind of information in writing diffuses some of the emotion that sometimes comes when discussing money matters.

It has always been helpful to me to remember that this is one of the reasons celebrities pay their agents an automatic ten percent commission. Safely navigating the choppy waters of salary negotiation is a major challenge and makes everyone uncomfortable, no matter who they are. I know an assistant who actually pays a lawyer to negotiate his deals, but this is uncommon in the world of professional assistants.

Another suggestion is that once you are employed for two or more years, you might propose a plan for salary increases in two year increments, thereby needing to have this discussion/ evaluation only once every two years rather than every year. This kind of arrangement highlights that a long-term commitment is being made by both the assistant and employer.

Finally, negotiate other things besides salary. Increased vacation days, health insurance, pension plan, parking space, transportation costs, phone reimbursement, use of the vacation home, etc. – all of these things have a dollar value and help to make you, the assistant, a satisfied, hard-working, and loyal employee.

CHAPTER 10

THE INSIDE SCOOP! SECRETS TO FINDING AND KEEPING THE PERFECT ASSISTANT

This chapter was written in the hopes of speaking directly to prospective employers – celebrities and other high-powered individuals whose lives would improve greatly from working with a terrific assistant. To all the assistants reading this book, I hope this information assists you in the journey towards building a mutually rewarding and healthy relationship with your employer.

George Carlin joked – who exactly is the worst doctor? There has to be somebody who is the worst, right?

The same goes for professional assistants. Most of us are experienced and hard-working, and we strive for excellence every day. However, yes, it's also true, there are a few assistants who just don't cut it or who aren't meant for you. Here is an insider's look at how to find and keep a great assistant in the shortest amount of time.

The given is, you, our employers, are extremely busy. The bottom line – following these suggestions will pay off for you big-time.

1. ***Be clear about your needs.*** It's okay if you don't know 100% about what you need from your assistants. If she is experienced, she will help you figure it out. To get started, it is important for you to identify the Top Ten things you feel like you need your assistant to do. Write them down.

2. ***If someone else is screening resumes before you get to see either the resume or the candidate, brief that person well.*** It might be your agent, business manager, lawyer, publicist, former assistant, or your mother. Even if you think they know what kind of a person you want and need in an assistant, take the time to discuss it with your "screener." If you do this, you actually stand a chance of getting the right person.

3. ***Be clear and realistic about your expectations.*** Do you prefer a male or female? Someone who needs to travel with you all the time, some of the time or not at all? Smoker or non? Computer geek or is low-tech okay? Do you need someone 24/7 who can leave town on an hour's notice, or can a person with some personal commitments (spouse, child, plants, dog) do the job?

4. ***Be prepared to get what you pay for.*** (Please refer to Chapter 9 regarding salaries.) We all know that New York and Los Angeles and most major cities, for that matter, are expensive to live in. Being a professional assistant usually does not allow for spare time to do extra income-producing work. Be fair and even generous. Respectful compensation will translate into your assistant going above and beyond the call of duty – all day, every day. In New York, an experienced, full-time assistant is paid on average $70K/year plus benefits.

5. ***Interview your potential assistants and present realistic scenarios of your work together.*** Ask your candidates how they would, for example, handle putting together a last-

minute dinner party or what they would do to arrange theatre tickets for seven people for the hottest show on Broadway. By spending some time talking, you will get to know if you would be able to be with them day-in, day-out. You will also learn if the sounds of their voices are grating to you or if you are getting a "weird vibe." Isn't it better to find this out immediately? If possible and if time permits, bring the candidates back another day to spend a couple of hours or even a day in your work environment.

6. *__Take all personal recommendations for assistants with a grain of salt.__* Only you know if you will be compatible. In addition to personal recommendations, request resumes from New York Celebrity Assistants. Since NYCA was founded in 1996, many celebrities have found their assistants through NYCA. There is no charge for this service. (www.nycelebrityassistants.com)

7. *__Communicate regularly and listen, especially in the first few weeks.__* Okay, you've hired your new assistant. There will be a learning curve but with most good assistants, it is short. Experienced assistants expect to have to hit the ground running with very little training; but when issues come up and, of course, they will, we urge you to express yourself honestly and clearly about the problem. Most assistants will try very hard to read your mind (I'm serious), but it is not always possible. Conversely, I encourage you, especially at the beginning, to check-in with your assistant at least once a week, preferably in person but even by phone, text, or e-mail, to ask, *"How's it going? Are you okay? Any problems?"* Really listen to the answers. Taking this time at the beginning will short-circuit long-term problems. Bottom line – your assistant can't fix it if he or she truly doesn't know a problem exists.

"For an assistant/employer relationship to succeed, people have to be committed to change, to grow, to evolve. It's got to be like life! And each person is different – you cannot jam an assistant into a pigeonhole or pre-conceived idea.

You have to carve it out together. My advice would be to find someone who wants to free you from those things you do not want to do, someone you can delegate to, and trust that they are going to be able to not only handle situations, but handle them in a manner that represents you well.

Figure out what you need and be clear about why you need it."

Olympia Dukakis

8. *Behaving irrationally and unreasonably does not serve you.*
   Assistants expect high-powered employers to have high
   expectations and to be needy, demanding, opinionated
   perfectionists. Even high-maintenance. That's fine, totally
   normal, and part of the deal. What is not as easy to work
   with are irrationality and unreasonableness, "acting out"
   your stress. These qualities are tough to negotiate around,
   nearly impossible. In your frantic life, there are things that
   are simply out of your (and your assistant's) control – the
   weather, construction on the Turnpike, and your mother's
   sudden illness. Life happens, and things are going to go
   wrong despite your assistant's best efforts. I urge you to
   understand this and be judicious about when you lose your
   cool to the person who is trying to help you the most.
   That said, all professional assistants know you are going
   to lose it sometimes, and that's okay, too. We know to not
   take it personally, but repeated temper tantrums get old
   fast, especially when they're unjustified. In that case, your
   assistant might just decide you are impossible to please
   and will quit. Some celebrities have a revolving door of
   assistants. Personally, that has always struck me as much
   more work for you, a busy person, to have to repeat the
   process of hiring and training someone new, as opposed
   to working with the able assistant you painstakingly hired
   in the first place. Finally, know that it is self-serving to the
   assistant if everything goes *perfectly* for you. That's your
   assistant's goal. Always.

9. *Two heads are better than one.* Give your assistant the
   permission to speak up if she or he has a suggestion, an
   idea, or sees a problem. She or he is in a prime position to
   hear and see things that you do not. Openly encouraging
   independent thinking and creativity will bring out the best
   in your assistant and ultimately, serve your goals and needs.

10. ***Ongoing communication is key.*** Communicate with your assistant however you feel comfortable. Face-time, notes, e-mail, telephone – do whatever you must to communicate what you need, what you want, what's important, and what isn't. If you have told your assistant that the kitchen must always be stocked with blueberries and then you decide you want melons instead, please tell him or her. If the bathroom needs a paint job before the end of the month and you realize it at 2AM, write your assistant a note. I promise you, your wishes are his or her commands as long as you communicate!

11. ***Last but not least, be a nice person.*** Decency and kindness go a long way. Offer feedback regularly. As a celebrity, chances are that you receive constant feedback from your fans, your reviews, your agent, etc. Not so with your assistant. Tell your assistant about the producer who commented on the great job he or she did. Show appreciation for a job well done. Say thank you. Send flowers or have someone else send them with an appropriate note. Give a generous raise or bonus. Offer an afternoon off. Remember your assistant's birthday. Give praise when deserved. Honest, positive feedback will come back to you exponentially.

Follow these suggestions and if you are fortunate, you will end up with a terrific assistant with whom you are extremely comfortable, compatible, and trusting.

On top of all of that, he or she will fulfill your every whim making your busy life a joy, enable you to maximize your earnings, and you will also have found your biggest fan. Does it get any better?

CHAPTER 11

GLAMOUR, GLITZ AND OTHER PERKS...SOMETIMES!

*T*here is no doubt about it – being a celebrity assistant can be tremendous fun and offer many rewards, tangible and non. For me, my ten-day trip to Australia was a fabulous perk, an experience I shall never forget, and a highlight of my career.

Over the years, I have met and spoken to famous and not famous actors, politicians, musicians, and directors. All very interesting people! Whoopi Goldberg, Armistead Maupin, Isaac Stern, Sally Field, Shirley MacLaine, Gov. Michael Dukakis (MA), Gov. Thomas Kean (NJ), Sen. Bill Bradley (NJ), Edie Falco, Diane Ladd, James Earl Jones, Christopher Reeve, John Kander & Fred Ebb, Marlo Thomas, Phil Donahue, and Frank Langella, to name just a very few. A favorite memory was a short phone conversation I had with Mike Dukakis just days before it would be decided whether to impeach President Clinton or not. That felt rather extraordinary to discuss politics with a former presidential candidate.

I had my most embarrassing moment with Phyllis Diller when I ridiculously mistook her for Carol Channing. I did this right in front of Olympia who just rolled her eyes and laughed. You cannot be in this business and not blow it once in awhile. Phyllis was totally sweet and even autographed a photo for my mother. I still cringe at the memory, though.

In 2002, I accompanied Olympia to Juneau and Fairbanks, Alaska for a speaking and teaching engagement. What an extraordinary trip! We went whale watching, stood on a glacier, and drank wine in our hotel's outdoor hot tub late at night. Equally if not more memorable, however, were our talks on the airplane, ordering room service, analyzing movies together, and my getting to watch Olympia teach acting.

I attended the Sundance Film Festival in Utah with Olympia when I was seven months pregnant. *"Moonstruck"* was going to open the Festival and Olympia was introducing the film. At the last minute, her husband Louis found out his soap opera would not give him the days off. I volunteered to accompany Olympia in Louis' place and was so excited when she said, *"Great!"* It was my first time to travel with Olympia. We made quite a pair in the ice and snow in January, 1988. Olympia was sure I was going to give birth in a snowdrift.

To top things off, I happen to be a Robert Redford fan, but I didn't get up the nerve to ask to be introduced to him until it was too late – he had left the grounds on the day we were flying out. The head of the festival asked me why I didn't ask sooner, that it absolutely could have been arranged. I am not terribly star-struck after all these years in the business, but I admit I have kicked myself ever since over that one. Life lesson – Take advantage of the unique opportunities that come your way. Sometimes you only get one chance.

In Sydney, Australia, I got my one chance to see the famous Opera House before we flew out. Despite horrendous jet lag, I woke up at 6AM and took a run through the Botanical Gardens, rounded a corner, and there it was! Majestic and shining in the early morning sun. It took my breath away and I started to cry at its simple beauty.

I'm glad I took my chance.

When we travel, I usually fly first-class with Olympia. Occasionally but not often, I'm in coach and she is up front. Even if this is the case initially, sometimes the airline personnel will make a change if there is room in first-class. An airport greeter can also be invaluable in this situation. The lesson here is – the world loves to help celebrities whenever possible, and the assistant is often the recipient of this "overflow" of generosity. We stay at four and five star hotels, often in the Presidential Suite if there is one, and travel by limousine. For those interested in these kinds of details, Olympia's preference is an understated black Town Car, not a stretch limo, and definitely *not* white.

It is a given that the world loves to do favors for celebrities. Celebrities get special treatment all the time in the form of tickets, clothes, gifts, beauty products, cruises – you name it. It is said that movie stars are American "royalty" and are treated accordingly. Because the gift-givers are usually communicating a great deal with the assistant, it is very common for the assistant to be the recipient of some of these gifts as well.

I remember one time when Olympia was sent about ten designer dresses to consider wearing for a special event. Anyone who has ever watched the Oscars or any awards show knows that fashion designers crave celebrities to wear their clothes. The deal was that she could have whatever she wanted at a steep discount. She didn't end up liking anything. But I did. I now own a great dress at a fabulous price.

One memorable trip was when Olympia and I went to London for three days to choose an apartment for her while she did a play there. We went on to Prague where she finished shooting the miniseries "*Joan of Arc*" with Peter Strauss and Leelee Sobieski. In Prague, our accommodations were in a real, honest-to-goodness castle converted into a hotel. One morning it was snowing on our castle. Amazing, indelible, unforgettable images.

Another great perk I enjoyed was during the few years that Olympia owned two villas on the island of St. Maarten. Olympia generously offered to let me take my family there on vacation, which was as fantastic as it sounds. (If you like beach vacations, this island has it all, in my opinion.)

Over the years, I have flown in several private planes with Olympia, but my favorite memory is of the first time. Olympia and I were getting settled in the back of an eight-seater plane when the pilot politely looked back at us and said, "*Ladies, can we leave now?*" We both burst out laughing, struck by the idea that no pilot had ever before asked for our permission to take off.

One of my most glamorous experiences was attending the People's Choice Awards with Olympia in 1989 when she accepted the award on behalf of the cast of "*Steel Magnolias.*" We were sitting at the front and center table with Jack Nicholson and Michael Keaton, who were accepting for "*Batman*" that year; Edward James Olmos, who was next to me; and an actress I had always wanted to meet, Meryl Streep, who was with her husband, Don Gummer. Place cards for Jane Fonda and Raquel Welch were on the table, but they never showed up. I loved the fact that from across the table, I could tell that Jack Nicholson, sunglasses and all, was trying to figure out who *I* was! Oh, and remember that designer dress I bought? I wore it at this event.

At a commercial break, I took my chance to talk to Meryl Streep, a fellow New Jerseyan, and tell her I had seen her off-Broadway in two one-act plays when I was a student at Rutgers University, and that when I wrote my review, it was all about her performance. Meryl's pleased comment, "*Hardly anyone talks to me about having seen me onstage.*"

I enjoyed meeting her. It was a magical night, and we had a great time. I had never seen so many celebrities in person in one place before. It was a bit overwhelming, but great fun. The more of these types of events you attend, the less strange they seem.

Another memorable night was when I found myself at a quiet, post-Broadway show dinner opposite Whoopi Goldberg and some other actors with Olympia. It was very normal but surreal at the same time. I had the chance to tell Whoopi that my ten-year old son had seen her film "*Corrina, Corrina*" at least a dozen times and her response was, "*Oh, I'm so sorry!*" We laughed and chatted about raising kids.

I did an informal poll of some of my colleagues about some of the most glamorous and cool perks they have received as celebrity assistants. Here goes. Richard Dreyfuss' assistant of twenty-two years, Audrey Bamber, received a Mercedes convertible which she named Humphrey. Maury Povich gave his assistant a trip to Colorado each year for her birthday. Maury's assistant also told me that when Jerry Seinfeld was doing a show in Atlantic City, Maury hired a limo and sent the assistant and four others to see the show and meet Jerry backstage. One assistant received a Labrador puppy as a gift and was asked to bring him to work with her so the dog could play with her employer's Lab.

Another assistant gets to drive her employer's Jaguar and Mercedes whenever she likes and was gifted with a membership to a dating service. Another was flown to her employer's wedding in Florence, Italy. How about a Christmas gift of a wine cellar starter kit – two antique wine decanters and $20,000 worth of fine wine? One assistant received a cash Christmas bonus of $4000 and another was given her honeymoon in Paris as a wedding present. Sometimes these perks can be mixed blessings – I was reminded that one assistant travels by yacht with his employer but is literally on the job 24/7. Another assistant organized and accompanied the celebrity's family on their vacation to DisneyWorld but also ended up working most of the time to make sure everything went off without a hitch. He had a great suite but didn't get to go on any rides.

Very usual perks are access to front and center "house" seats for popular shows, concerts and sporting events and access to frequent flyer miles. You often receive hand-me-downs – gifts your employer doesn't need or want. These can be truly awesome. My favorite sweatshirt came from the "*Mr. Holland's Opus*" shoot complete with the John Lennon lyric, "Life is what happens when you are busy making other plans."

Time for a reality check, though. The not-so-glamorous parts of the work are how you spend the majority of the time. That's a fact for me and for all of the other assistants I know. *The events I've shared in this chapter occurred over a twenty-two year period.*

An assistant needs to know that he or she might be invited to a star-studded party, but could end up working part or maybe all of the night. This has happened to me. I enjoy my work very much and don't need it to be glamorous most of the time. I like making things happen behind the scenes, and that's a good attitude to have if you are going to succeed in this work. My desk is my headquarters; and armed with my two-line phone, computer, modem, scanner, and fax machine, I can make a lot of things happen. Nobody is around to watch. I can talk to a hundred people in a day via phone, fax and e-mail and not leave my office. The bottom line – working as a celebrity assistant is definitely not glamorous most of the time.

This is what Max Szadek, former assistant to the late Luther Vandross, had to say. *"Here's the bad side. World tours overlap with major holidays, which means you are never home for the holidays. Friends and family always stop understanding after the first year. Traveling means you are not only packing for yourself but someone else and also unpacking for someone else. A lot of the time, you live on your employer's schedule, especially on the road. People associate you with your employer, so your life can be seen as a reflection of theirs, which may or may not be true."*

Dealing with difficult people with big egos can be emotionally draining. Working long hours for several days or weeks straight on a tough project can be satisfying but also hard on your body and spirit. Burnout is a big risk factor in our work. It's a fact that no one can sustain an overly extended period of relentless stress and activity. If you are working for a reasonable person, it makes sense to take an extra day or two off after a particularly long project has been accomplished.

Two common downsides of this work are having to handle

intrusive personal questions about your employer and being asked special favors because of your access. I know some assistants who lie to strangers about what they do for a living in order to avoid the inevitable questions borne of the curiosity which surrounds their celebrity employer. Assistants also understand that they need to be watchful for people who have hidden agendas, and are, in effect, trying to manipulate their way to the employer through the assistant.

Sometimes the job involves doing tasks that can be downright humdrum and menial – picking up prescriptions, taking the dog to the vet, cleaning up after the dog, handling dry cleaning, returning books to the library. I've done them all, as have my colleagues. But this is definitely a "do what it takes" kind of job. You do it and it's over, and you move on to the next thing.

It's never boring and no two days are ever the same. I've heard this from dozens of assistants as the main thing they love about the work. I think it is very telling about the kind of people who are drawn to this work. We all love variety!

Here's my idea of a satisfying time. When Olympia and Louis were out of town for several weeks doing a play, I assigned myself to re-organize every closet and file drawer, and then to re-organize every book, video and CD. In the end, it serves me to know where everything is. Sincerely gratifying. How about you?

This next point is very important. Don't expect to be thanked profusely, even when you pull off miracles. It's not necessarily that your employer is not grateful; it's usually that life is moving so fast, we move on to the next crisis or next event. There isn't a lot of time to dwell on successes…or failures. This took me awhile to get used to, but it is the norm in our profession. So much for the non-glamorous. In my opinion, it's all in your attitude. It also helps a lot if you like who you are working for!

"A sex symbol becomes a thing. I hate being a thing."
Marilyn Monroe

*"Celebrity was a long time in coming.
It will go away. Everything goes away."*
Carol Burnett

CHAPTER 12

CELEBRITY ASSISTING: THE DARK SIDE

*W*ebster's Dictionary defines ***Abuse***: (verb) To use wrongly, misuse, to hurt by treating badly.

I would be remiss if I did not address the issue of abuse in our profession in this book.

I am referring to verbal abuse, mental abuse, physical abuse, sexual abuse, and drug and alcohol abuse. My goal is not to sugarcoat, but to present a balanced view of a complicated and difficult subject. Yes, abuse does exist – celebrities abusing their assistants and assistants abusing their celebrity employers. Yes, some relationships are toxic and play out in dramatic ways. The not-so-sexy or publicized fact is that most celebrities value their assistants and treat them well.

The difference is that we hear about abuse more in our profession because it involves celebrities, and the media is only too happy to sensationalize and capitalize on people, especially famous ones, behaving badly and being "difficult." Also, much like life, situations are often shades of gray – not simple, not black and white.

A celebrity and his or her assistant both have built-in issues which cause pressure and anxiety, and can lead to abuse. Fame, money, and status can be frightening, even terrifying, for a celebrity. That fear can cause a person to behave in extreme ways towards his or her assistant. The assistant's issues have to do with the lack of definition in the job description since it is a "do what it takes" position. This lack of definition can be crazy-making and agitating for the assistant. The boundary between being an employee and a friend gets blurred very easily and can cause confusion and disappointment. Is the friendship real or not? Furthermore, an assistant should not be dependent on the employer to define self-worth or feeling of well-being, but many assistants fall into this trap because of the power and charisma of the employer.

A resentful assistant might choose to be abusive in the form of intentionally letting things fall through the cracks or even stealing from the employer.

The truth is we *all* have bad days – employers and assistants alike. Days when you just don't want to be there or do your best. Days when you don't feel well or when you are cranky because you had an argument with your brother. Days when you feel like you want to strangle the next person who crosses your path! Life happens.

That said…you've read in the tabloids and seen on television and in films the sensational stories of lawsuits, sexy nannies turned assistants, stun guns, sexual harassment of both men and women, and celebrities who clobber their assistants with telephones. In 2003, E-Entertainment TV produced a one-hour show called *"Revenge of the Celebrity Assistants,"* which highlighted the darker side of this profession, complete with all the pending lawsuits and counter-suits between celebrity employers and their former assistants.

My problem with this show and other coverage by the media about celebrity assistants is how unbalanced and sensational the depictions are. Of course, the shows do it for ratings since dysfunctional and abusive relationships attract more attention than healthy ones. They make it seem as if all celebrity/assistant relationships are filled with high drama, violence, and emotional upheaval every day. It's just not like that. My fondest wish is that they would at least show the viewer some contrasting relationships – examples of close working relationships which are healthy and functioning well, featuring big-name stars. Without the contrast, the perception out in the world of the celebrity assistant is demeaned, skewed, and inaccurate.

Psychology Today (Mary Loftus, "The Other Side of Fame," June 1995) conducted a survey among celebrities asking their primary sources of stress. The top ten were:

- the celebrity press
- critics
- threatening letters/calls
- the lack of privacy
- the constant monitoring of their lives
- worry about career plunges
- stalkers
- lack of security
- curious fans
- worries about their children's lives being disrupted

"The celebrities' reactions to this stress were: depression, loss of sleep, crying over nothing, bad moods, lack of concentration, stomach problems, paranoia, overspending, and lack of trust. With a support staff comes a payroll, employees and associates who depend on the celebrity for their own livelihood. That puts a celebrity under constant pressure to be famous."

The article continues – *"Solutions to stress included talking to friends or therapists, beefing up security, having friends outside the business, protecting their kids, laughing as much as possible, and finding faith."*

This information helps us understand why the following sometimes occurs, but it most certainly does not excuse it.

- **_Verbal abuse._** Your employer screams and yells, uses profanity, and generally speaks in a demeaning and disrespectful way. Also commonplace is verbal abuse from others involved in the lives of your employer. When this occurs, I encourage assistants to discuss this calmly and directly with their employers. Most employers feel that they need and want to know when their assistants are being treated badly. Furthermore, the assistants need to understand how their employers want them to deal with these situations.

There are assistants who verbally abuse others in the name of the employer. Some conclude that the assistant wants to *be* the employer. This is a dangerous and complex dynamic which can create animosity and tension among everyone involved.

- *Mental abuse.* Vindictive behavior, mean-spiritedness, promises not kept, and irrationality are the characteristics of mental abuse. One colleague shared that she would arrive for work and her employer would say that he "didn't feel like working" and told her to go home. She would not get paid for that day. Another colleague related that he was often asked to lie for his employer and it made him uncomfortable. Still another assistant was replaced in her position while she was still working for the employer. The uncomfortable situation caused the assistant to quit as opposed to being fired.

  This area of abuse can be very subtle. The test of severity is usually found in how often the situations occur.

- *Physical abuse.* You are physically assaulted in some way. This is the most clear-cut example of abuse and completely unacceptable under all circumstances. Your choices include filing charges and/or quitting your job, or attempting to work out the problem with your employer. The worst thing would be to do nothing at all. As with any abuse, if it happened once, it could happen again. For the record, I don't personally know any assistants who have been in this situation.

- ***Sexual abuse.*** This area of abuse might be the grayest of them all. It can be subtle or overt, but sexual nonetheless. One example involves a female assistant to an actor. She would arrive at her employer's home for a meeting, and he would sometimes greet her naked and conduct the meeting as if nothing was unusual. She had trouble expressing her discomfort and eventually quit.

  I don't know anyone – woman or man – who has not had to deal with sexual harassment in one form or another. This can mean dealing with sexual jokes, explicit sexual advances or innuendoes, blunt comments about parts of our bodies or our clothing. Whatever it is, it is extremely tricky to decide if it is "abuse" and when it is time to take any action such as:

  A.   laughing it off
  B.   getting furious, yet saying nothing
  C.   confronting the offender
  D.   pressing charges

  Sometimes the boundary between what is funny and what is hurtful is very difficult to define.

- ***Drug and alcohol abuse.*** Your employer might try to involve you in some way in his or her own addiction(s). Assistants also try to manage and work through their own addictions. The following is an excerpt about drug abuse from the same *Psychology Today* article.

  "For celebrities, the pressure is always on to turn in a perfect performance, to be better than before, to constantly hit the mark. At the same time, artists tend to be sensitive souls, in touch with naked emotions they mine for our perusal. Artists are the lenses

through which life is transmitted. They show us what we think and feel in a way that is profound, intense and highly emotional. They experience life more clearly than the rest of us. Drugs are a way to mute these feelings, which threaten to overwhelm. And with the riches that accompany their fame, drugs are an escape-route celebrities can afford – at least for awhile. The list of celebrity deaths from drugs is long, and continually updated – Elvis Presley, Judy Garland, Marilyn Monroe, Jim Morrison, Janis Joplin, John Belushi, and River Phoenix."

Over my years of working, I can report that my skin has thickened quite a bit from dealing with difficult people. For example, I remember a situation early in my career feeling defenseless and horrified when a theatre director was convinced I had lied to him, and, of course, I hadn't. He made a scene in front of many people and it was very embarrassing. Nothing I said made any difference at all to him. Fortunately, my employer backed me up in front of everyone. It's a terrible feeling to be looking at the same situation, and you see it as a white rabbit and the other person sees it as a pink elephant! How can you possibly find common ground? It takes courage to walk back into the room and continue working with such a person, but you don't always have a choice. I learned quite a lot through these kinds of tests.

Here are a few other things I've learned the hard way about human nature which help me in my work.

- The first thing out of someone's mouth is the most important thing to him or her. And if he or she repeats it, it is a red flag yelling "Pay attention!"
- Everyone has an agenda, including you. This is not bad, just a good thing to keep in mind as you move through situations.
- If someone is upset, it's usually about him or her, not

you. Don't assume you are the problem. Ask. Simply ask, "*What's wrong? What can I do to help?*" I believe those are eight of the most useful words in our work.

- A psychologist helped me with this one – People do things that serve them. That applies to behavior, work, hobbies, etc. So if a person seems to create chaos everywhere he or she goes, that behavior serves him or her in some way.
- Assume that there is always something that you don't know about any given situation, and it might very well be these unknowns that control the outcome.
- Selective hearing and selective memory are very real. People often hear what they want to hear and remember only what they want to remember because it serves them. Understanding this can help you. Tip: keep great records.
- Denial is one of the most powerful forces of human nature. Example: If someone does not want to acknowledge a drug problem, the chances of you convincing him or her is very small.

Abuse is about *power*, power to control another human being. The best advice I can give you is to trust your instincts. Only you know if you are being asked to do something which is against your better judgment, illegal, or that makes you feel uncomfortable. It is true that some famous people think they are so powerful that they are above it all and don't think they should ever hear the word "no."

It is a well known fact that celebrities can get away with reprehensible behavior simply because they are celebrities.

Bottom line – You have a choice. You are an employee and have rights, especially the right to say "no." You also have the right to leave if a situation seems beyond your control. Unfortunately, these abusive situations do exist as much as we would like them not to, but both the assistant and employer have an opportunity to set boundaries and ground rules starting at the first interview. Be sensitive to what you are being told is your job description, and be sure to do your Internet research homework on your prospective employer.

I shall end this chapter about the darker side of our business with an article I wrote which appeared in OfficePro magazine (March, 2008 issue) published by the International Association of Administrative Professionals.

officePRO

How to Stand Up For Yourself Without Losing Your Job
Bonnie Low-Kramen
March, 2008

The country was stunned on October 30th, 2007 by the murder of celebrity realtor Linda Stein allegedly by her personal assistant in New York City. Ms. Stein was beaten to death. The media reports that the assistant was provoked by having marijuana smoke blown in her face repeatedly, being "yelled at all the time," and being hit with a piece of yoga equipment. How could this have happened? And more importantly, how could it have been avoided?

"*The Devil Wears Prada*" boss from hell comes to life? Life imitating art, only worse?

Every administrative professional understands and relates to being disrespected and abused in the workplace. It is the proverbial "elephant in the room." Everyone knows it's there but no one wants to talk about it or deal with it.

But we *are* dealing with it – with silent rage, with passive-aggressive acts such as calling in sick when we aren't really sick and by acting out our anger on everyone, anyone other than the abuser. The targets of this unexpressed anger can include our co-workers, spouse, children, or the dog. The cycle of abuse continues in this way.

The future of our profession is at stake. It's not easy, but let's do it anyway; take on the elephant, that is.

Administrative professionals possess the power to find solutions to this problem. We need not be victims unless we choose to be. We are in a unique position because of the very nature of the work we do "in support of" our employers. However, at its most basic level, abusive behavior has no place in the workplace, is wrong and we need to participate in the solutions.

The givens: 95% of the 4.1 million administrative professionals in America are women. Women are socialized as young girls to not assert or be confrontational. To assert and confront are nearly impossible assignments for many women. Just ask. What you'll literally hear is, "*I would do anything to not have to confront someone.*" The reason for this is because our societal training is so deeply rooted.

The good news is the word "nearly." Women in the workplace, especially ones who have been promoted into management, have learned the ways to positively confront people. The results? They get what they want and need and instead of making people angry, everyone is calmer because of the clarity which comes as a bi-product of honest communication.

Respect from others in the workplace begins with self-respect.

<u>**Ways to Garner Respect**</u>:

1. Begin with your cover letter and resume. These materials are your first contact with the workplace. Make clear that being an administrative professional is your "career" rather than your "job." Include a Professional Objective. The words you choose matter in order to communicate your professionalism, your desire to seek excellence and the seriousness with which you view your role.

Take great care with these documents because they paint a picture of who you are and offer a first impression before you even get a chance to walk through the door. No typos, no grammatical errors. Letter-perfect materials are the first step to achieving respect.

2. E-mail communications. All e-mails to managers and co-workers should be professionally written. You will be judged on every one. Can't you tell so much about someone you've never met face-to-face by how they communicate in e-mail?

3. The interview(s). Your prospective employer's HR staff was impressed enough by your materials to bring you in for an interview. You will be evaluated by how you dress and conduct yourself. Self-respect is evidenced by the way you speak, what you say and how you say it. Practice. Prepare a story for everything on your resume. These stories reveal your values and what matters to you.

Self-respect is about viewing yourself as the solution to someone else's problem and presenting yourself as such. You bring experience, skills, and intelligence to the table and you get to evaluate whether their assignment is a good match for your talents and vice versa.

Interview them as much as they are interviewing you. Ask questions such as: *Why did the last assistant leave? Is this a non-smoking office? Will I be on-call 24/7? Is any travel involved? How are expenses reimbursed?* Asking these questions will help you to better evaluate the position and at the same time, communicate self respect.

You will probably have more than one interview. Handle each one as a top priority and be prepared with stories which communicate the ways in which you do your best work. Say things like, "*I enjoy being part of a team where the primary agenda is getting the job done. I have a hard time in an environment where there is screaming and gossip.*" See the reaction.

4. Your manager. You have opportunities from your very first interaction with him or her to command respect. It is possible to command respect without being abrasive or unpleasant. In fact, it works better to be simple, honest, pleasant and direct. Use humor. Kiddingly say, "*You're not a screamer, are you?*"

He or she will ask you about former situations which will help you garner respect. Be honest and state the ways in which you work well such as; *I am very self-motivated. If you give me access to you and let me know what you want the end result to be, I'll run with it.* Or - *How do you prefer we communicate on a daily basis? How about when we are on deadline and in a crunch? Do you prefer some other way in those situations?* These discussions set the groundwork for reasonable expectations and mutual respect.

5. Day to day behavior. Respect is garnered by taking initiative and being a part of the solution, not the problem. Offer a suggestion or an idea about something you have observed or know is a burning issue. If you are going to raise an issue, be prepared with one or more possible solutions. Present this to your manager in writing or verbally. Setting a high standard for you garners respect from co-workers and managers. Make others look good and it will come back to you. Be generous with praise, credit, information and resources. Helping others even when it is not your job garners respect as does being the "go-to" person in a crunch.

6. When abuses occur. As unpleasant as this is, handle it immediately. Don't assume it is an isolated incident. In general, if abuse happens once, it will probably happen again.

<u>Verbal Abuse</u> – Your manager using profanity, is screaming, or is otherwise demeaning towards you.

<u>Response Options</u>: Calmly get up and say, "*I cannot work with you if you are screaming. I'll be at my desk.*" Or - "*I know you are stressed out, but you cannot speak to me in that way.*" Then leave the room or the space for a few minutes. You are clarifying your limits and boundaries in this way. Do you risk being fired? Of course, but it's worth the risk if you are a valuable assistant. Give your manager a chance to cool off and see what happens.

<u>Sexual Harassment</u> – This can be subtle or overt, but it is very common. Harassment can range from seemingly innocent comments about the way you look in that outfit to blatant demands for sex.

<u>Response Options</u>: Respect comes from confronting the offender by directly saying, "*Your behavior is inappropriate and unacceptable to me. I'm going to give you the benefit of the doubt that you didn't know how I would respond. However, that will be the last time. If it happens again, I will report you. Any questions?*" Wait for an answer and walk away.

<u>Physical Abuse</u> – Your manager or a co-worker assaults you in some way.

<u>Response Options</u>: Yell, run and call security or the police.

Other methods of dealing with abusive language and behavior are to write a note expressing your feelings, to ask a peer of your supervisor to speak to him or her on your behalf, or to raise the issue with the HR staff. Resigning and/or pressing charges is always an option, albeit a wholly unpleasant, time-consuming, emotionally draining and potentially expensive one.

Abusive behavior is rooted in having power and wielding that power in a disrespectful way. Administrative professionals possess great power to affect the workplace and their own experience in a positive way by standing up for what is right and commanding respect. Not only will you not lose your job, you will probably end up being promoted.

It could be murder to wait.

"Networking is essential. If it had not been for NYCA (New York Celebrity Assistants), I would not have had the opportunity to be introduced to the position I am in today – which is the most incredible, amazing experience of my life!"
Libby Moore, Chief of Staff,
Personal Assistant to Oprah Winfrey

CHAPTER 13

HOW DO YOU GET THE JOB?

*A*h, the burning question! Here are the answers in order of importance.

- Networking
- Skills & Personality
- Timing
- Networking
- Great cover letter & resume
- Great interview(s)
- Networking
- Good references
- Luck
- Networking

Did you notice "**_Networking_**?" Networking is the process of getting to know your colleagues – their areas of expertise, *their* contacts and vice versa. They get to know you and everyone uses that information in all kinds of ways, certainly for job searches. We live in a "who-you-know" world; and in the business of job searching, it is absolutely essential to network effectively and constantly – to figure out who can help you get those theatre tickets or get the phone number of so-and-so. I add to my Rolodex/computer almost daily with names, numbers, and e-mail addresses of people who I think might be helpful to me someday, and I know they do the same with me.

Networking – using your connections to maximum effect is a key way of helping you find work as an assistant to a celebrity or any high-powered person.

You must exploit (in the best sense of this word) every contact you possess and tell everyone you know that this is the work you desire. Even if you know that a particular person cannot directly help you find a job, perhaps that person knows someone else who can help you. People love to talk, so get the word out there!

So, how will you find the job you want? The truth is, there is no simple answer. You must get yourself in a "celebrity environment" with people who regularly deal with celebrities. If you love pop music and know a great deal about it, you might want to target work with a music company. If you are a fashion maven, target design houses or modeling agencies. If you love film, consider starting as an assistant at a top talent agency like William Morris Endeavor, or a public relations firm like PMK, or a film company like Miramax. These are great places to gain experience and to hear about jobs with individual celebrities. Many entertainment companies list positions on the website www.showbizjobs.com.

In the Preface, I described how I came to work for Olympia Dukakis, how I had a front-row seat for her rising fame since I began working with Olympia more than a year before she made the film "*Moonstruck.*" My story is about timing, luck, and being in the right place at the right time. But my story is also about having an extremely compatible background for Olympia (my college majors of English and Theatre) and my genuine love for and interest in the arts in general, drama in particular. Taking it a step further – we've been together for all these years because our personalities and chemistry are right. We both feel very fortunate about that. We're good roommates – neither of us smokes, we both like it really warm in the apartment, we're both neat freaks, and we both like to throw away stuff we don't need. Things like that. And, yes, we have become friends and do socialize. We go out to dinner several times a year, and the whole Dukakis/Zorich family attended my son's Bar Mitzvah; but make no mistake, I know our business relationship is first and foremost.

After getting to know many other assistants over the past few years, I can tell you that no two stories are the same – they truly run the gamut. The assistant to a world-renowned violinist found his job at a cocktail party. The assistant-to-be's friend was talking to another friend who worked for the artist's manager about the maestro needing an assistant. The friends talked, a few interviews took place, and he got the job. This story is about who you know, taking initiative, and luck. This assistant's background was also extremely compatible with the artist's because of his interest in and knowledge of classical music. The assistant to the best-selling author, James Patterson, came to interview for a job at a publishing company as the assistant to the Editor-in-Chief; but upon arrival she learned that, based on her resume, they wanted her to interview for another job as the assistant to one of their authors (Mr. Patterson).

To writers they say, write what you know. To aspiring celebrity assistants, I say, target a celebrity employer in a field you enjoy and are knowledgeable about. Think of yourself as the perfect solution to another person's problem. You will be filling a need.

Sometimes, a celebrity is desperate for an assistant and will reach out for the closest, trusted person. This desperation stems from the intense pressure celebrities are under; and it can result in knee-jerk, and sometimes unhappy, decisions. On Broadway and on film sets, this has often resulted in dressers and drivers getting promoted. I know of one celebrity who hired the man who was doing her fan mail to be her new assistant. None of the people I have just told you about had ever before been an assistant to a celebrity.

Rarely does a celebrity put an ad for an assistant in the classified section. Celebrities look to the people they trust – some hire family members or personal friends. The trust factor is very important. Very often, the issue becomes that while the celebrity can trust family and friends most easily, those people don't necessarily possess the myriad of other skills required for this demanding job. That issue has created the need for experienced celebrity assistants. More often, celebrities will seek help from their agents, managers, publicists or lawyers to find a professional assistant.

Also, there are several employment agencies that screen carefully and have job listings for celebrities and/or entertainment companies. In New York, celebrities and their representatives have turned to New York Celebrity Assistants for help.

Another option is to contact Broadway producers like the Shubert Organization and the Nederlander Organization. Sometimes when they bring a show into New York from out of town, a star needs a temporary assistant. If you have a celebrity in mind for whom you think you want to work, you can do your research, find his or her agent or manager, and make contact. The easiest way to find contact information for actors is to call the Actors Equity Association or the Screen Actors Guild. Believe it or not, this tactic of directly contacting a specific celebrity has worked. This truly is the case of being in the right place at the right time.

If you have no experience at all and you can afford it, you might consider an internship at one of the networks or a radio station in order to get your foot in the door and be in the celebrity environment. Understand that internships pay very little, if anything at all, and some are only available to college students. Still, it is an option for some. Once you are in the celebrity environment, it will be much easier to find work with an individual celebrity. Once you have a job with a celebrity, it is easier to find more work because of your expanded experience.

Education matters. Many of my colleagues hold one college degree and a few have more than one. An MBA is especially desirable. Others have gone back to school for additional computer training on the newer software products and also for public speaking and foreign languages. Your desire and willingness to improve your skills can be a factor in being chosen for a position.

So, how you get a job as a celebrity assistant can be complicated and more than a one-step process. It will be very much about networking, taking initiative, being creative, timing, and luck. It will equally be about evaluating your own skills and interests, doing your homework, and creating a strategy for getting a job with a celebrity employer with whom you will be compatible.

I know several celebrities who have gone through many assistants. It's been a revolving door because for whatever reason, they were not compatible. I know assistants who have used their positions as stepping stones to other jobs in the entertainment business or who have taken their skills and experience out of the profession altogether. There is a high burnout rate for assistants because of the intense nature of the work. Some assistants might only last a year or two. For all of these reasons, there can be a big turnover in jobs. If you are in the right place at the right time, you can capitalize on that and fill a need.

COVER LETTER AND RESUME

Your cover letter should be professional yet tailored for that particular celebrity if you know with whom you are interviewing. You don't always know on the first round of screening. If you know who it is, do your homework on the celebrity, which is very easy to do on the Internet. Find out whatever you can about him or her and include a fact or two in your letter. State why you believe you should be considered for the position based on your background and what you know. It is important that you not come across as starstruck or overly impressed by fame. Yet, you need to find a way to *make it personal.* Strive to make an authentic connection. Celebrities want and need to be normal people in their relationships with their assistants.

The look and content of your resume is critical. Most often, your first contact with any celebrity will be in writing via faxed or downloaded cover letter and resume sent to the celebrity's agent, manager, or employment agency. Only after they have reviewed these materials will you be called in for an interview.

Important Note: Do not send your resume to a celebrity's home mailing address unless you have been given express permission to do so. This may be viewed as an invasion of privacy.

The look of your letter and resume say a great deal about you, especially how computer literate and how detail-oriented you are. As with all business correspondence, there should be no spelling or grammatical errors. Any resumes with more than one spelling or grammatical error usually end up in the recycle bin. Have someone knowledgeable proofread your work because the spell-check and grammar features on computers are not foolproof.

Regarding the "look" of your resume – Your resume should be easy on the eye – literally, easy to read. This means it should not be too dense and the font should be no smaller than eleven point. Help the reader by using enough white space around your content. If the reader has to work too hard to read your resume or has to struggle to understand who you are, those pages will be discarded. If you are presenting a "hard copy" of your resume, use excellent quality, heavy paper of white, gray or off-white color only.

Regarding the content – This is where the resume for a position as a personal assistant varies from any other kind of resume. In addition to your work history, you should highlight all skills and hobbies you enjoy doing. For example, one of my colleagues enjoys flower arranging so he included it on his resume. He worked for a Broadway star and was paid additional money to do flower arranging. Same situation for another colleague of mine who did catering before she began working for a TV star. Now she caters dinners for her employer in addition to being an assistant. In our work, it matters if you can drive a car, speak a foreign language, have extensive experience in international travel, train dogs, plan parties, have taken a class in CPR and first-aid, do bookkeeping or publicity, etc. Do *not* include any skills that you have no interest in doing in this job. This part of your resume can make the difference between hiring you or another candidate. Including that you are a dog-lover on your resume may spark an entire conversation about the celebrity's pets. Ideally, a resume should paint a picture of who you are and what your experience is, as well as some clues to reveal your personality.

I believe in not wasting anyone's time. I know it is not required that you reveal your age or whether you are married or have children, but I think these facts are a real time-saver when considering someone as a celebrity assistant. I recommend including them on your resume. This information is going to matter, just like whether you are a cigarette smoker or are an Aries. (See Sample Resume, Pg. 132)

I've read hundreds of cover letters and resumes and most are not specific enough. These important documents should create a clear, living, breathing picture of the experience, education, gender, age, skills and interests of the candidate. This impersonal electronic "introduction" via download should answer the question for the reader – How can (<u>candidate's name</u>) be the solution to my staffing problem?

<u>Regarding your interview</u> – Your appearance matters a great deal. Be logical. If you are interviewing with a rock star, you don't want to show up in a corporate business suit. In this situation, it is okay to dress a bit funky. By all means, dress in a way that you feel comfortable because when you are interviewing to be a celebrity assistant, it is *personal.* You will be evaluated on every basis – your appearance, the way you express yourself, your resume and your cover letter. You will be an extension of your celebrity if you are hired, therefore, you will need to look the part. One celebrity dismissed a prospective assistant because he did not like her "karma." Another felt really comfortable

with the candidate, especially after learning her astrological sign.

__*Advice from the recruiters*__ – Don't go overboard with perfume/cologne, jewelry, or make-up. Express your personal style in moderation. It's a balance worth attempting. Keep in mind that you want the interview to be about you and what you can do for the employer, not about your overwhelming fragrance or stiletto heels.

__*True Story*__ – Here's one story of a successful personal connection at the interview. A prospective assistant had a first interview with a TV star on the day after the actress was nominated for an Emmy Award. The interview was at 7:30AM (the only time the actress had), so the candidate decided to buy the newspapers with the Emmy news and arrive with them as a little congratulations gift. The gesture was thoughtful, helpful, and showed that the prospective assistant knew what was going on in the celebrity's life – just the thing a celebrity assistant would do. She got the job on the spot.

Because this work is so personal, be sure you interview your prospective employer as much as he or she is interviewing you. Ask questions such as: "*Why did the last assistant leave?*" "*What's the most important thing to you about what our relationship should be?*" Share personal information. "*I am allergic to smoke – is the office a smoke-free environment?*" "*I try to attend church each week. Will this job require me to work on Sunday?*" It is not uncommon for first interviews to be conducted by a celebrity's agent or manager. Once you pass that screening, you are sent to the celebrity for an interview.

Be yourself. Don't be afraid to reveal who you are because potential employers need something solid to hold onto and remember you by. You actually have an advantage at interviews because you know more about them than they know about you. Give them a reason to hire you over someone else. Listen to what you are hearing about their problems and specifically explain how you would fill that need and solve those issues. Be honest about your skills and work history. For every skill or responsibility listed on your resume, have a story to accompany it so you are ready when you are asked a question.

What I hear from the recruiters is that enthusiasm, a willingness to learn, and a good, positive attitude is even more crucial than having the perfect experience. These qualities often create the difference between candidates.

A FINAL NOTE

Work hard on your cover letter and resume. Listen to feedback and learn from it. Network! If this profession is what you want, don't give up. ***Go for it!***

RESUME TEMPLATE – Sample

What follows on the next two pages is a fictional sample resume to be used as a model. It contains the key elements you should include to apply for a position as a Personal Assistant. My thanks to recruiter Margaret Kennedy for creating it.

- Professional Objective
- Skills
- Education – Be specific about the years because your age can be a factor
- Personal – This section helps paint a clearer picture of who you are

Note: The fonts suggested for the resume are: TIMES NEW ROMAN, ARIEL or CENTURY GOTHIC, in 11 or 12pt type. They are clean and easy to read. The following resume is formatted to fit this 6 x 9 book. Your resume on 8.5 x 11 paper will look different of course.

JENNA PUDDLEDUCK
1234 Madison Avenue New York NY 10002
(Ph) (212)555-1212 (Cell) (917)555-1313
jennapuddleduck@netscape.net

PROFESSIONAL OBJECTIVE
Seeking position as the Personal Assistant to a high profile individual. Highly dedicated, trustworthy and responsible professional with the aptitude to oversee a project from its conception to completion with superlative results. Committed and diligent with strong organizational and interpersonal skills. Capable of handling multiple tasks simultaneously, with talent to acquire and apply knowledge rapidly. Proficient in written and oral communications. Work well with minimal supervision and enthusiastic to contribute in a team or solo environment.

EMPLOYMENT
3/98-Present   Personal/ Social Assistant

          Smith Residence, New York, NY
          Jones Residence, New York, NY
          Harris Residence, Poughkeepsie, NY

- Organize/expedite financial aspects of household
- Supervise household staff and contractors
- Coordinate activities and appointments for the family
- Schedule business, social and personal commitments
- Administer property management at multiple residences
- Purchase online and acknowledge receipt
- Analyze budgets through monthly reports
- Arrange all travel including but not limited to air, car, hotel and land excursions

11/96-3/98   Personal Assistant   PseudoArt Gallery, Palm Beach, FL/New York, NY

- Coordinated daily affairs, private and social events
- Arranged international and domestic travel
- Organized meetings/appointments/legal matters
- Assisted in negotiating sales of contemporary art with private clientele
- Provided diplomacy and independent judgment to confidential matters
- Attended art shows to network with gallery owners and prospective buyers

1/95-11/96   VIP Coordinator   Hilton International Corp.,
                                    Duluth, WI, & NY, NY

- Oversaw the orderly arrangement of International/VIP matters
- Used strong interpersonal skills
- Worked under pressure with great skill and patience
- Provided high volume telephone assistance and customer service

8/89-1/95   International Account Executive
                                    Right Royal Rip-Off
                                    Cruise Line, Bahamas

- Created weekly and monthly productivity reports for Vice President of International Marketing
- Trained international representatives and top producers of the Midwest region with online computer system and tracking/analysis of usage
- Served as liaison between Vice President and top producers/ international representatives
- Traveled extensively – international/domestic
- Produced high volume letter/memo/e-mail writing

SKILLS
- Fluent in Spanish. Proficient in MS Office, WordPerfect for Windows, QuickBooks, Quicken, and Internet use, smartphones, Wi-Fi tablets, Dictaphone. 55 wpm.

PERSONAL
- Passions include film history, plays, opera, and poetry. Gourmet cook. Can drive both automatic and stick-shift. Speak fluent Spanish and some German. Have traveled extensively through Europe, Canada and the Caribbean. Dog lover and non-smoker.

EDUCATION
2000-Present   City University, Seattle – Masters Program online,
                 Economics and Finance
1993   Iowa University, Sioux City – Bachelor's Degree
                 in Hospitality Management
1989   Palm Beach Community College, Florida – Associate's
                 Degree in Business

References Available Upon Request

This piece hangs on the wall in front of my desk.
It inspires me. B L-K

By Marianne Williamson

"Our deepest fear is not that we are inadequate.
Our deepest fear is that we are powerful beyond measure.
It is our light, not our darkness that most frightens us.
We ask ourselves, who am I to be brilliant,
gorgeous, talented and fabulous?
Actually, who are you not to be?
Your playing small does not serve the world.
There's nothing enlightened about shrinking
so that other people won't feel insecure around you."

CHAPTER 14

GENDER IN THE WORKPLACE

*A*ccording to the U.S. Department of Labor, 95% of America's four million administrative professionals are women. Celebrity assistants are a subset of this larger group, and my own observation is that the same percentage is true for us as well. Given these numbers, the subject of gender is a very important one to explore in this book, and I hope to inspire a positive dialogue about the many workplace issues that are impacted by the interaction between women and men. For the record, I am privileged to know many male assistants, two of whom were particularly helpful with this chapter.

Speaking engagements have given me the unique opportunity to meet and talk with female and male assistants from New York, New Jersey, Boston, Philadelphia, Miami, Kansas City, San José, Los Angeles, San Francisco, and London. (My audiences have been 95% female on average.) I have also heard from others in Mississippi, Nebraska, Germany, Japan, and Malaysia via the Web. These assistants work for celebrities, CEOs, and middle managers. In addition, I have listened to, learned from, and debated with my NYCA colleagues and the leaders in our profession who generously shared their views with me. What follows are ideas, observations, and conclusions, as well as confusions and frustrations, and finally, a genuine optimism about the future.

Of this I am certain – today's professional assistants have an image problem, which is directly tied to obsolete ideas of what an assistant/secretary does. If I've learned anything from all these years in show business, it is that *perception is reality*. Behavior and language can help or hinder that perception. For example, when women in the workplace are perceived as the stereotype of being "catty," that perception hurts their image and directly relates to the level of respect and compensation they receive from co-workers and employers. "Catty" can get translated to "unprofessional" which can then get translated to "not worthy" of promotion or a salary increase. It is not always a "glass ceiling" holding women back, but rather a "sticky floor."

By definition, our roles are behind the scenes and supportive. No longer though, does this mean invisible and unheard. Successful assistants are now confidently voicing informed opinions and ideas, matter-of-factly touting their accomplishments, and negotiating six-figure compensation packages.

One motivation for writing this book was to help change the perception of celebrity assistants, most of whom you now know are women. The print and electronic media often paints us in extremes – we are either ditzy go-fers or brow-beaten slaves or we spend our days shopping on Fifth Avenue and our nights on the red carpet. We have been referred to as a frivolous indulgence and the ultimate luxury. These are warped perceptions, far from the way things really are. But if that is the perception, that is the reality – unless we keep working to alter the image.

Consider our image on film. My colleagues and I agree that *"The Devil Wears Prada"* (2006) is a painfully accurate portrayal of the tyrannical employer/assistant relationship, as is the television sitcom *"Ugly Betty"* (2006). Other films which mainly promote the old stereotypes about secretaries are *"Nine to Five"* (1980), *"Working Girl"* (1988), and *"America's Sweethearts"* (2001). I find it ironic that one of the strongest, most positive portrayals of our profession on film is from 1957 – in *"Desk Set"* with Katharine Hepburn. One of my favorite scenes in a movie is from *"Air Force One"* (1997) in which

Harrison Ford plays the President, and one of his administrative assistants saves the situation by speaking up when she realizes that the Russian terrorists only cut *one* of the fax lines on the plane, not both. Problem-solving, thinking on her feet under pressure – now that's the way it *really* works.

Language and the words we use have a profound impact on our image. Words have the power to inspire, but also to undermine. Our words, whether written or in conversation, cannot be underestimated or dismissed as unimportant. For example, by referring to ourselves as the "girls" in the office, rather than the "staff" or "co-workers" or the "admins," we minimize and diminish the work we do. Further, referring to our work as our "profession" or "career" commands more respect than speaking about it as our "job." We promote a climate of respect when we show respect for ourselves and one another with the words we choose.

Titles are a hot topic in today's workplace. In the same way that most are relieved that the job title "Secretary" is being phased out, we should also retire the use of the word "boss" which is archaic, inaccurate, and demeaning and replace it with the less loaded words, "manager," "employer," and "executive." I have listened to assistants stress the importance of titles and their impact on the respect they are given within their organizations. Assistants want their titles to accurately reflect their job descriptions and level of responsibility, and most feel "Secretary" does not accomplish this. "Legal Secretary" is a title that is still generally accepted although a shift towards replacing it with "Legal Administrator" or "Legal Assistant" is currently underway. The dialogue will continue, and it will be an ongoing process.

Our behavior, our actions, speak even louder than words. Think about a woman who is assertive, confrontational, and opinionated versus a man who exhibits these same qualities. They are often judged, *perceived*, differently. It isn't fair, but there it is. Only if we acknowledge that this phenomenon exists can we change any double standard.

The ways women and men interact in today's workplace are changing. Why? <u>One reason</u>: Current statistics say that one in every two marriages ends in divorce. <u>The result</u>: Women in the workplace are as serious as men about their professions because many are supporting families on their income. Fewer women are working just to make "extra money" – women *need* to work. The two-career family has become a necessity in many parts of the country as a result of the economy. Furthermore, there is increased respect in the workplace for parenting. It is no longer considered only a mother's job to accompany children to doctors' appointments and attend baseball games. <u>Another reason</u>: Workplace volatility – frequent downsizing and outsourcing. <u>The result</u>: Fewer people are doing more work. This situation causes high stress and creates the need for a "team" mentality. Gender has become less important than whether or not someone can get the job done. <u>One more reason</u>: 9/11/01 and the resulting war. <u>The result</u>: Tremendous movement and change in office personnel across the country. We have seen massive layoffs in some areas and increased hiring in others. For example, computer technology, clean energy, Internet marketing and ecologically-friendly green products are areas where hiring is strong. <u>Still one more reason</u>: More women hold college degrees now than at any other time in history. <u>The result</u>: Women are competing intellectually with men and with each other. They are being increasingly viewed as important and respected members of their executive teams, complete with improved salaries. In addition, more employers require an assistant to hold a college degree to be considered for a position. As salaries increase, more men view the profession as a viable career option.

As the guest speaker at an event celebrating Administrative Professionals Week, I was seated next to a high level executive of an international Fortune 500 company and his assistant of twenty-five years. We were discussing the changing face of American business as it related to his assistant, and he bottom-lined it for me. *"Do you want to know what 'global' really means? Global means that I travel constantly. I am running through foreign airports many days out of the month, communicating with my assistant and fellow executives by cell and teleconferencing. I am exhausted much of the time, but that is the way business has to happen. I depend on my assistant to run my life and act on my behalf when I am away. Her work is vital to keeping everything moving forward and running smoothly."*

We are living in a time of flux and rethinking old models. This climate creates opportunities for change. The stereotypical ideas of how women and men interact in the workplace have been thrown into the air much like a deck of cards. Women are CEOs, executives, department heads, and decision-makers who are networking and making deals in airport lounges and at day spas. We now have "flex-time" – an arrangement for staff, both women and men, to share a position, working either full- or part-time from home with flexible hours. Working from home saves substantial overhead for employers. Technology is turning out to be an equalizing force between the sexes.

More and more substantive work is being handled by telephone and e-mail where gender is a non-issue. Many executives are handling their own correspondence which frees the assistants to focus on project management.

Historically, female assistants have worked for male employers. Today, it is equally common and accepted that female assistants work for female employers. The newer trend is for male assistants to work for either male or female employers. Post WWII society asked: "Where is a woman's place?" The answer used to be: "In the home." Today's society is answering: "Everywhere." That is a radical change in sixty years.

The piece that precedes this chapter by Marianne Williamson speaks to me because it is about self-esteem. Confidence is something many people, women and men, have in short supply

– something I had in short supply and continue to confront. The issue of self-esteem is important because it directly relates to how we succeed at our work. It has to do with identifying what gives us confidence, strength, and dignity, and what can throw us off the track and cause anger, resentment, and insecurity.

All of us have had obstacles to overcome in our lives. For me, it was the loss of my father when I was fifteen. It was being the only Jewish person in my grade throughout my school years and experiencing harsh prejudice because of it. These are undeniable factors in making me who I am today. Olympia Dukakis had to overcome bigotry growing up as a first generation Greek-American in Massachusetts, and she speaks openly about how that resulted in her fierce determination to succeed. Self-esteem has to do with how we view ourselves which impacts how we function at work and in life. Looking honestly at our personal histories – our strengths and our limitations – is the only way to move toward positive transformation both in our work and our personal lives.

Unfortunately, there is a prevailing paradigm that says that women do not help other women, in part because we are insecure. I say no. It does not have to be that way if women decide not to tolerate particular behavior and language from ourselves or others. For the most part in my career, my own experience has been very positive.

I have received enthusiastic encouragement and support from women, and I reciprocate every chance I get. That said, I cannot disregard what so many women – leaders in our profession and assistants from all over the country – have told me is true. The good news is that *women are onto it*. When I speak about this issue, I see some discomfort in the audience, but also tremendous recognition and a determined acknowledgement that a single individual has the power to inspire others toward change by example.

Current research says that teamwork is the key to the future in the workplace, teamwork not only with our co-workers but with our employers. This mindset is starting to take center stage, but it's not an easy shift. Women are socialized as young girls to compete against one another – physically and mentally – to be chosen by boys and then later, by men. These old, ingrained habits die hard, but women know this behavior does not serve us. Instead of feeling threatened, we can choose to look to one another as resources and use each other to the advantage of the whole. Here's the payoff if we make the shift. The perception of our profession will improve – respect, salaries, and benefits will increase – and we will raise the bar of excellence in our high-tech, fast-moving profession.

Vitally important is organized mentoring. A big part of being an ultimate assistant is to share what we know. It is not an overstatement to say that the future of our profession depends on it. Mentors can positively influence and inform the young women and men entering our profession. We understand the uncertainty they experience. We can teach them best practices and let them in on the "unwritten rules." Think about someone who has been a mentor in your own life, and how motivated and inspired you felt when encouraged, supported, and challenged. A mentor can make the difference between success and superior achievement.

In addition, the perception of our role as assistants improves even further when we distribute professional business cards with our own names and titles on them. A deceivingly small and low-cost detail, business cards are as vital to have as an e-mail address. They contribute to our professional image.

And finally, there's the issue of balance, with which we all wrestle every day. It will be my lifelong challenge to achieve balance between my work life and my personal life. Striving for balance can create uncertainty and stress. Some days I feel as if I am not doing anything well and everything is out of balance. When that happens, I do the best I can, take it one day at a time, and work to make tomorrow better than today. My male colleagues assure me it is the same with them.

One regret I have at this point in my own career is not having taken enough vacations. Through the years, I remember often thinking I was indispensable and would wait until a better time. What I've learned the hard way is that there is no better time. An issue for both women and men, taking time away from work is extremely important, even if for only a long weekend. If you can relate to this sentiment, there is no time like the present to do something about it.

In general, women strive to do it all. Studies show we are champion multi-taskers and often risk burnout, depression, alcoholism, illness, and being physically out of shape. We live in a world that celebrates both women and men practicing workaholism, but minimizes efforts towards renewal and recovery, both of which are necessary for sustained high performance. Hopefully, years of experience can teach us that we need to be realistically optimistic about what we can achieve from day to day.

We are living and working in a very exciting time when old norms and stereotypes are being shattered daily. Assistants are being promoted to management positions. More women than ever hold high positions in business and, as a result, wield tremendous power. Think of someone like Oprah Winfrey and the power she has to influence great numbers of people. Think of yourselves, the assistants to high-level employers, and the power *you* possess. Professional assistants, women and men alike, now have an unprecedented opportunity to effect positive changes for themselves and their colleagues, and move towards true and healthy peer-ship and partnership, both in attitude and compensation.

Tackling the subject of gender in the workplace is a fascinating and satisfying challenge. I've wanted to grapple with these issues which have confounded me and work to find the words to communicate them. It is a topic that we think about but don't say out loud or discuss very much, in part because we don't want to "open a can of worms" or make waves, and also because there are no quick fixes or foolproof answers that work in every situation.

Let's do it anyway.

Given these issues, I believe we need to take a fresh look at our work situations and continue to ask questions. Join and get involved with professional organizations and share articles that help us keep our eye on emerging trends and opportunities. Where problems exist, we can choose to be part of the solution. Each of us *can* make a difference.

As Mahatma Gandhi said, *"We must be the change we wish to see in the world."*

"The number one resource assistants have is one another.
Two heads (or more) truly are better than one when it comes to our business.
Two of my favorite words are 'open' and 'options.'
Open, as in the opposite of rigid and unyielding.
Using resources effectively and creatively is immensely rewarding, not to mention time-saving. If you are open to new ideas and possibilities, that creates options. And when you have options,
you have many ways to go about solving problems.
The result of solving problems easier and faster is more free time, work satisfaction, and less stress.
Works for me!"

Bonnie Low-Kramen

CHAPTER 15

RESOURCES-TO-GO

New York Celebrity Assistants (NYCA) is the single most important resource I have in my work as an assistant. Whether you work for a celebrity or not, I encourage you to seek out a professional organization to enable you to network with your peers.

Founded in 1996 by eight assistants including myself, NYCA was designed to be a professional network and resource organization serving the unique needs of celebrity assistants. Prior to NYCA, there was no formal resource for this profession in New York. When we started, and by then I was already doing this work for ten years, I could count on one hand the number of assistants I knew personally. There was no organized way, no mechanism in place, for us to know one another.

Kerri Campos, former assistant to Sally Field and others, commented, "*If we are lucky enough to manage the lives of some of the most influential people in the world, then we must be considered some of the most organized and efficient people in the world, right? If so, then why aren't 'the most organized and efficient' individuals organized as a professional group and recognized as a true profession?*" Of course, she was right, and fortunately, the situation has changed for the better. Kerri became president of her own training and recruiting firm for personal assistants in Los Angeles.

NYCA has more than one hundred members in New York now, and I like to think about it this way. Before NYCA, there would never be a situation where I could be in a room and socialize with the assistants to Kelly Ripa, Sarah Ferguson, the Duchess of York, and Itzhak Perlman. Our worlds are different but our work is so similar. Also, like every assistant, I know I have a terrific Rolodex, but just imagine the contacts of *all of us* put together. There are no limits to the possibilities and no one we can't find.

NYCA holds monthly meetings on issues that are relevant to our work, such as *Celebrity Security, Event Planning,* and the annual *Unique Gifts* meeting. We are hosted by venues all over New York City such as the Le Parker Meridien Hotel, Royalton Hotel, St. Regis Hotel, Carlyle Hotel, Soho Grand Hotel, and the Waldorf Towers. We are hosted because the management of these venues understands the influence and power of the assistants to celebrities. Very often it is the assistant who decides which restaurant or hotel with which to do business. The personal connections are invaluable.

In addition, NYCA members are connected electronically by group e-mail. Communication happens daily over e-mail, solving problems and sharing information – and it happens within minutes and with the click of a mouse. The beauty of this system is that the information is trustworthy because we know the source firsthand.

Membership in NYCA requires that you be working full-time for a celebrity for a minimum of one year. Members need not be based in New York, although that helps for attending meetings. Dues are $150/year. Contact information for NYCA is on the Resource list at the end of this chapter.

West Coast-based celebrity assistants can join the ACPA, the Association of Celebrity Personal Assistants in Los Angeles. London-based celebrity assistants can join the UKACA, the United Kingdom Association of Celebrity Assistants. Contact information for both the ACPA and UKACA is on the Resource list. If you are an assistant interested in joining an organization but not working for a celebrity, consider IAAP, the International Association of Administrative Professionals. Contact information for IAAP is on the Resource list.

RESOURCES FOR THE PROFESSIONAL ASSISTANT

A word of caution regarding the Internet…take what you read with a grain of salt. Anyone can put __anything__ on the Web, so if you have any doubts about the facts, double-check your information on another website.

Books

The New Executive Assistant by Melba J. Duncan

Managing Up: How to Forge an Effective Relationship With Those Above You by Rosanne Badowski & Roger Gittines

The Essential Handbook For Personal Assistants: Tools For Becoming Or Hiring The Ultimate Personal Assistant by Craig Copeland

The Organizer, Secrets and Systems from the World's Top Executive Assistants by Anna-Carin Jean

Etiquette by Peggy Post

The Power of Respect by Deborah Norville

How to Win Friends and Influence People in the Digital Age by Dale Carnegie

Greet! Eat! Tweet! 52 Etiquette Postings to Avoid Pitfalls and Boost Your Career by Barbara Pachter

Organizing from the Inside Out by Julie Morganstern

It's Not A Glass Ceiling, It's A Sticky Floor by Rebecca Shambaugh

How to Make Peace With Anyone by David Lieberman

The Four Agreements & The Mastery of Love, both by Don Miguel Ruiz (These two books contain great wisdom regarding professional and personal relationships.)

It's All Your Fault by Bill Robinson (about being an assistant in Hollywood)

Be a Kickass Assistant by Heather Beckel (about being an assistant in Washington, DC)

Where to Find It, Buy It, Eat It in New York by Gerry Frank (updated annually)

Virtual Assistant by Diana Ennen and Kelly Poelker
Who Do You Think You Are... Anyway? by Robert Rohm, Ph.D.

Magazines

OfficePro Magazine – Published by the International Association
of Administrative Professionals (IAAP) www.iaap-hq.org
More Magazine – Smart talk for smart women over 40
Daily Variety – Great for research on what movies are in
production, where and feature which actors
Backstage – Great for information on what is happening in the
New York theatre
New York Magazine – Every major city has its version of this
magazine
Time Out New York – Every major city has its version of this
magazine
Zagats Guide – Restaurant listings & descriptions, updated yearly
Online version – www.zagat.com
Ross Reports – Individual booklets listing contact information
for entertainment Publicists, Agents, Directors, Managers,
etc. Online version – www.rossreports.com

Online Administrative Professional Newsletters and Blogs
Note: Join LinkIn Discussion Groups — a great source of information

www.careerealism.com
www.eatyourcareer.com
www.assistantstellall.com
www.executivesecretary.com
www.thegrindstone.com
www.proassisting.com
www.Personal-Assistant-Tips.com
www.deskdemon.com
The Effective Admin www.admin-ezine.com

Association of Executive & Administrative Professionals
www.theaeap.com

Truly Useful and Favorite Websites

Search Engines – Info on Everything!

www.google.com
www.igoogle.com (Dashboard & Groupware program)
www.yahoo.com
www.ask.com
www.dogpile.com
www.ehow.com
www.bing.com

Job Search

www.showbizjobs.com
www.estatejobs.com
www.indeed.com
www.monster.com
www.craigslist.com
www.careerbuilder.com
www.womenforhire.com
www.simplyhired.com
www.theladders.com
www.glassdoor.com
www.brightsideresumes.com (Resumes)
www.personaltouchcareerservices.com (Resumes)

Work-at-Home Jobs / Virtual Assistants

www.simply-virtual.com
www.yourextrahand.com
www.assistu.com
www.assistantmatch.com
www.ivaa.org

Travel Planning

www.trip.com

www.travelocity.com

www.expedia.com

www.orbitz.com

www.traffic.com

www.kayak.com

www.travelzoo.com

www.bestparking.com

www.globalentry.gov

Door-to-Door Directions & Maps

www.mapquest.com

www.randmcnally.com

www.mapblast.com

www.maps.google.com

www.maps.yahoo.com

Check Airline Seating

www.seatguru.com

Check Flight Status

www.flightaware.com

www.fly.faa.gov/flyfaa/usmap.jsp

www.flightstats.com

Passport Overnight

www.itseasypassport.com

Foreign Currency Exchange Rates

www.xe.net/ucc

Translation from one language to another
>   www.babelfish.altavista.com/tr
>   www.travlang.com/languages

Find time zone and current time for anywhere in the world
>   www.timeanddate.com

Restaurant Finder
>   www.zagat.com

**Great prices on all things to do with your computer
& general shopping**
>   www.ebay.com
>   www.overstock.com
>   www.pricegrabber.com
>   www.mysimon.com

Great prices on used items
>   www.craigslist.com

Microsoft Office Templates, Forms & More
>   www.office.microsoft.com

Technology Training & Consulting
>   www.redcapeco.com

Find Any Book
>   www.amazon.com
>   www.bookfinder.com
>   www.abebooks.com

Left-handed Products
>   www.leftyscorner.com

Dig Up Movie Info – Internet Movie Database
www.imdb.com

Dig Up Broadway Info – Internet Broadway Database
www.ibdb.com

Get Health Info
www.intelihealth.com
www.webmd.com

General Research
www.britannica.com
www.dictionary.com
www.wikipedia.org
www.encarta.com

Look up people
www.facebook.com
www.people.yahoo.com
www.infospace.com
www.linkedin.com

Find a Zip Code
www.zip4.usps.com/zip4/citytown_zip.jsp

Etiquette and Protocol
www.emilypost.com
www.etiquettesurvival.com

Unique & Very Cool Gifts

www.cookiesbydesign.com	Custom cookies
www.fretzels.com	Designer & themed pretzels
www.petography.com	Pet photography
www.puppypurse.com	Clever pet carriers
www.wallmonkeys.com	Custom removable wall art

Professional Associations

NEW YORK

New York Celebrity Assistants (NYCA)
www.nycelebrityassistants.com

LOS ANGELES

Association of Celebrity Personal Assistants (ACPA)
www.acpa-la.com

LONDON

United Kingdom Celebrity Assistants (UKACA)
www.aca-uk.com

NATIONAL

American Management Association (AMA)
www.amanet.org
American Society of Administrative Professionals (ASAP)
www.ASAPorg.com
Domestic Estate Managers Association (DEMA)
www.domesticmanagers.com

INTERNATIONAL

International Association of Administrative Professionals
(IAAP) Check the website for a chapter near you.
www.iaap-hq.org
International Association of Private Service Professionals
(IAPSP) www.iapsp.net
International Virtual Assistants Association
www.ivaa.org

This hangs on my wall too.

Success
Ralph Waldo Emerson

To laugh often and much
To win the respect of intelligent people
To earn the appreciation of honest critics,
To find the best in others
To leave the world a bit better
whether by a healthy child,
a garden patch or a redeemed social condition,
To know even one life has breathed easier
because you have lived –
This is to have succeeded.

CHAPTER 16

ASSISTANTS IN THE NEWS...

"After Luther Vandross, the R&B singer, had a stroke last year, his assistant, Max Szadek (eight years) did not have to send out an e-mail message to get a call from another assistant he had met in the ticket line for the NYCA's night at 'Urinetown.'

She worked for a doctor who headed a hospital rehabilitation unit. 'That referral was just a breakthrough,' said Mr. Szadek, who was able to get Mr. Vandross into the unit."

—New York Times

"All celebrities have an assistant in their lives. That is, if they know how to pick one. You must possess an obsession with lists, a love of the memo form, a head like the Yellow Pages, and a knack for plumbing, mechanics, botany, and simonizing."

—Vanity Fair Magazine

"The life of a celebrity is very unusual, and that's what's created the need for highly skilled assistants. The non-profit NYCA offers professional development opportunities to its members. It provides them with networking, job referrals, social events held at posh locales, and monthly meetings with special guest speakers."

—Real People Magazine

"A celebrity assistant, simply put, is the person you'd want to have around after the apocalypse. Or at least the person a celebrity would want around after the apocalypse."
—Vanity Fair Magazine

"There is a new breed of resourceful, won't-take-no-for-an-answer personal assistants who coordinate every move for the rich, famous, and powerful. You get the feeling she could coordinate a political campaign or run a company. Developing the capacity to pull off the near-impossible with panache and a sense of humor is a talent required along the way."
—London Times

This New York Times article appeared on June 8, 2004.

The New York Times

June 8, 2004 Tuesday — Late Edition - Final

SECTION: Section E; Column 1; Pg. 1;
The Arts/Cultural Desk
HEADLINE: Celebrity Assistants Keep the Stars Twinkling
BYLINE: By PATRICIA COHEN
Unedited text

When Their Wish Is Your Command

There is a moment in the documentary *"Elaine Stritch at Liberty"* when this Broadway legend is tromping through her hotel room at the Savoy in London, raised fist shaking, berating her assistant for failing to get tickets for someone.

"You didn't succeed with it yesterday, so do it right now," Ms. Stritch yells in her sandpapered rasp.

At Wednesday night's screening of the film at HBO's private theater in Manhattan, the audience gave a knowing laugh. It was, after all, also the monthly meeting of New York Celebrity Assistants – a "survivors meeting," as someone called it – and who there had not had to wrangle tickets for a finger-tapping boss?

If diaper launderers have their own association and cosmetics chemists have their own society, why should celebrity assistants not have their own organization, a place where they can confide, consult and kvetch?

At least that is what Bonnie Kramen (Olympia Dukakis's personal assistant for 18 years) thought when she helped found the group with a handful of colleagues eight years ago. "*Most of us run one-person offices, and you're in a vacuum,*" said Ms. Kramen, who does everything from picking up prescriptions to reading scripts. "*But we have such a need to know each other, such a need for resources, contacts who we trust.*"

Where else could you find out the best place to get a 50-pound beaded gown cleaned or who is owed a favor by the maitre d'hotel at Nobu or how you ship a dog from New York to Africa? It's all in the spirit of "*Why shouldn't my plant man become your plant man?*"

"*It's a wonderful source,*" says Audrey Bamber (Richard Dreyfuss, 21 years), whose 24/7 job has meant spending weeks on location in places like "*ravingly hot and sweaty*" French Guiana, and bone-chilling Libby, Mont., where there were "*not enough rooms in the town to house the crew.*"

One thing that it is not, though, is gossipy, Rick Borutta (Ms. Stritch, four years) insists. Assistants know secrets you would not want to share with your therapist; the lipo that was suctioned, the bills that went unpaid, the herpes that was transmitted.

"*It's one of the most difficult relationships in the world,*" said Ms. Stritch, outfitted in a fisherman-style rain hat, sweater vest and silk-dotted tie, in varying shades of beige and tan. "*I'm the new assistant,*" the actress Stockard Channing announced as she arrived with Ms. Stritch. Her prospective employer retorted, "*You wouldn't last 15 minutes.*"

Ms. Stritch complimented Mr. Borutta, whom she called an *"adorable pain,"* on his blue-and yellow-dotted tie, one she had given him. *"She would like me to dress how she's dressed: a sweater vest, a tie, a shirt and everything matching,"* he said.

For a while Mr. Borutta and Ms. Stritch lived in the same Sag Harbor house, where they watched late night television and sang show tunes. *"She'd even call my mother on Mother's Day,"* Mr. Borutta said.

The job requires walking a fine line between intimacy and professionalism, a bit like the nanny who is paid to feed, bathe and hug your child. Ms. Kramen has attended weddings of the Dukakis children, and Ms. Dukakis was there for Ms. Kramen's son's Bar Mitzvah. Still, she knows, *"we're friends, but our business relationship comes first."*

Karen Palmer (Itzhak Perlman, 15 years) said, *"We have a very clear understanding that his life and my life are two separate entities."*

That does not mean there is not some dish. No names please, but Ms. Kramen does know of stories like the one about the A-list actor traveling in London who called his assistant in New York at 4 a.m. to say *"the toilet paper was running out in the bathroom, and could she call the hotel and handle it?"* One assistant can attest to the rose petals that Barbra Streisand insists be strewn over her bathroom.

Those are the stories that are making some former assistants money from tell-all books, like *"The Devil Wears Prada"* (Broadway), a thinly veiled fictional account of working for the "boss from hell" by Laura Weisberger, a former assistant to Anna Wintour of Vogue.

Yet much of the work of longtime assistants is usually less juicy; people with bosses like the supermodel Naomi Campbell, who cracked her assistant in the head with a telephone, usually don't make it to "longtime" status. Much of the time it's business as usual. And that is when New York Celebrity Assistants is most helpful to its 90 members.

"We can send out a group e-mail to our members, and answers come back in five minutes," Ms. Kramen said. For instance there was the time that she needed someone to teach Ms. Dukakis to fake playing the trumpet for her role in the 2000 television movie *"The Last of the Blonde Bombshells."* Out went the e-mail request, and within minutes a former assistant to Isaac Stern hooked her up with a trumpet player from the New York Philharmonic. The tutor carried an extra trumpet and made house calls.

After Luther Vandross, the R&B singer, had a stroke last year, his assistant, Max Szadek (eight years) did not have to send out an e-mail message to get a call from another assistant he had met in the ticket line for the organization's night at *"Urinetown."* She worked for a doctor who headed a hospital rehabilitation unit.

"That referral was just a breakthrough," said Mr. Szadek, who was able to get Mr. Vandross into the unit.

To join the New York group, assistants have to have a year's experience. Dues are $150 a year, and everyone must sign a nondisclosure statement. Members are listed next to the names of their employers, a bit like 50's-era wives who are introduced by their husbands' names at society functions. The perks of membership include special movie screenings, theater premieres, four-star restaurant banquets and seminars on topics like security and hiring a stylist. (A Los Angeles group originally was associated but now is independent.)

Ms. Kramen, who teaches a course at the Learning Annex about becoming a celebrity assistant, tells aspirants that they should consider how much they like cleaning out closets, color coding files and organizing books, not to mention phoning and getting.

After Elton John sent Ms. Stritch an orchid when she was in London, she asked if he would send one to every hotel room on her national tour. Immediately he signaled his assistant. For months afterward a bigger and bigger orchid awaited her, till the one sent to her home base at the Carlyle Hotel in New York was so large that it is now sitting in the lobby.

As for her own assistant, Ms. Stritch was notorious for giving out Mr. Borutta's number to Stephen Sondheim, Dixie Carter, William Goldman – people, Mr. Borutta, said, with whom you *"know that 'no' was not the word you could use"* – who wanted last-minute tickets to her Broadway show.

These sorts of demands do not phase Ms. Kramen, who happily considers herself "a lifer." Other assistants, though, often use the position as a stepping stone. Ms. Channing said she had just hired an assistant after going years without one. *"I didn't want to get too dependent on someone,"* she said.

"They will grow up and leave you," Ms. Stritch said. Mr. Borutta, for instance, is now studying documentary filmmaking at Hunter College.

As for their relationship now? *"Now I am going to school only 10 blocks from the Carlyle,"* he said. *"I run into her on the street, and we walk together. 'One of these days,' we say to each other, 'we are going to have dinner together.'"*

CHAPTER 17

IN THEIR OWN WORDS
Assistants speak...

"Long hours, heavy responsibility. I sometimes dream about the job. Sometimes there is so much going on, there is a fear of overload and I'll miss something."
"Cartier watch, mink coat." (Gifts received from employer)
Susan Zito, former assistant to author Barbara Taylor-Bradford

"My employer has become so dependent on me that he suffers, and I feel guilty whenever I'm out and he's in...which isn't often."
Mary MacDonald, 26-year former assistant to publisher Jann Wenner

"I had never heard of my celebrity employer, and didn't even know him when we met for the first time. However, after being hired by Howard Stern back in 1989, I told someone who I was going to be working for. They obviously knew who Howard was and dropped their plate of food. I should have known at that moment the person I agreed to work for was not a 'normal boss.' However, Howard is a really good person. The job has been exciting, challenging, and even though I work very long hours and have little time for a personal life, I still wouldn't trade it for any other job in the world."
Laura Lackner, 16-year assistant to radio's Howard Stern

"I'm meticulous with details. I take morbid pleasure from getting things right. This quality has helped me immensely over the years working with a perfectionist duchess! She is quick to credit my attention to detail as one of my strongest skills."

**John O'Sullivan, 10-year assistant
to Sarah Ferguson, Duchess of York**

*"When a curve is thrown, unexpected and fast, there is a 'high,' a joy, a satisfaction in making the catch! The challenges that stretch the imagination, that bring out the drive, that get the adrenaline flowing are the ones that are most exciting. Working for Itzhak Perlman is a dynamic lifestyle. I am never bored.
The job is never tiresome as there is always something new on the horizon."*

**Karen Palmer, 16-year assistant
to Maestro Itzhak Perlman**

"As far as perks, I've traveled all over the world on tour, attended the GRAMMYs and the American Music Awards, went to the Super Bowl, and even met the President."

**Max Szadek, 9-year former assistant
to the late Luther Vandross**

"I get beeped or phoned whenever I am needed. Recently I was beeped at 9AM and told I was needed to go on a business trip at 1PM the same day, pack a bag, etc. One can look at this either way – the glamorous side (leaving on a moment's notice for St. Thomas for five days) or the downside (having to cancel all personal plans)."

Joseph Viggiani, Personal Assistant

"People always ask me, 'Where do you see yourself in five years?' My response is always the same, 'Where am I going?' Linda trusts me with her life, literally. Not many people can say that about their job while walking out of the office toting a new handbag, shoes, jewels, or other fabulous items that their employer just handed them."

Holly Eardley, 6-year assistant to Linda Ellerbee, journalist & TV producer

The celebrity 'community'...

"There are some client assistants with whom I very seldom communicate. However, when an assistant is an actively participating member of the team, it invariably enhances what can be accomplished. Schedules are better coordinated, everyone is in the loop and things go more smoothly."

Gene Parseghian, Talent Manager, Parseghian Planco Management, NYC

" Assistants? Don't leave home without one! My experience in running a 24-hour bi-coastal luxury ground transportation company that caters to celebrities and executives is challenging to say the least. Without the support of the assistants, it would be virtually impossible to provide the level of service my clients have come to expect. I often interact with a client's assistants exclusively. I can't even imagine what my business would be like without them. I suppose one could compare it to operating a company in today's business environment without a telephone."

Gail Ricketts, President, Ready to Roll Limousine, NYC

"A good celebrity assistant is invaluable in keeping every aspect of your client's life in order. I find this to be one of the most important partnerships to make in order to perform my end as a publicist effectively."

Donna Daniels, Donna Daniels Public Relations, Entertainment Publicity, NYC

CHAPTER 18

"IT'S A WRAP"

So that's it. As they really do say at the end of a film shoot, it's a wrap. This book is my take on this wonderful, unique profession called Celebrity Assisting, and its application to all professional assistants. It's most of what I know about it, and is certainly what I love about it.

However, this is only my "wrap" *for now.* I am excited by the future and the progress being made by our profession. I am optimistic about the organizations which are being driven by passionate, visionary people who are working to raise the bar, to strive for excellence, and ultimately, to help us succeed in all areas of our work.

There is more work to be done though – from the broad concerns of how professional assistants are perceived and the methods with which we communicate with one another to the minutia of the importance of carrying business cards. I envision a time when the profession of being an assistant is widely understood to be a highly respected and valued career path in and of itself, sought after by both women and men, and complete with excellent compensation and benefits.

My most fervent hope is that as a group, we use our vast talents to effectively share information with one another. Information not only about the work itself, but the trickier issues of office politics, salary negotiations, career advancement, stress management, and people-skills, to name just a few. We need to work towards mentoring which is organized, authorized and enthusiastically supported rather than haphazard and intermittent. There is simply no reason why anyone must reinvent the wheel anymore.

I sincerely hope this book and my presentations to administrative professionals take steps in these directions.

What do *you* think?

I would be pleased to hear from you. Let me know what you think about the book, what it still needs, the reasons you wish to know more, and your own experiences as an assistant. Please e-mail me at Bonnie@BonnieLowKramen.com.

Thank you in advance for your time, your interest, and your feedback.

I want to again express my deepest thanks to Olympia Dukakis and Louis Zorich because without their support, this book could not, would not, have ever been written. Their generosity is a gift in my life.

Lastly...I believe in what Marianne Williamson said. Don't play small. Dream large!

I wish you all the best.

LOUIS ZORICH
Photo by Blanche Mackey

BONNIE LOW-KRAMEN
Photo by Jillian Nelson

OLYMPIA DUKAKIS
Photo by Christian Oth

ABOUT THE AUTHOR

*B*onnie Low-Kramen has been the assistant to celebrity couple Olympia Dukakis (Academy Award, "*Moonstruck*," "*Steel Magnolias*") and Louis Zorich ("*Mad About You*") since 1986. She is also a co-founder and former President of New York Celebrity Assistants (NYCA), a networking and support organization for celebrity assistants.

Ms. Low-Kramen is a passionate spokesperson on issues concerning celebrity assistants, and she enjoys setting the record straight. As a result, she has been quoted in the *New York Times, Wall Street Journal, USA Today, NY Post,* and *Vanity Fair.* She has been interviewed on *Entertainment Tonight* and *Good Day New York,* among others. She teaches "Be the Ultimate Assistant" workshops nationally, and is a guest speaker at executive assistant conferences and events in the United States, United Kingdom, and Canada.

Ms. Low-Kramen worked to create NYCA in 1996 with seven

fellow celebrity assistants. It is the only organization of its kind on the East Coast and has grown to over one hundred members. In 2003, she was honored by her peers for career achievement at a ceremony in Beverly Hills.

Ms. Low-Kramen's work with Olympia Dukakis has included close involvement with the Academy Award win for "*Moonstruck*," the 1988 presidential campaign of Michael Dukakis, travel around the world to places such as Sydney, London, Alaska and Prague, and numerous awards shows and benefits.

A New Jersey native and current resident, Ms. Low-Kramen holds a B.A. degree from Rutgers University in English and Theatre. She worked in public relations and marketing for not-for-profit theatres in Chicago, Atlanta and Houston before returning to New Jersey where she became Public Relations Director at Olympia Dukakis' Whole Theatre in Montclair, NJ.

She lives in New Jersey with her high-school sweetheart, Robert Sanders, and her son Adam Kramen.

ACKNOWLEDGEMENTS

With tremendous gratitude, I wish to thank and acknowledge my talented and smart friends and colleagues who so generously helped me with this book. They are; Claudia Allon, Leslie Ayvazian, Audrey Bamber, Kerri Campos, Angelica Canales, Donna Daniels, Mark Dettle, Olympia Dukakis, Kathryn Eaker, Holly Eardley, Susan Fenner, Dr. Maddy Gerrish, Jonathan Gullery, Micki Hobson, Mary Jordan, Nick Katsoris, Margaret Kennedy, Laura Lackner, Mary MacDonald, Toby Mack, S. Lynn Matsumoto, Jillian Nelson, Susan McTigue, Scott Michaels, Leni Miller, Libby Moore, Janice Naehu, John O'Sullivan, Karen Palmer, Gene Parseghian, Dolores Phelan, Tom Reidy, Gail Ricketts, Adrienne Rogove, Bruce Rogove, Lisa Romero, Robin Rose, Cliff Rubin, Robert J. Sanders, Laura Schreiner, George Shepherd, Barbara Sprechman, Rick Stroud, Max Szadek, Joseph Viggiani, Eric Weinberger, Anthony Zelig, Susan Zito, Christina Zorich, Peter Zorich, Stefan Zorich, and Louis Zorich.

I wish to thank my family for their love and support. They are; Adam Kramen, Ruth & Sol Low, Jen & Ron Weisenthal, Andrea & Jason Weisenthal, and the kids – Matt, Stephanie, Rachel, and Zachary.

For their part in my journey, I thank; Sharon Arthur, Jacques Boubli, Susan Collings, Jim DeSheppar, Patricia Diana, Melba Duncan, Karla Hodge, Jonathan Holiff, Mark Kramen, Donna Lee, Douglas Meyer, Gilda Moss, Gail Newman, Tom Spray, Rita Tateel, Michael Tiknis, and my friends from the Whole Theatre.

To discuss booking a presentation by Bonnie Low-Kramen
for your organization or company, please contact
Bonnie through her website:

www.BonnieLowKramen.com

Recommendations are available from
but not limited to the following:

AMA – American Management Association

Amgen Corporation

AstraZeneca

DEMA – Domestic Estate Managers Association

Honeywell International

IAAP – International Association of
Administrative Professionals

IAPSP – International Association
of Private Service Professionals

Johnson & Johnson

Merck Pharmaceuticals

NYCA – New York Celebrity Assistants

Rutgers University

Schering-Plough Corporation

Siemens

SVCA - Silicon Valley Catalyst Association

Women in Film

Rev It Up!

The Lifestyle Diet that Puts YOU in the Driver's Seat

Tammy Beasley, RD, CSSD, LD

Rev It Up!

The Lifestyle Diet that Puts YOU in the Driver's Seat

Written by Tammy Beasley, RD, CSSD, LD
Registered, licensed dietitian, certified specialist in sports dietetics, certified Spinning instructor

Cover design by Emily Martinez, www.thebigpix.com

Distributed by Rev It Up Fitness, LLC. Printed by American Printing Company, Birmingham, Alabama,USA.

ISBN 978-0-615-33769-2

This publication is designed to provide information in regard to the subject matter covered. It is distributed with the understanding that the writer, editor, and publisher are not engaged in offering medical advice. Medical Warning: This manual proposes a program of physical and dietary recommendations for the reader to follow. However, before starting this or any other wellness program, you should consult your physician.

Visit us on the Web: www.revitupfitness.com

Rev It Up! is dedicated to all the clients with whom I have worked over the last 25 years. Thank you for sharing your lives with me. Each of you has contributed to this manuscript, and I am grateful and blessed to have had the privilege to work with you.

To my parents, thank you for setting the example of following your heart and never giving up. And to my husband, Dan, and sons, Adam and Luke–you have never failed to support my dream to one day, indeed, put in print the message of "Rev It Up!" that I have learned to live and share over the years. It's been an eight year journey to see this through, and thank you for walking it with me!

Contents

What the Experts are Saying

"Tammy Beasley is eminently qualified to help improve the overall health and well-being of individuals with a wide range of nutrition–related issues. Her rigorous and comprehensive technical education and clinical training in the field of dietetics, as well as her unique professional and personal experiences, have positioned her as a leading authority in the art and science of 'eating and living well'."
    Dean June Henton, College of Human Sciences
    Auburn University

"Just the guidance you need to put into action strategies for life! Tammy Beasley, Licensed Registered Dietitian, has easily translated evidence-based science for you into a meaningful, realistic roadmap for a life-long journey of healthy living. Tammy lives the life that she is sharing in this book–and serves as a living example both professionally and healthfully as true testament that the route you take next will be forever life-changing. Now....full speed ahead!'
    Susan C. Scott, RD, LD
    President and CEO, SCS Nutrition Consulting
    2008 Outstanding Dietitian, Alabama Dietetic Association

"I love Rev It Up! and have found in it the one source for most all the information I need to help my patients get beyond 'I'm on a diet' thinking to 'I can live a healthy lifestyle' thinking. Rev It Up! has solid nutritional information presented in a creative, incremental, organized and timely way. It is comprehensive, yet easily understandable for my patients. The program has a built-in schedule and logbook to assist my clients in tracking their progress through the program. After working through the program, my clients are well-equipped to become independent 'non dieters' who are able to make healthy lifestyle decisions for themselves. I like the analogy drawn between a car engine and our 'metabolic machines' and predict Rev It Up! will become a household word across the country. I think of it as my personal wellness assistant."
    Ginger Ryan Combs, RD, LD
    Clinical Dietitian

"Rev It Up! is not a fad diet; it's an eating strategy and fitness prescription for healthy living that is essential for regaining control of your life. This book is a must have if you are serious about changing your eating habits, losing weight and getting fit."
Officer Chris Hluzek
Police Academy and S.W.A.T. Fitness Instructor

"I started teaching Rev It Up! in January 2007 as part of my employee wellness program. Interesting note from a participant after the first week as he said, 'You haven't told me what to eat yet. That's different and I LIKE IT!' Rev It Up! is about overall real-life changes and not following a strict diet. It's a very positive program."
Janelle Campbell, MS, RD, CDE
Clinical Dietitian

"Tammy's expertise in re-teaching clients to trust their bodies, understand hunger and fullness, and accept and appreciate their bodies' needs has been invaluable to my clients. Her personal warmth and caring commitment to clients as well as her approach to wellness have been an integral part of my clients' ability to succeed."
Dana Summers, LPC, NBCC
Licensed Professional Counselor

"Tammy Beasley is an excellent clinical nutritionist. I am impressed with her knowledge and great communication skills. She has created a fantastic tool in the Rev It Up! program for achieving a safe and effective approach to weight loss."
Raetta Bevan Fountain, MD
Gastroenterologist

"As a physical therapist, I was excited to find such a dynamic and comprehensive health and wellness program. Having been through several nationally recognized weight-loss programs in the past, I feel this program is far superior in helping the client truly make a lifestyle change. This catch phrase is often alluded to in other programs, but Rev It Up! addresses all aspects of a healthy lifestyle including nutrition, fitness, and tackling the tough psychosocial components. Education is a cornerstone of the program, providing

sound, in-depth nutrition and fitness information in an easy-to-understand, easy-to-follow format which allows the client to make smart health decisions in real-life situations. The program is safe, effective, and more importantly, empowering."
　　Janine Nesin, PT, DPT
　　Physical Therapist

What Rev It Up! Alumni are Saying

"I have dieted my entire adult life–literally moving from one to the next searching for the 'one' that works. I heard about Rev It Up! and thought, 'Maybe this one will work?' My goal was no longer just weight loss. I wanted to eat like normal people. I can't express in words the difference this program has made in my life. No longer is a food or food group off limits. I eat-REAL food! I have gained so much confidence in myself and my choices. People see change in me, not just in size, but in my smile, too."
          Rebecca

"This program is a real eye opener. Can't believe what I did not know! We (my wife and I) can't stop talking about it. Probably the most dynamic program I've ever experienced. Rev It Up! makes sense, and really works…(written in 2002)
(and again in 2007)…*"Many if not all of the Rev It Up! principles have been incorporated in our everyday living experiences and our lives. I cannot believe I 'did not know' how much I did not know about nutrition, exercise, and the value of how you eat and what you eat. Barbara and I have lost approximately 15 and 24 pounds, respectively, from the beginning of the program and we have managed to maintain 100% of that loss (five years later!). The program had a tremendous positive influence on our lives in terms of overall health and wellness. We learned the positive benefits of exercise and more specifically eating right, i.e. fuel for the body (I will never forget that session!)."*
          Al and Barbara

"Thank you for introducing me to my new life! Until now, I didn't know what it was like to have any self-confidence or look in the mirror and be able to think… 'you look pretty good today!'"
          M.H.

"In our search for a diet and exercise program, my wife and I were interested in something different. We wanted something that stressed the science of diet and weight loss more than scales and calorie counting. We wanted to know how best to integrate exercise with correct eating habits. We wanted a program that was interesting and

worthwhile. We found Rev It Up! to fill these needs and more, and we recommend it as an excellent foundation for healthy living."
>   Dr. R.W.

"I do not consider myself on a diet or doing without any foods I want at times. Rev It Up! is a way of life for me. I am mentally feeling in control again and physically am without the health problems that the 60's usually bring – no heart problems, no diabetes, and no cholesterol problems."
>   Joyce

"Rev It Up! has taught me that there is a smart way to eat those foods I love and not feel guilty. It's also taught me to exercise smarter, too!"
>   Mary

"Because of what I learned from Rev It Up!, I was able to apply the principles even while I was pregnant. I ate healthy (with the exception of just a few cravings!) and only gained 25 pounds during my entire pregnancy."
>   Nikki

"I can't tell you how much I am enjoying Rev It Up! It seems to be giving me the freedom to eat healthy, eat when I'm hungry, eat without remorse, eat until I'm full. It has quieted the sugar cravings and stopped the binges in the evening. If just those two things can be conquered for the long haul, it is a miracle! No one has put it in a comprehensive, step-by-step format for me before. I can understand it, follow it, and there's really no desire to deviate–something I always felt the urge to do with other plans."
>   Rose

"Rev It Up! is a more realistic and natural approach to changing my eating habits instead of a 'rigid denial' or chemical driven method like so many others. I also like the concept of the challenges, allowing me to focus on one aspect of change at a time."
>   Julie

"Rev It Up! is the best money I have ever spent. I tell everyone about the program. The best benefit I received was freedom from cravings. I lost 10 pounds while working the program and have maintained 34 pounds of weight loss since then!"
Cheryl

"With all the gimmick and fad diets out there, this is actually a wellness program that doesn't make me feel deprived or that I'm on a diet."
J.D.

A Note from the Author

Rev It Up! was created after years of counseling hundreds of clients on two different ends of the wellness spectrum and hearing myself sharing the same information with all of them. These clients ranged from those with eating disorder struggles on one end to the elite athletes on the other end, and the chronic dieters and recreational athletes who were in the middle somewhere. The clients struggling with disordered eating needed to look inside out–to understand how and why their bodies were responding to their eating and exercise obsessions-and learn how to communicate with their bodies again through hunger, fullness, and embracing the goal of wellness vs. a specific body weight. The chronic dieter and recreational athlete-male, female, young and old–were in the middle of the spectrum with their own struggles about weight and fitness. And on the opposite end, the dedicated, competitive athletes came wanting to know as many hard facts, figures, and specific meal plans as possible to meet their fitness demands.

The great majority of consumer information available to the two opposite ends of the spectrum does not often overlap. Yet I found that the competitive athlete benefited from looking beyond meal plans to the "why" and "how" of metabolism-and slowing down to explore hunger/fullness cues completed the wellness picture. At the same time, I found that the eating disorder client benefited from knowing some simple, practical but specific guidelines on when and what to eat to help reduce the fear of food while exploring the emotions behind specific choices. And the chronic dieter and recreational athletes also gained new confidence learning and practicing these same principles-and broadened their perspective of wellness in general, their own bodies in detail.

Thus, Rev It Up! was born as a program for women and men that approached wellness by looking at metabolism first – HOW the body works-and WHY the traditional way of "doing diets" isn't enough. Is the educational component of the program new in the truths that are presented? Not really-to live well, an individual must fuel and move the body appropriately. But is it new in its approach? YES! The body as a car, metabolism as the engine, and food and fluid as the fuel–

with all the specific nuances of car maintenance and parts, from the fuel gauge, rear-view mirror, battery charge, oil change, and more. The car analogy runs throughout the entire program, which is progressive from week to week, building on the principles learned in a step-by-step approach. It's user-friendly, simple in presentation but complex in its power to change a person's perspective of living well!

I invite you to experience Rev It Up! for yourself. Join the hundreds before you who have made a difference in their own life by learning and living the Rev It Up! principles. I look forward to partnering with you to make a difference in your health, and welcome any opportunity to hear from you as you work the principles, see the changes, and feel the difference.

In health,

Tammy

Rev It Up!

The Lifestyle Diet that Puts YOU in the Driver's Seat

Introduction

Welcome to Rev It Up! Congratulations on investing in your future by learning how to lead a new lifestyle-not just follow a diet plan. You may be wondering how this program is different from any others. Can it make a lasting difference? Can you really learn to LIVE a new healthy lifestyle, or will this be another temporary change that won't last?

If you have ever felt that you and your body are moving in opposite directions from each other, this is the program for you! Rev It Up! is designed to help you take an inside look at your relationship with your own body and learn how to get on the same track again. Learn how to communicate with each other again. You may be surprised to discover how many ways your body "talks" and responds to your messages every day.

How do you get on the same track again with your body? Your health? Let's begin by thinking about your favorite car. What model is it? Do you have a specific color in mind for the exterior? The interior? Pretend you have been given this specific car, and it is yours to care for and maintain. You can make changes to the exterior, and the outside of your car will look better for awhile. But "outside" changes only cover up and disguise any real problems inside the engine. A new set of tires or a brand new coat of paint can dress things up but a neglected engine will stop your car in its tracks every time. You don't have to read the driver's manual or follow the maintenance guidelines, but if you want your "dream car" to perform as long as possible, you will.

You probably know where this is going now, don't you? Of course you might not agree that your body is the "dream car" you have always wanted, at least not now, but it is a special car, the only one of its kind. Designed specifically for you. And it is yours to keep, care for, and maintain.

So here's the analogy: Your body is the car, your metabolism is its engine, and food is its fuel. Consider this program your driver's manual, full of instructions, suggested tools to use, and reminders to guide you along the road. You CAN understand what your body's signals mean and how to respond. You can KNOW the signs of wear and tear, when to slow down or speed up, and when a tune-up is necessary. And you can keep your body in good, even excellent, condition to keep performing at its best.

Program Principles:
How to Use This Driver's Manual!

Rev It Up! is an eight week wellness program designed to help you develop a healthy partnership with your body. It incorporates eating and exercise strategies to achieve a more balanced healthy lifestyle and a more efficient metabolism rate. Sounds great, right? But before you can learn how to make simple changes to improve your metabolism rate, you have to understand what "metabolism" means.

The "official" definition of metabolism is "the process in which the body breaks down the fuel (proteins, carbohydrates, and fats) you eat and uses the products to generate the energy required for growth and life." In other words, metabolism is how efficiently (or fast) you use (or burn) energy (or calories). Now, hopefully that makes more sense!

The two main strategies for a more efficient metabolism are "MOVE IT" and "FUEL IT". A fitness combination of aerobic exercise and strength training burns calories and builds muscle, and the more muscle you have, the more calories you can burn. That's the MOVE IT part. But, if you do not feed your body the right kind of fuel at the right time, your muscles will run out of energy before they have reached their potential. Inadequate food, and even insufficient fluids, can slow down, even reverse, the benefits your body can gain from exercise. And that's the FUEL IT part! The two go hand in hand.

So it's a balance between food, fluid, and fitness. Maybe you know the food components of a healthy lifestyle, but just can't get your fitness plan in order. Or maybe you are consistent with your workouts, but the food and fluid components do not match your fitness efforts. It's a three-sided triangle, and if one side is out of balance, the other two sides will pay the consequences. But even if all three sides are in balance, if the foundation on which it rests is shaky, things will eventually fall apart.

Consider this: when a new car is under construction, the majority of the work effort is spent laying a strong foundation, making sure the engine, brakes, carburetor and all the intricate parts can support the functions of the car itself. Lots of effort, labor, and engineering skill are required to create a working model that will withstand the test of time and not be shaken by weather changes, daily wear and tear, and the inevitable aging process. These details are not visibly seen when the car is finally ready to go and on the lot; however, the ability of these "hidden" details to work together is what determines the success of the car's functions. So it is with your body's foundation, too. Your ability to read your body's hunger and fullness signals, the way your emotions support or sabotage your fitness efforts, and how you think about your body and its progress are all part of the foundation that can make or break your efforts.

Rev It Up! is designed to address the four "F's": Foundation, Food, Fluid, and Fitness, working together. Phase One (Weeks 1 through 4) presents weekly challenges for each of the four "F's", one for Food, one for Fluid, one for Foundation, and one for Fitness. You can choose to do just one or two challenges a week, but the program is designed to provide four weekly challenges that work together, with each week building on the previous week's progress. During Phase Two (Weeks 5 through 8), each week will focus on a single "F", like Foundation OR Fitness, to help you accelerate your progress. After completing both phases, Rev It Up! guides you through a maintenance plan (the rest of your life!) for your short and long term goals.

"I think the program really works because it's little changes every week instead of being overwhelmed by trying to make huge changes all at once." Sabrina

You are encouraged to keep a journal in which you can write your specific daily goals, record your progress, and begin developing a strong, solid foundation to support your lifestyle changes. You may choose to write in the Maintenance Log, the journal pages starting on page 213 found in the back of this book-or simply use a blank notebook you already have on hand. Regardless of your choice, you will get the most out of this program if you journal regularly. As each week progresses, take a moment to summarize your progress on the "A Look in the Rearview Mirror" page located at the end of each week's lesson. These pages will help remind you of all the positive changes you have made, step by step, as you move through each phase of the program. Soon, you will be able to "hear" your engine running stronger, feel the difference it makes in your daily life and know that you are on your way to living well for a lifetime. So, ladies and gentlemen…..

START YOUR ENGINES!

Are You Ready to Rev It Up?

It is the mission of Rev It Up! to *"empower you to change from the inside out: find hope in your body's ability to change, feel confident in yourself and your body again, and live well-strong and balanced - through nutrition, fitness and behavioral modification education."* That sounds good, but not everyone may be ready to make the commitment to start living the Rev It Up! way.

Is Rev It Up! the right program, at the right time, for you? Only you can know for sure, so take this opportunity to assess *your* readiness for revving it up by answering the following questions:

1.   What other programs have you tried in the past?

2.   Which program worked best for you and why?

3.   On a scale of 1 to 10 (1= not at all, 10 = extremely important), how important is changing your eating/exercise habits to you?

4.   On a scale of 1 to 10, how confident are you in your capability to make the necessary changes?

5.   What is going on in your life right now that might "get in the way" of making changes in your lifestyle?

6.   List all of the positive benefits that you will receive by making healthy lifestyle changes.

7.   List all of the negative consequences that might occur by making healthy lifestyle changes.

8.   List all of the negative consequences that might occur by "staying the same".

9.   Do the positive benefits (Question #6) outweigh the negative consequences (Questions #7and #8)?

Now take a moment to look over your responses. If your reasons for change, and commitment to do so, are based on the positive benefits you expect and your internal motivation to see the journey through, you are ready. If your willingness to make these changes in your current home and work environment is stronger than a 5 out of 10 (see Questions #3 and #4), then you are more than ready!

PHASE ONE:
Let's Get Started!

Week 1: Start Your Engine

Week 2: Move Your Car
Out of the Garage

Week 3: Get In Gear

Week 4: Tune Up

Week 1:

Start Your Engine

"Rev It Up! has changed my life! By losing the weight I did on this program so far, I had the proof I needed that I could lose weight by simply changing my eating habits. I always thought that to lose weight, one had to eat very little, no snacks between meals, give up the food I love, and never leave the gym. Thanks to Rev It Up!, I know that's not true! For the first time in my life while trying to lose weight, I am not always hungry or craving things I "can't" have. This program is something I know I can follow forever."   Mona

Chapter 1

Headlights on Foundation:
Check the Fuel Gauge

You are about to take the first step towards a Rev It Up! lifestyle-learning to communicate with your body. If you feel like your body is moving in one direction and you are moving in another, this is your opportunity to begin moving together. Your body is designed to do just that – to communicate with you so that you are going in the same direction. Your body can tell you when it needs fuel, but do you know how? How it tells you when it is running out? How it lets you know when it's had enough? If you are not sure, think about how your car communicates its need for fuel-the FUEL GAUGE.

How critical is your car's fuel gauge? If you have ever ignored the fuel gauge and ended up out of gas on the side of the road, you realize what important messages it sends, and how stressful it can be when you are not paying attention to the warning signs. The fuel gauge tells you when your gas tank is nearing empty and needs refueling. It also tells you when the gas tank is full and cannot hold any more without spilling out of the opening, wasting not only fuel but also money.

Just as important, your body's fuel gauge is the HUNGER and FULLNESS cycle. Hunger or fullness is how your body "talks" or communicates its needs for food and fluids. Do you pay attention to your body's fuel gauge or do you usually ignore or overlook its signals? Hunger tells you when your body is almost out of "gas" and needs refueling. Can you hear it, or do you wait for the yellow or orange panic light to come on or the beep to sound, and find yourself frantically searching for a quick fix, angry with yourself that you did not stop a few miles back when a gas station was convenient and you were not rushed? Fullness tells you when your tank is filled but not overflowing. Do you stop when you are full, or do you forget to pay attention and keep the fuel flowing in until it spills out, wasting your money and putting you and your car at risk?

Knowing *when* to eat and *when* to stop is the key to a truly "revved up" metabolism. When are you really hungry, and how hungry are you? At this point, you may be saying, "I don't even know what hunger feels like!" Maybe you have ignored the signals over the years, and now you no longer know how to "listen to" or read your fuel (hunger) gauge. Maybe you eat simply out of habit regardless of your body's need for fuel. Or you may have confused true physical, or stomach, hunger with "emotional" hunger needs. Are you really hungry for that chocolate candy bar on your way home from work? Or are you *emotionally* hungry for the comfort and stress relief that the chocolate candy bar provides?

Determining your *level of hunger* and the type of hunger takes time and practice, but the results are worth it. No other habit is more important to a lifelong change in the way you eat and the way you feel about what you eat. Knowing your hunger and fullness level allows you to work with and understand your body instead of feeling like you are "the last one to know" what your body really needs and, therefore, at the mercy of your food cravings. Being able to tell the difference between physical hunger and emotional hunger is a powerful tool that relieves you from food guilt and helps change your relationship with food from a constant battle to a trusting partnership.

So how do you begin learning how to read your fuel gauge? It starts with simply recording your hunger and fullness levels before and after you eat or drink. A scale from 1 (starving!) to 10 (stuffed!) is provided to help you learn to decipher your body's signals. At first this will feel awkward. Compare this to learning to drive a car using a gearshift system for the first time when all you have driven before is a car with an automatic transmission. The issue is not IF you can drive but HOW you drive.

If you have ever challenged yourself to learn how to shift gears, you remember that initially you had to concentrate constantly in order to shift to the right gear at the right time. You may have felt that the change was too difficult at first, but in a short time you were shifting gears easily and with confidence. A new habit was born through practice and concentration that expanded your driving potential.

Likewise, a new habit that will expand your own metabolism's potential is learning to know when and what to eat by listening to your body's communication signals, hunger, and fullness.

In the beginning, you may not be able to tell the difference between a "3" and a "7" and may record a "5" before and after every meal or snack. Don't give up! Little by little, you will begin noticing a change as you take the time to become more aware of your body's signals. And the emotional hunger will also begin to separate from the physical hunger so that you can "see" what your body really needs. This step is the most important Foundation challenge you will face. But the benefits are amazing: *The ability to control your food choices instead of food choices controlling YOU!*

The following list provides a hunger scale from 1 to 10. Use this list when you think about how hungry you are, and record that number in your Maintenance Log in the back of this book. If your Log isn't handy, simply jot it down anywhere. Don't think too much about your answer. Record what first comes to mind! Repeat this same procedure after you finish eating by choosing another number between 1 and 10 that signals how full you feel.

Your Hunger and Fullness Fuel Gauge: Scale of 1 (starving!)-10 (stuffed!)

1. You're dizzy and unable to think clearly. "I'm going to pass out if I don't eat right this minute!"
2. You're very irritable, and your stomach feels like an empty pit. Where IS that food...*any* food!?
3. You need to eat, but you aren't going to pass out... at least not yet!
4. You feel a little hungry, and your body is sending signals to fuel your engine.
5. Your stomach is in neutral. If you stop eating now, your fuel tank will need more fuel (food) in a few hours.
6. Your stomach knows that food has arrived, but you still want to eat a little more.

7. Your stomach is getting full now. If you stop eating, your fuel tank will not need more fuel, or food, until about 4 hours later.
8. You are full-that "deep, dark hole" has been filled to the top!
9. Your stomach is completely stretched to the point of discomfort, and one more mouthful may not even fit!
10. Help! Fuel overload! You really cannot eat even one more bite.

> *"The most beneficial part of Rev It Up has been*
> *learning to eat healthy without having to feel*
> *as if I was dieting, and understanding the process*
> *of when your body is hungry or full as (a guideline) to eat*
> *or not to eat. It is amazing how Rev It Up*
> *references our bodies needing food for fuel like a*
> *vehicle needs gasoline to run."*   Michelle

Your **FOUNDATION CHALLENGE** for Week 1: Before eating and/or drinking, stop and check your fuel gauge. How hungry are you before you eat? How full are you afterwards? **Record the level of hunger (H) and fullness (F)** in your Maintenance Log before and after each meal and snack. Begin noticing what your body is trying to tell you, look for any patterns of behavior and start to follow your body's lead.

Chapter 2

Headlights on Food:
Turn the Key

You have turned your headlights on your body's fuel gauge and taken a look at hunger and fullness. Now, it's time to turn on your body's engine! You know how to start your car's engine: simply put the key in the ignition and turn it! So how do you turn on your body's engine? Just as simple – fix BREAKFAST (the "key") and EAT it (the "turn" that starts the engine)! Breakfast is the meal that is most often ignored, but it is the most important.   It's not called "break" the "fast" for nothing!

You may not feel that you have been "fasting", especially if you ate a second serving of dinner last night or lost control with a late-night snack before going to bed. You feel guilty, so maybe you should just skip breakfast. Surely your body can still find some fuel for this morning from your indulgences last night, right? Or maybe you just never eat breakfast because you don't wake up hungry. Or eating something in the morning makes you queasy. One meal cannot be that important, right?

Think again! Whatever fuel you put in your body the night before, it is either burned or stored by morning. As you sleep, your body is burning fuel to keep the heart pumping, blood circulating, lungs breathing, brain functioning-get the picture? Whatever fuel is available in excess, the body will store it (as fat) for future needs. So, your fuel tank is empty when you wake up even if you still feel full. What do you do?

You would not even think about backing your car out of the garage without first turning the key in the ignition. So why do you ask your body to "back out" and get moving, without starting its engine? Your fuel gauge is on empty in the morning, but your energy demands are increasing. You have about 1 to 1 ½ hours after getting out of bed to turn the key in the ignition and start the engine so that your car, or body, has fuel to move down the day's road. If you ignore the fuel gauge's "I'm on empty!" message, your body begins looking for other ways to take care of your fuel needs. It reacts to an empty fuel tank in ways that protect your body from burning fuel, since fuel is scarce. But do you really want your body protecting you from burning fuel, or calories? What your body does to help you store energy actually hurts you, and your metabolism, over time.

Let's look at what happens when you ignore your fuel gauge, do not eat, and your body feels threatened by the lack of available fuel, or calories, to meet the energy demands of your daily activities. Five changes begin to occur. The degree of change *varies* in every individual, and *depends* on how severe the restriction of energy (or calories) over time and how much activity is required. Regardless, all of the changes happen because your body is trying to take care of itself; however, the results end up hurting instead of helping your metabolism.

FIRST: Your body will start to lower the rate it burns calories, or fuel, to conserve as much energy as possible.

SECOND: Your body will begin to protect its extra fuel stores, your stored body fat, just in case you decide to skip the next meal, too. (Remember, it's not sure when you will fuel again!)

THIRD: Your body may burn some of its own muscle tissue for extra energy if burning less calories is not enough to make up for the lack of energy fuel. (Your own muscle tastes like chicken to an empty tank!)

FOURTH: Your body will trigger your brain to send signals to make LPL, or lipoprotein lipase. LPL is an enzyme that's main purpose is to encourage your body to store fat. More LPL in your body means more of the next meal's calories can be stored as fat instead of used immediately for energy.

FIFTH (and finally!): Your body will probably crave fats and/or sugars when it feels overdue for fuel: Fats, because this fuel group has the most calories per serving size, and sugar, because this fuel can be broken down very quickly. Who craves lettuce and carrots now? Don't be surprised if you cannot resist a quick drive through the fast food window!

At this point, your *willpower* is not the issue. Your fuel gauge has sent out its warning light, and your body has responded. It just so happens that its responses are geared to slow your metabolism instead of revving it up! So what can you do to start changing your body's response? Eat breakfast within 1 to 1 ½ hours after getting out of bed. It is as simple as that!

Do you already eat breakfast regularly, and within the right time frame? Good for you! And good FOR you! Did you know that regular breakfast eaters have less difficulty maintaining weight? Make healthier food choices throughout the rest of the day? Think clearer, and are more productive at work or school? Are less irritable when life throws a curve? If you fall into this category, you will find this week's Food Challenge easy. No problem, you can spend more time concentrating on the other challenges coming up! In the meantime, just keep eating breakfast, and record how hungry you are before, and how full you are after, you eat. Don't worry-you will learn more about what to eat, not only for breakfast but other meals, next week.

Caution Sign for Morning Exercisers

Do you exercise regularly in the early morning hours, and wonder how you can fit in breakfast? If you are an early bird that hits the gym or pavement before the sun comes up, simply plan on eating breakfast within 30 minutes AFTER finishing your workout. Eating within that 30-minute window is the ideal time for your muscles to recover this fuel level. This fuel helps re-fill the energy stores in your muscles so you are ready to go again the next morning. And if you are training for a competitive event, you may want to consider eating a small carbohydrate snack right before you work out to start the motor running, such as a banana, a small glass of juice or a handful of dry cereal. However, if weight loss is your goal, the pre-exercise snack may not be necessary.

However, most people find themselves in the category of a breakfast-skipper. It's time to look at some common excuses for not eating breakfast and decide to skip the excuses instead of the morning fuel! Do these sound familiar?

"I never really eat breakfast because I am never hungry when I wake up."

Hmmm, you have just been challenged to "eat when hungry and stop when full". Since you aren't hungry in the mornings, wouldn't it be contradictory to eat? What's the deal?

Take a moment and imagine someone is trying to get your attention and calls your name repeatedly, but you ignore them, repeatedly. That person will eventually stop trying. Likewise, a body whose signals to eat have been ignored time and time again has probably learned to stop trying to get your attention. It will stay quiet, which means that your metabolism may stay asleep. It will remain so until you decide to "wake it up" or turn it on by eating. If this is not until lunch, you have lost those hours that your body could be burning calories more efficiently. The body changes that result in a slower metabolism have started to occur because the fuel tank is empty yet the car, your body, has been asked to perform.

To break this negative cycle, a new pattern must be established. Eating something in the morning begins to re-activate your fuel gauge. As your body adjusts to having fuel available on an everyday basis, your metabolism adjusts, too. Instead of slowing down, it will begin to rev up since your gas tank is full! No more muscle being mistaken for chicken, less LPL enzymes running around waiting to store extra body fat, and fewer cravings that you cannot control. In other words, breakfast turns the key in the ignition, which starts the engine running, which starts fuel burning!

"I don't need breakfast in the mornings because I tend to overeat in the evenings, and therefore wake up feeling full, and guilty!"

You are nervous, because you know that you always overeat during the day, especially at night. Surely adding more food (calories!) at breakfast can only make matters worse, right? You have gained weight over time by not eating breakfast, so how will your body not gain even more weight if you add morning calories, too? Your concern is understandable. But, remember, NOT eating breakfast has not helped you maintain a desirable weight. It has not worked! It is time to change the way your body responds. Wake up your metabolism!

At first, eating something in the mornings may feel like you are just forcing calories in without eating any less through the rest of the day. And in fact, your evening meals may not be much smaller during the first week or two. Habits are hard to break! But remember that at least your body is arriving at that evening meal burning more calories during the day because you have eaten instead of skipped meals. As you continue concentrating on hunger and fullness signals, you will notice when a change begins.

You will stop eating out of habit and begin eating out of need. You will begin eating fewer calories in the evening because you do not like to feel a "10" on the fullness gauge-you are definitely no longer comfortable being that full! In turn, you will begin eating more during the day, and your energy level will take notice. Your meals will balance out as you begin to communicate with your body and use your fuel gauge. When your fuel tank is nearing empty again, you will be better able to listen and take action, choosing a healthier snack or meal instead of just whatever you can grab fast!

So no more excuses! If you are not a regular breakfast eater, start out simple and plain. Try a piece of whole-wheat toast with jam, or a cup of low-fat vanilla yogurt with fresh fruit, or a small bowl of cereal with low-fat milk. Remember to make a quick note of how hungry you are *before* eating, and then how full you are *after* eating. Watch for this to gradually change and improve, once your fuel gauge, or hunger cycle, starts matching up with your body's needs again. It's not being ignored any longer! And in about 3 weeks, you may notice that you wake up hungry for the first time in your life. That's a great sign of a metabolism that is up, burning calories, and ready to go!

"I was not a breakfast eater, but I have stuck with
the challenge of having breakfast within 1 ½ hours
of awakening. Just wanted you to know, for the first time

I was SO hungry for breakfast this morning! I can't ever remember being hungry for breakfast before!"   Sabrina

Your **FOOD CHALLENGE** for Week 1: **Eat breakfast within 1 to 1 ½ hours** after getting out of bed in order to turn on your car's engine and break the fast. In your Maintenance Log, record what you eat and drink, noting hunger (H) and fullness (F) levels before and after each meal.

WARNING: Your first week does NOT provide you with an easy way out! No list of specific breakfast meals from which to choose is given… just yet. You are being asked to concentrate on hunger and fullness levels, and how different food choices affect these levels. Do NOT proceed unless you want to begin making a difference in how you relate to your body. Do NOT proceed unless you want to begin experiencing control over your hunger and fullness levels. Do NOT proceed unless you truly want to gain ownership over your body and its weight changes. But if you DO, then keep going!

Chapter 3

Headlights on Fluid:
Watch Your Water Level

You may have heard that everyone needs a minimum of eight cups of water a day, but do you know where this originated? The amount of daily water you need is determined by how much daily water you lose. You lose water in your sweat, your urine, and even through breathing. To maintain water balance in your body, this fluid must be replaced. A general guideline is one liter of water (which is close to 1 quart, or 4 cups) for every 1000 calories you consume. If the average person consumes about 2000 calories every day, this translates to about 8 cups.

So do you need to actually drink this amount? Let's think about this a minute. Metabolism itself releases water back into your body-and can replace about 10% of your water losses. The foods you eat every day can replace about 20 to 40% of your water losses. So does this mean that you only need to drink up to 4 or 5 cups more? It IS true that metabolism of foods, and food itself, can give back about half of the water you lose every day. But you cannot stop there and assume that you only need 4 or 5 cups more until you look at the whole picture.

The typical American eats only 1 ½ servings of vegetables or fruits in any given day. Therefore, the foods that provide the most water are the least consumed. Furthermore, the typical American eats one out of every three meals at a sit-down or fast food restaurant and these meals are more processed and quite often much higher in sodium (or salt). Our bodies can function well on less than 2000 milligrams (mg) of sodium each day, but the average American eats two to four TIMES this amount, mostly from the processed or restaurant foods consumed. And it is a known fact that increased sodium in food increases fluid needs. So, your food choices have the potential to give back up to 40% of your water needs, but does today's lifestyle, with few fruits and vegetables and excessive amount of sodium, really include the foods that meet that need, on a daily basis?

What other factors influence your need for water? Your age helps determine fluid needs, since young children as well as older adults' needs are greater because they have less sensitivity to thirst and often become dehydrated. Your geographical location plays a part, since high altitudes or high humidity increase the need for more water. Your body size is a factor, because if you are overweight, your water needs are greater. And, if you choose to begin an exercise program, like you will in Rev It Up!, your water needs increase even more. The average American will typically only replace about 65% of the water lost in sweat if the decision is left up to perception of thirst only.

Let's keep looking at the role water plays in our health and our metabolism. Your body is about 60% water, and ALL energy reactions in your body, including the burning of fat calories, require water. Are you aware that water carries nutrients through the body and waste products out of the body? That water lubricates your joints to keep them moving? And water acts like a radiator to cool your body off when your temperature begins to rise, such as during exercise? And, finally, *more* water is the best solution when you are bloated? When the body gets less water than it needs, it senses this shortage as a threat and begins to hold on to every drop. The result? You feel, and are, bloated! Drink more water, and then your body will not feel threatened and will release the stored water it is holding.

Is water a factor in the process of metabolism itself? You bet! Water plays a role in the body's ability to metabolize, or burn, stored fat. Your kidneys cannot work properly without enough water. When they cannot carry their workload, they hand over some of their job responsibility to the liver. Since one of the liver's jobs is to turn stored body fat into energy that can be used (burned) by the body, the liver may have trouble operating at full speed if it has to do some of the kidney's work. If so, it may break down less fat, which means more fat remains stored in the body and weight loss potentially slows down. So, water keeps the kidneys working properly, which helps keep the liver doing its job of breaking down stored fat. So water has a role in the fat-burning process of metabolism.

Next benefit? Water helps maintain good muscle and skin tone. Did you know that water gives the muscle its natural ability to contract? A muscle that contracts is a muscle at work. A muscle at work means energy burned. Energy burned means your metabolism is revved up and doing its job! A "revved up" metabolism usually results in weight loss if your body is carrying more weight than it needs. Since weight loss can leave skin looking loose, water helps reduce this sagging by supporting your shrinking cells and keeping the skin plumped and healthy.

Last but not least, water can help remove waste produced when extra body fat is burned. So it would make sense that more water is needed to help flush out the extra waste caused by weight loss itself. Once again, it seems water is important for a more efficient metabolism and for optimal health.

But the real question comes down to this: What counts as "water"? What about those flavored or fitness waters? Can coffee count? Regular or decaffeinated? What about sodas – regular or diet? The Dietary Guidelines for Americans 2005 say that all of these fluids can hydrate because they all contain water; therefore, caffeine containing drinks can count towards your daily fluid needs.

What does Rev It Up! say? You will take a closer look at each one of these fluid options, including newer products like fitness or flavored waters, in Week 3. But for this week, if you are willing to take the Rev It Up! challenge *all the way*, let's try to stick with the tried and true fluid, water itself, to meet your first FLUID challenge.

Need some strategies to help you drink more water? Try one of these ideas:

1. "Don't leave home without it!" Keep a water bottle chilled and ready to go, and when you grab your car keys, grab a water bottle, too! Keep a water bottle in your car…and try to finish it off before you reach your destination. Fill it back up and drink more water on your way home.

2.   Purchase the 8-ounce individual bottles of water and put eight of these in your refrigerator as a reminder of your day's goal. You can "see" the full challenge, but it is in smaller increments. An 8-ounce portion may be easier to handle at one time than a big 24-ounce water bottle!

3.   Let a glass of water be the door that opens and closes a meal or snack. Before you begin eating, open the door by drinking 4 to 8 ounces of water. After you finish eating, close the door by drinking 4 to 8 ounces more.

4.   Add a little lemon or lime juice to give your water more pizzazz.

5.   Freeze a water bottle that is half full of water overnight. In the morning, fill up the remainder of the bottle with water. This will guarantee that your water stays cool for a longer period of time.

Your **FLUID CHALLENGE** for Week 1: Dive in and try to **double the amount of water you drink, up to 8 glasses a day**. If one glass is 8 ounces (or 1 cup), that's 64 ounces (or 8 cups) daily. In your Maintenance Log, check off one cup for every 8 ounces consumed.

Chapter 4

Headlights on Fitness:
Warm Up Your Motor

You have learned the "fuel it" strategies for the first week of Rev It Up!. Now it's time to use the fuel to "move it"! Think about your car again. It's no surprise that all the parts to your car are designed for movement-movement that's efficient and consistent to take you where you need to go. Likewise, your body is designed for movement, too. Take a moment to remind yourself about all the benefits of moving your body.

How Does Exercise Benefit Your Body?

You may know that exercise can lower your blood cholesterol, reduce your blood pressure, strengthen your bones, and stabilize your blood sugar. Exercise may even help reduce your risk of developing diabetes and some types of cancer. And you know that exercise burns calories. What you may not know is that exercise actually improves your body's ability to burn stored body fat. Remember the enzyme LPL, whose job includes moving fat from your blood into fat cells for storage? Exercise counteracts LPL's fat-storing activity! It slows down LPL's activity in fat tissues, making it harder to store fat. And it increases LPL's ability to move fat into muscle cells so that it can be burned for energy instead of stored as more body fat. Sure, exercise burns calories, but it does so much more for you because it can literally change your fat-storing system into a more productive fat-burning system!

How Does Exercise Benefit Your Brain?

Exercise benefits your physical body in many ways, but it also benefits your *emotional* body. Many studies have shown that exercise not only increases your energy level but also helps relieve depression, improve self-esteem, and balance mood swings. Exercise triggers your brain to produce certain "feel good" chemicals called endorphins. These chemicals are related to the opium family and can produce a natural high that calms moods, lifts spirits, and improves self-confidence. With a stressful, fast-paced lifestyle, you need the emotional benefits alone that make regular exercise worth your time.

What Type of Exercise Do You Need To Do?

There are lots of reasons why moving your body is beneficial. But what kind of exercise is best? To rev up your metabolism, a combination of aerobic exercise and strength training is the goal. The first Fitness Challenge targets aerobic exercise, like walking, jogging, cycling or participating in a group exercise class like step aerobics. These types of exercise are called "aerobic" because you use a lot of "air", or oxygen, as you work. The key is to move your body in an activity that increases the number of heartbeats and the number of breaths you take per minute and keeps these numbers there for a steady period of time. And over time, your heart muscle grows stronger and larger, so that each beat is more efficient.

With more "powerful" heartbeats, the number of beats needed to do the same amount of exercise decreases. And your body learns to deliver oxygen to your muscles at a faster pace, so your heart does not have to work as hard since each beat is stronger and more oxygen is available to your working muscles. What a great tradeoff!

How Often and How Long Should You Exercise?

Of the two types of exercise, aerobic exercise should be done more often. Three times a week for 20 minutes each in your target heart rate range will help lower your risk of heart disease for sure, but to really rev up your metabolism, your body needs to exercise "more often than not." That translates to about 4 to 5 days each week. **Check with your doctor first** if you have not been physically active or have a medical history that might be affected by exercise. When you have your doctor's permission, start slowly and work up to 30 to 45 minutes each time at a pace that forces your heart to work harder.

Caution Sign:
This is the Moment when the
Rubber Meets the Road!

Stop and check out how you are feeling right now, at this very moment. Did you balk at reading the word "should"? Cringe at the mention of that "E" word (exercise) in general? Feel tired at the thought of 20 minutes, 3 days a week, let alone 30-45 minutes for 4 days a week?

In today's crazy-paced world, it's no wonder exercise can seem so difficult. How do you honestly fit it in? Is it worth it if you can only make time for 10 minutes a day, and not even every day? Especially when the calorie charts tell you that would only burn the equivalent of an apple? What if you literally hate to exercise? You do not even like to sweat?

These thoughts are real and can feel like permanent roadblocks. Sometimes it may be best to forget about the calories burned and the "I really should exercise" thinking. Start over, back at the beginning. The key is to begin a new *pattern*, even if it's just 10 minutes at first. Once the pattern of moving your body is set, it is easier to add more time later. So think about setting a new pattern of just moving more. Who knows where it might lead? Studies have shown that moving your body (exercise) has a healthy synergistic effect. Move your body regularly, and you actually begin choosing, better yet, desiring healthier foods. Consistent activity tends to change taste preferences from the typical high-fat fare to more lower-fat favorites. And that can happen without looking at a nutrition book or reading a calorie list!

If you are someone who struggles with even the thought of exercise, try one of these simple steps. Think small, set a pattern for this week's routine, and see if it doesn't begin changing your perspective!

1.   Concentrate on only the next 24 hours. Decide to take 10 to 15 minutes out of the entire 24-hour day to purposely move your body. (By the way, that leaves 23 hours and 45 minutes to do all your other routines!)

2.   Set clothes out the night before if getting up early to move, or if planning to move after work. Having a comfortable set of clothes ready to go, or already packed in the car, waiting for you to

leave your office, helps keep the pattern in place. Better yet, change at work – whether going to a gym, an outdoor track, even if going straight home. You will be ready to move when you walk into your own front door!

3.   Plan a distraction if you choose to move inside a gym or your home, such as on a treadmill. Read that magazine that came in the mail last week (most magazines can be read in about 10 to 15 minutes!). Read those journal articles stacked up on your desk. Choose five energetic songs and make a plan to move for those five songs only (five songs usually last about 15 minutes). Watch TV, or better yet, rent a movie DVD and play a 15-minute segment each time. If it is a really good movie, you will want to get back on that treadmill again just to see what happens next!

Now you have your body moving. One day planned at a time. A new pattern of lifestyle is in place. Feeling better now?

Is There Anything Else To Know?

Yes, there is-the **warm-up**. Take a minute and picture yourself getting in your car on a cold morning. You know you need to take a few minutes to allow your engine to warm up, so when you DO start driving, your car is ready to go and less likely to stall in the middle of traffic. Likewise, you also need to warm-up your body first. It may be easier to just jump into exercise-it saves you time, right? Well, eliminating the warm up may save a few minutes, at that moment, but you risk losing a lot of time later by decreasing your body's performance and increasing the risk of injury. An injury can put your body in the repair shop for a long time. Is it worth the risk?

Starting your activity ever so slowly allows your heart rate to increase slowly. It also helps change the direction of your blood flow away from organs like your stomach, where it is needed for digestion, towards your working muscles, for exercise. If you start moving too quickly without warming up, blood has to move VERY quickly to your muscles. This can not only make you nauseated because of the abrupt interruption of digestion but also rapidly increase your heart rate and your breathing. You will get tired more quickly, which cannot help but affect your desire to continue.

To warm up your muscles, allow for an extra 5 minutes to do the same activity but at a slower pace. For example, if you want to walk on the treadmill, warm up by starting out at a slower pace. Gently swing your arms by your side and very gradually increase the speed over 5 minutes. This plan works for ANY activity! The extra 5 minutes also give your mind a chance to relax, rid itself of the day's stress, and focus on your exercise goals.

Is That All?

"What goes up…must come down!" If the warm up is so important, so is the **cool-down.** Stopping abruptly stresses your muscles, and that includes your heart. It can increase your blood pressure, cause muscle cramps and soreness, make you dizzy, and increase your risk of injury. So always plan for some cool-down time, when you begin slowing down your pace and decreasing your heart rate-while you continue the same activity. Allow the cool down to gently take your muscles back to where they started so that they are ready to go again when YOU are!

The second part of a proper cool-down includes time to **stretch** those warm, flexible muscles! Exercise works your muscles, and during those contractions that you repeated over and over as you moved your body, your muscles have tightened. Tight muscles are shorter muscles. Stretching takes advantage of the warm muscle's flexibility, lengthening that same muscle, helping you relax, and improving your range of motion. This helps take away that soreness you may feel the next day, too.

Another reason? Stretching helps prevent the natural effect of aging! As you age, your muscles and joints lose flexibility, which may eventually affect your enjoyment of many daily activities. Stretching, done consistently, helps keep your muscles more flexible. And if your muscles are already warm from working out, you are able to receive the most benefit from each stretch.

Begin your stretches with the muscles you used the most. For example, if you walked, stretch the front and back of your thigh, and your calf muscles, first. Begin with the biggest muscles in that area and move to the smaller (i.e., thigh muscles before calf muscles). Next, stretch the upper body: torso, back, chest, shoulders, and arms, since they have helped balance and stabilize you during exercise.

Sample Stretching Routine

QUADRICEP (FRONT OF YOUR THIGH) STRETCH:
While holding a chair or other object for balance with your left hand, bend your right leg at the knee while bringing your right foot up behind you. Reach back with your *right hand and grasp the middle of your right foot or your right ankle. Your knee should be pointing straight down towards the floor and your hip should be relaxed. Do not lift your foot higher and pull your knee out of that straight down alignment. Remember to keep your opposite knee unlocked. Hold for 10 to 15 seconds and repeat on opposite side. You should feel this stretch in the front muscles of your thigh. For a more advanced stretch, let go of your stabilizing chair or wall and lift the opposite arm (from the leg being stretched) out to the side so that you add some benefit to the balancing muscles during your stretch.

*People with knee trouble may wish to use the opposite hand and reach behind the back to grasp the foot of the bending leg in order to protect the knee from possible injury.

HAMSTRING (BACK OF YOUR THIGH) STRETCH:
Place your right foot on a chair or elevated object that is lower than your hips. Do not lock your knee. Gently "sink" into the stretch by bending the opposite knee and lowering your body. Hold for 10 to 15 seconds, and repeat with the opposite leg.

CALF STRETCH:
Facing a wall, press your right foot against the wall, keeping your heel stationary against the floor and a slight bend in your knee. Hold for 10 to 15 seconds and repeat with your opposite foot.

TORSO:

Stand with feet hip width apart and slowly lift straightened arms out in front of you until they are reaching straight up and your elbows are just in front of your ears. Hands should be open with palms facing inward. Take a deep breath and as you exhale, slowly bend to the right and hold while you take slow, deep breaths for 10 to 15 seconds. Return to center and stretch upward for 10 to 15 seconds. Repeat to the left side.

CHEST STRETCH:

Clasp your hands behind your back. Extend your arms up and out, as if you are trying to pull your shoulder blades together. Hold for 10 to 15 seconds.

BACK STRETCH:

Clasp your hands in front of your chest, arms extended. Reach forward as if you are pulling your shoulder blades apart. Hold for 10 to 15 seconds.

SHOULDER STRETCH:

Stand up straight and tall. Bring your right arm across your chest, supporting with your left hand. Feel the stretch in your right shoulder. Consciously drop, or relax, the right shoulder even more if you can. Hold for 10 to 20 seconds, and repeat with other arm.

There are many more stretches you can do, but these target the major muscles and will help you begin a routine that will keep you flexible and help prevent injuries down the road. Remember to breathe deeply and slowly during each stretch!

The "Anything Else?" is definitely "something else," isn't it? *A warm-up, AND a cool-down including good stretch time.* Can you still keep your workout commitment to an amount of time that is realistic? Sure! A 5-minute warm-up can be followed by 30 minutes of aerobic exercise and concluded with 10 minutes to cool down and stretch. So, yes, you can. The big question: Is it worth it? Absolutely! It's an investment in your body's ability to KEEP on exercising!

Your **FITNESS CHALLENGE** for Week 1: **Choose an aerobic activity you enjoy, and commit to move your body (with your physician's permission).** If you are new or just resistant to regular body movement, start small with simple goals. Get a new lifestyle *pattern* set. You can add to your pattern as the weeks pass, but try to commit to include a warm-up AND cool-down each time. It doesn't really matter what time of day you choose-if you are not a morning person, do not plan to attend a 5:30am aerobics class! Find a time that works with your schedule-and commit to moving your body, consistently, with a long-term goal of 4 days out of every week. Use your Maintenance Log to record your progress (what you do, when you do it, and for how long).

A Look in the Rearview Mirror

Week 1: Start Your Engine

Foundation: Before eating or drinking, stop and check your fuel gauge. Record the level of hunger (H) and fullness (F) in your Maintenance Log before and after each meal and snack.

Food: Turn the key by eating breakfast every morning within 1-1 ½ hours after rising.

Fluid: Dive in and try to double the amount of water you drink, up to eight glasses daily.

Fitness: Choose an aerobic activity you enjoy, and commit to move your body (with your physician's permission), working up to four different days. Gradually work up to 45 to 60 total minutes, which includes warm-up and cool-down.

Record any changes you notice this week:

Date	Thoughts, Feelings, Body Changes?

Week 2:

Move Your Car
Out of the Garage

"With all the gimmick and fad diets out there, this is actually a wellness program that doesn't make me feel deprived or that I'm on a diet. This may seem like a small thing, but it's been the most important: using 'ping pong ball' portions from the fat group and using the size of my hand as a guide to the right size in meat or protein portions. That helps keep me on a healthy track." A.R.

Chapter 5

Headlights on Foundation:
Align Your Fuel Timing

You are on your way to building a new foundation by checking your fuel gauge, or your hunger/fullness levels, before and after each meal or snack. The next Foundation strategy for a revved up metabolism that goes hand-in-hand with your fuel gauge is the alignment, or balance, of meals and snacks. In past attempts to lose weight, have you tried to balance the amount of fuel (*what* you eat and drink) but ignored the need to balance the timing (*when* you eat and drink)? The "what" and "when" are both important steps to moving on out!

Let's start with the "when". To turn the key in the ignition, you have started eating breakfast within 1 to 1 ½ hours after getting out of bed. Now, let's take it one step further and align the rest of your meals and snacks to keep your engine fueled throughout the entire day.

Think back to your car again. You know it's time to fuel your car when you see the needle on your fuel gauge nearing the empty level, right? Most cars are equipped with reminders to warn of a low gas tank-either a light appears or a beep is heard. Some even have a programmed voice telling you fuel is needed. Wouldn't it be nice if our bodies had the same clear warning features?

If you are paying attention, you hear the warning before you reach empty, stop, and fill your gas tank. Sometimes you may accidentally find yourself on empty without realizing it because you ignored the signals or did not stop long enough to notice. In more of a panic now, you quickly rush to find a gas station, hoping you make it before you run out of fuel. Often you will not have the time to locate the best price or your favorite brand-you're just lucky to find anything and find it fast!

Once at the pump, it makes sense to go ahead and fill the fuel tank completely. Saves you time in the long run. But occasionally you may have to put in just a few dollars-maybe that's all the cash you have available or you don't have enough time to fuel the entire engine at that moment. The extra few gallons of fuel will give you the boost you need to buy some time until you have an opportunity to fill it up.

How do you know when your tank is full? The nozzle clicks off, right? (if only our bodies were that easy!) Even if you are on a long trip to one of your favorite destinations and know that you have hours to go before you are there, you still cannot add any more fuel once the tank is full. Well, you *could* override the pump and force more fuel into the tank, but the gas has nowhere left to go. It spills out, on to the car, down to the ground, and is completely wasted. Or you could buy the extra tank of gas and store it in a container, but you still would have to wait to use it, and storing gas in a moving car has its consequences! Whichever the circumstance, the gas cannot be used then, but you still have to pay for it, right?

"I would never overfill my tank like that and waste gas and money!" Yes, you are right. You *do* know your tank's limitations and how to meet your car's fuel needs depending on your daily plans. But do you know that much about your own body, and how to meet its fuel needs without overflowing?

Pumping gas into a fuel tank is like fueling your metabolism with regular stops at mealtimes. Let's compare the two:

Your body's fuel tank holds <u>about 4 hours worth of fuel</u> at any given time. Your fuel gauge is your hunger and fullness cycle. As your hunger approaches a 3 out of a 10 on the hunger scale, your body's warning light, hunger, lets you know that it's time to look for fuel. Ideally you have some time to look around and find the best price and brand of "fuel" (food) for your "car"(body), either at a restaurant or at home. When you find it, you stop, fill up the tank by eating a meal, and hit the road again, fueled and ready.

As the day continues, you notice your hunger is approaching a 3 out of 10 again. You have several commitments and know it's going to be a few more hours before your next meal, so you stop and refuel with a snack, or a few dollars worth of fuel to buy some time until you can fill it up.

What if you don't pay attention to your hunger cycles, and you realize you are a 1 out of a 10 before you had a chance to look for the nearest fuel (food) station? You will be very quick to choose something fast and easy, regardless if it is the best choice in health and price or not. Fast food restaurants or convenience store snacks become too hard to pass up when you are out of fuel and out of time!

Or maybe you know you are going to your favorite restaurant for dinner. So you plan to skip your lunch so you can eat more calories at dinner without feeling guilty. *Not a good idea!* First of all, you will be so hungry that your cravings will increase and your ability to make healthy, balanced choices will be compromised. Secondly, it is inevitable that you will overeat at that meal. That is no different from standing at the pump with your hand holding the lever down as gas continues to flow even after the nozzle clicks and the pump reads full. You keep filling beyond the amount that your tank can hold. This wastes calories and ends up inevitably being wasted and stored as body fat. *Somehow it is a lot easier to see the consequences of over-fueling your gas tank than it is over-fueling your body's tank.*

The important lesson here is meal timing! So follow these simple guidelines:

1) Breakfast needs to be eaten within 1 to 1 ½ hours of getting up and going (You are doing this already, right?).

2) All other meals or snacks need to be eaten within 4 hours of the previous meal or snack. *Example A*: You ate breakfast at 6:30 a.m. and lunchtime will not arrive until around noon, so you eat a snack at about 10 a.m. to keep your engine fueled! *Example B*: You ate breakfast around 8:00 a.m., so you will not need to eat a morning snack since your lunch break is at noon. But plan ahead for that long afternoon stretch! *Example C*: You eat lunch at noon, but dinner is not planned until after 6:00p.m. Therefore, an afternoon snack around 3:00 p.m. will be necessary to keep

your engine running efficiently and prevent cravings before dinner.

3) What about snacks *after* dinner? Late-evening snacks are not mandatory and probably not necessary for most people. Your body will begin slowing down in its preparation for sleep and does not need any additional energy. But, in certain situations, an after-dinner snack may be necessary if you are going to remain active for a long period of time after your dinner meal. *Example A*: You are a student staying up late to study for an exam. You had dinner at 6 p.m. and it is already 10 p.m., and you are not finished. A snack is probably a good idea to keep you energized to continue studying and to prevent that late-night refrigerator raid! *Example B*: You are a business person and up late completing a project. Yes, the same suggestion applies to you. Do not be afraid of eating later in the evening if you are busy with work or an event and you find yourself hungry again after 3 or 4 hours have passed since dinner. But, if you are just sitting and watching the evening news before you go to bed, your body does not need an energy boost. There is no hard and fast rule that prohibits evening snacking-listen to your body, check out the situation, and respond according to your needs. But if weight loss is your goal, be cautious about fueling your tank when your car is parked in the garage!

So, that is how you take the next step to align your meals and snacks. You have already started eating breakfast. Now just watch the clock and make sure that you fuel your engine within 4 hours of each meal or snack. As the availability of fuel stays consistent, you will notice that your hunger, or fuel gauge, begins to match up to the clock. And as you become more aware of your hunger and fullness levels, you will not need to watch the clock-you will simply be able to listen to your body and respond to your brain's signal to eat.

Do you hear yourself saying, "*I just don't know about this? You tell me to follow my hunger signals but then you ask me to eat every 4hours. I am NOT hungry every4 hours! What gives?*" Initially, you may feel that you are a slave to Father Time, having to eat based on a clock without feeling or knowing you are really hungry. And if you have always eaten a big dinner meal, you may not quickly decrease the quantity at that meal just because you've eaten more throughout the day. Habits are difficult to break! But don't forget several truths:

1. If you have eaten more throughout the day, your body will arrive at that dinner meal burning more calories than it used to burn at that time.
2. You will have a well-fueled, clear mind so that you can make conscious decisions about how much and what to eat.
3. Gradually, but consistently, your three meals will begin lining up so that each meal is no bigger or smaller than the other.
4. Because you are now eating from hunger and fullness signals, you will notice that you are not as hungry and will begin eating less at dinner based on your own decision.,
5. At this point, you OWN your body changes! Congratulations!

If these five reasons do not provide enough assurance, try this. Repeat the following four-word sentence, with confidence, when you feel the need to keep eating even though you know you are not really hungry anymore: **I CAN EAT AGAIN!**

Now repeat it again, emphasizing the first word: **I** can eat again. Now the second word: I **CAN** eat again. Then the third word: I can **EAT** again. Finally the fourth word: I can eat **AGAIN**. There is something strangely comforting about saying "I can eat again!" You may know it intellectually but do your actions often reflect something different? Somehow it's easier to eat each meal as if it is the last, rather than be willing to put the fork down when your fuel tank is full but the rest of the lasagna is still sitting on your plate, or the last half of that slice of pie is calling your name.

No one is telling you not to have it, but just have it later, when your fuel tank actually needs more fuel. Then the body can and will use it, not when it overflows from a tank that is already full but when it flows into a tank that is empty and ready for more!

Once you align the timing of your meals and snacks, you may start to notice that your cravings begin to lessen. This may be most apparent in the afternoon if you have never stopped to eat a snack even though your lunch and dinner are always more than 4 hours apart. When your body is fueled consistently, and is not allowed to get too hungry between meals, the cravings for fats and sugars begin to disappear. Isn't that a wonderful benefit of eating a snack?

If that is not enough, keep an eye on changes in your energy level, too. With consistent fuel, you will see your energy level become more consistent. And you will feel better! Both energy increases and craving decreases are evidence of a changing metabolism. You are on your way!

> *"I really feel that I know so much more about my body now than ever, and feel 100% better than I have felt for years. I know part of it is because I know I look better but much of it is that I have so much more energy. Tonight I actually crossed my left leg over my right one, and I cannot tell you how long it has been since I did that comfortably."* Doris

Your **FOUNDATION CHALLENGE** for Week 2: Eat breakfast within 1 to 1 1/2 hours after rising, and **do not wait longer than 4 hours between each meal or snack.** Record the times you eat in your Maintenance Log.

Chapter 6

Headlights on Food:
Balance Your Fuel Content

See how it all begins to work together? Now let's examine the other important step to meal alignment-the "WHAT":

A.   A balanced meal needs to include 3 to 4 fuel (food) groups to qualify.
B.   A balanced snack needs to include 1 to 2 fuel (food) groups to qualify.

What exactly is a fuel group? Although more than 40 different nutrients with many different functions are required for good health, these nutrients can be divided into just five food groups-all of which provide fuel for your body. Hence the term, fuel group! One single fuel group is not more important than another because each group has different "jobs" or priorities in the body. Our body is an amazing machine that requires fuel from all the food groups to produce its best work. And these same fuel groups can be divided into those that provide ENERGY (to specifically fuel the brain and all your body's functions and movement) and those that provide PROTEIN (for replacing and building cells, hormones, enzymes, and muscles among other jobs!) The five fuel groups that you will use to build a meal or snack include the *energy* fuel groups: Grains and Starches, Fruits and Vegetables, and the *protein* fuel groups: Animal/Plant Proteins and Dairy Proteins.

You need both energy and protein at all three meals-breakfast, lunch and dinner. For snacks, it depends on the time frame. If you have just an hour or so before lunch, a mid-morning snack for only energy gives you that little boost you need. But since you usually need more fuel in the afternoon to break the six or more hour time span between lunch and dinner, your afternoon snack needs both energy and protein from two fuel groups. Protein, when eaten with an energy fuel, helps make the energy from that grain or fruit or vegetable last longer, and also helps prevent cravings. Therefore, energy and protein fuels work together-whether eaten at meals or snacks-to provide more lasting energy and a healthier balance of fuel.

A complete table of what foods go into each fuel group is right around the corner, but before you read any further about what to eat, you may have already noticed that certain well-loved foods have not been mentioned yet. Are you asking yourself, "Where are those desserts hiding? What about a glass of wine? And I don't see any French fries!" Indeed they have not been mentioned specifically yet, but do not panic! These "other" foods do have a place, but the other fuel group is just that-OTHER. It does not count as one of the fuel groups from which to build a meal or snack. The "other" foods simply *complement* your meals and snacks. So look at how to build a meal or snack from the five basic fuel groups first, then you will discover how the "other" group fits in.

Are you ready to learn how to build a meal? You will need to remember the following guidelines:

A MEAL = 3 to 4 fuel groups (for both energy and protein)

A SNACK = 1 to 2 fuel groups (depends on time of day)

    Mid-morning snack = 1 fuel group for energy only

    Mid-afternoon snack = 2 fuel groups for energy and protein

Next, you will need to know how much a portion is for each fuel group. Does this mean you have to weigh and measure your foods? No! Does this mean that you have to keep a food reference handy that lists portions and calories for each food? No! So, what does this mean for you, someone who desires to lose weight but needs a road map that guides your path without becoming unrealistic, demanding, or complicated?

In Rev It Up! terms, you'll need only three simple tools to keep you on the right road: a baseball, a ping pong ball, and the palm of your hand. Breathe a sigh of relief and throw out that old calorie-counting book! Toss the fat gram counter! For a reference, study the following:

1.   A **baseball** is approximately 2.94" wide:

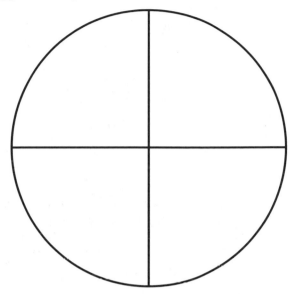

2.   The **palm of your hand**…you should have one of these with you!

3.   A **ping pong ball** is approximately 1 ½ " wide:

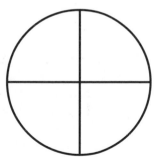

Now take a closer look at each of these:

Visualize a baseball on your plate. Technically, you could cut a baseball in two and fill each side with mashed potatoes-and both sides would equal one full cup (It's true!). However, "technical" does not always represent "realistic." Who carries around a measuring cup and levels off a serving perfectly? And if you had to technically represent a true serving of every grain or starch, fruit or vegetable, the differences can vary from a tennis ball to a softball size, depending on the density of the food you are measuring. So, stay simple and realistic. Think baseball circumference, and count one-half baseball as roughly the size of 1 portion of grain or starch, and one baseball as roughly the size of 1 portion of fruit, vegetable or soft dairy protein like cottage cheese. (Other liquid-based dairy products, like yogurt or milk, still need the typical 8-ounce or 1-cup portion).

The palm of your hand is the amount of protein you need at each lunch and dinner. A palm is usually about 3 to 5 ounces, depending on the bone structure and size of the person; therefore, a large-boned, taller person will need more protein than a small-build, petite person. Your palm answers the question for lunch and dinner, but what about breakfast? Typically the size of half of your palm is equal to one egg, for women, and two eggs, for men. It's doubtful you will eat, or even need, eggs every day, which is why the breakfast meal proteins are unique. Dairy products, even nuts and seeds, fit well at breakfast, too. Answers to more of your breakfast questions can be found shortly when you look at examples of breakfast meals.

A ping pong ball is roughly the size of 1 portion of snack proteins, like peanut butter (1 tablespoon = 1 ping pong ball), nuts/seeds (1 tablespoon= 1 ping pong ball) or block-style cheese (1 ounce "block" = 1 ping pong ball). A ping pong ball is also about the size of 1 portion (1 tablespoon) of fat, like salad dressing, mayonnaise, butter, margarine, sour cream, cream cheese, oil…in other words, the fats you add to foods to increase flavor and texture. Again, think ping pong ball *circumference*. Nuts certainly vary in size, and peanut butter is denser than vegetable oil, so "technically" a serving might vary between a large marble and a golf ball. But stay simple, and realistic, and count one ping pong ball as roughly 1 portion of snack proteins and 1 portion of higher-fat condiments.

Overwhelmed? Take a slow, deep breath and repeat: "I solemnly swear that I will NOT panic until I have read through this entire chapter." You will see how it all works together in just a few minutes. Right now, simply read each fuel group that follows, and note the recommended portions for each, depending on if it's a meal or a snack. *Please note:* Portion guidelines are specific for general weight loss and may need to be individualized. See a registered dietitian for a more individualized plan if needed.

ENERGY FUEL GROUP	PORTION GUIDELINES FOR WEIGHT LOSS
GRAINS and STARCHES (WHOLE GRAIN OR 100% WHOLE-WHEAT preferred) • Breads, including pita, bagels, tortillas, roll/bun • Beans/peas, like lentils, navy, pinto, lima, garbanzo • Corn, including tortillas and popcorn • Crackers • Oats and cereals, hot or cold • Pastas • Potatoes, white and sweet • Pretzels, low-fat chips • Rice, brown preferred	For **meal**: 1 baseball (*women*) or 1 ½- baseballs (*men*) For **snack***: 0- ½ baseball (*women*) or 0-1 baseball (*men*) (*"0" means you can choose another energy fuel like vegetable or fruit for a snack instead of choosing a grain) Note: 1 bread slice/roll = ½ baseball

ENERGY FUEL GROUP	PORTION GUIDELINES FOR WEIGHT LOSS
FRUITS • All fresh fruits • All canned fruits, NO sugar added • All frozen fruits, NO sugar added • All dried fruits*, NO sugar added	For **meal** or **snack** (*women and men*): 1 baseball *2 ping pong balls for dried fruits

ENERGY FUEL GROUP	PORTION GUIDELINES FOR WEIGHT LOSS
VEGETABLES • All fresh vegetables • All frozen vegetables, without cream sauces (Canned vegetables are not preferred due to high level of sodium and low level of fiber)	For **meal** or **snack** (*women and men*): 1or more baseballs

PROTEIN FUEL GROUP	PORTION GUIDELINES FOR WEIGHT LOSS
DAIRY PROTEINS • Cheeses, part skim or 2% milk based preferred • Cottage cheese, 1% • Milk, fat free or 1% • Yogurt, fat free or 1% Try to include at least 2 servings (*men*) or 3 servings (*women*)* of dairy daily to get the calcium needed to maintain strong bones.	For **meal** or **snack** (*women* and *men*): 1 ping pong ball of cheese (block style, or 1 slice prepackaged) 1 baseball of cottage cheese 1 cup (8 ounce) yogurt or milk *If you do not include this amount consistently, consider taking a calcium supplement with Vitamin D.

PROTEIN FUEL GROUP	PORTION GUIDELINES FOR WEIGHT LOSS
ANIMAL / PLANT PROTEINS **Animal Proteins:** • Beef, lean cuts preferred • Canadian bacon • Deli sliced meats, lean • Egg or egg substitutes (Continued on next page)	For **breakfast meal** (*women and men*): 1/2 palm size (Example: 1 egg for women, two for men) For **lunch and dinner meals** (*women and men*): palm size

• Fish, fresh, frozen, canned • Pork, lean cuts preferred • Poultry, without skin **Plant Proteins:** • Beans/lentils (NOTE: These are also grain fuels.) • Soy products, including tofu • Vegetarian meats	For **lunch and dinner meals** (*women and men*): palm size
Snack Proteins: • Peanut butter, natural preferred • Nuts and seeds	For **snack** (*women and men*): 1 ping pong ball Note: These plant proteins are best for snacks because of the higher calorie content.

[As stated, these recommendations are for weight loss for most individuals. Discuss these guidelines with a registered dietitian if you feel they do not meet your specific needs or circumstances. If your goal is sports performance, you will need to increase the recommended number of servings depending on your exercise level.]

So all you need is a baseball, a ping pong ball, and the palm of your hand. Can it really be that simple? Yes! Each day is different, and hopefully you eat a variety of grains, fruits, and vegetables for your energy fuel, and a variety of animal, plant, and dairy proteins. It will all balance out in the long run, but only having three real-life objects as portion guides make it simple. You can go anywhere and keep your portions in control, without a calorie guidebook or fat gram counter, when you visualize a baseball or your palm as your guide. Likewise for a ping pong ball!

Is it time for another deep breath? All of this discussion about energy fuel, protein fuel, and portion guidelines can seem overwhelming at first, especially if you are used to receiving simple lists of "correct" foods to eat with specific measurements or recipes for each. A long list of "good and bad" foods is certainly easier in some ways-especially initially-because you do not have to think too hard to follow the plan. But is it realistic? What if you don't *like* most of the foods on the "good" list-what do you choose then? What if you make a mistake and eat the "wrong" thing? You have failed the plan and feel like giving up instead of embracing the opportunity to learn how your body's fuel gauge responds to different types of fuel. And what happens when you get tired of that list-how do you maintain control over your weight then?

OWNERSHIP of the changes your body makes-whether it is in weight loss, increased energy or decreased cravings-is so important. An easy "good and bad" food list takes the ownership away from YOU, and any success achieved is usually temporary. So you quit. But when you want to lose weight again, you pick up the list and try again. The problem? You have not changed the patterns and habits that got you there in the first place. Ownership of your food choices leads to ownership of your body's successes-that truly makes the long term difference!

Let's talk through another example. When you are looking at a map to a new city, many different choices exist, and the route you choose will depend on your priorities. Do you want to take the scenic route, or do you need to take the interstates in order to save time? It's up to you. Regardless of your reasons, you have to study the map to find the route that works best for you. And, inevitably, you might make a few wrong turns, but you realize your mistake when the landmarks you are passing do not match up to the ones you expect. Your unexpected detour slows you down, but it also makes you pay more attention. And you will probably not make the same mistake again since you are more focused now!

But if someone is driving *for* you, your responsibilities change dramatically. It's doubtful that you will pay attention to the roads you are traveling, since riding as a passenger is much easier and requires little concentration on your part. This works well for you as long as the driver is available-but what happens if you are required to drive yourself the next time? You have no one to depend on but yourself to find your way back home, but you don't know the right way to go. You did not pay attention to the turns that you needed to make and now you find yourself lost and confused about what direction to take.

If you know that feeling of being frustrated with yourself when you cannot remember simple turns, get lost, and waste valuable time in the process, then you can hopefully relate to how it feels if you have been following a "good and bad" food list, without having to think, until all of a sudden it's not working for you anymore. The diet is over, the list is gone, and you are on your own. You find yourself going in circles, or just going back the way you came and giving up. A diet that tells you exactly what food to eat at every meal is just like someone driving *for* you. Ownership of your body is following guidelines but having to make your own food choices, some good and some bad. Ownership of your body is learning from every good and not so good choice and feeling more confident as you get closer to your goal.   And as you own your mistakes as well as your progress, you can take 100% credit for your inevitable success!

Convinced that you want to give this ownership thing a try? Great! Let's put the Rev It Up! guidelines together and see how it works. At each meal-breakfast, lunch and dinner-you need both energy and protein-from 3 to 4 fuel group choices. At each snack, which is designed to give you a few extra "miles" before you stop for a fill-up, you need less fuel than at your meal times, so select only 1 to 2 fuel group choices. At your morning snack, you probably need just energy (1 fuel group) unless you work out in the early morning, then you can consider adding protein, too. At your afternoon snack, you definitely need energy and protein (2 fuel groups).

How about some examples of different meals and snacks using the different fuel groups? Check out the following ideas:

Breakfast Examples:

An example of a balanced breakfast, using 3 fuel groups, is cold cereal like Raisin Bran (amount of 1baseball for women, 2 for men), small grapefruit (1 baseball), and 1% milk (1 cup).

3 fuel groups = GRAIN (cereal) + FRUIT (grapefruit)
+ DAIRY (milk)

Did this provide both energy and protein? Yes! Energy from the grain and fruit, and protein from the milk. A good example of a balanced meal providing energy and protein that meets the 3 to 4 fuel group goal. A second example, using 4 fuel groups, is a toasted English muffin (2 halves for women, 3 halves for men), served "sandwich style" with slices of tomato (amount of 1 baseball), a scrambled egg or two (1/2 to 1palm size portion) and reduced-fat (2% milk) cheese (1 individual slice).

4 fuel groups = GRAIN (muffin) + VEGETABLE (tomato) + ANIMAL PROTEIN (egg) + DAIRY (cheese)

Did this meal provide energy and protein? Yes, energy from the grain and vegetable, and protein from the egg and cheese. A balanced meal providing energy and protein that meets the 4 fuel group goals. If you were wondering how a vegetable could fit at breakfast, you can see that tomatoes or other choices like bell peppers, mushrooms, and onions work great! You can even sauté them, adding them to your scrambled egg for variety.

Lunch or Dinner Examples:

An example of a balanced lunch or dinner is a whole-wheat pita pocket (1 pita for women, 1 ½ - 2 for men) stuffed with deli-sliced turkey (palm-size portion), lettuce shreds and tomato slices (at least 1 baseball), with strawberries (1 baseball) on the side.

4 fuel groups = GRAIN (pita) + VEGETABLE (lettuce/tomato) + FRUIT (strawberries) + ANIMAL PROTEIN (turkey)

A second example: How about a grilled pork tenderloin (palm size portion) with steamed asparagus (at least 1 baseball), a small baked sweet potato (size of 1/2 baseball for women, 1 baseball for men), and a whole grain roll (1/2 baseball)?

3 fuel groups = GRAIN (sweet potato and roll) + VEGETABLE (asparagus) + ANIMAL PROTEIN (pork)

You can add a ping pong ball-sized amount of butter or margarine to flavor your potato and roll. More on those OTHER foods coming up soon!

If you prefer combination type foods, a third example is thin crust vegetable pizza. The crust is your grain (1 baseball = 2 slices thin crust for women, 3 for men), the cheese (about 1 ping pong ball per average pizza slice) is your dairy, and the vegetables (hopefully enough for 1 baseball amount) speak for themselves! Adding a side salad (another baseball) with "light" vinaigrette dressing (up to 1 ping pong ball amount) will top it off.

3 fuel groups = GRAIN (pizza crust) + VEGETABLE (tomato sauce with vegetable toppings, salad) + DAIRY (cheese)

Snack Examples:

A "1 fuel group" snack, ideal for a midmorning pick-up, can be graham crackers (1/2 baseball = one large rectangle, or 2 "squares") *or* an apple (one baseball). Carrot sticks (one baseball) can certainly fit as well. The grain, fruit or vegetable fuel groups provide the energy you need for that midmorning boost. A dairy fuel, like one cup of low fat (1%) yogurt or milk, also fits well.

1 fuel group = GRAIN *or* FRUIT *or* VEGETABLE *or* DAIRY

A "2 fuel group" snack, ideal for the afternoon stretch when dinner will be much later, can be whole-wheat crackers (1/2 baseball amount equals 6 to 8 crackers) and a mozzarella cheese stick (about 1 ping pong ball). Another example is low-fat vanilla yogurt (1 cup, or 8 ounces) with banana slices (1 baseball) added. How about apple slices (1 baseball) with peanut butter (1 ping pong ball amount)? Or even whole grain cereal (1/2 to 1 baseball size amount) and 1% milk (1 cup or 8 ounces)?

2 fuel groups = GRAIN + DAIRY *or* FRUIT + DAIRY *or* FRUIT + PLANT PROTEIN

Other snack examples will be provided soon. But in the meantime, hopefully this helps you see how you can build a meal or snack, using the fuel groups to enjoy lots of variety while keeping your metabolism boosted! Even though giving a list of ready-to-go snack choices would be easier to follow, it takes away from your ownership of what you decide to eat. The list is purposefully delayed until Chapter 14 (Week 4) so that you can experiment with your own combinations and use your own hunger and fullness signals to decide what works for you or doesn't. The same principle holds true for meals, too. A ready-to-go list of lunch and dinner choices is easier but takes away the learning process. Remember, you want to drive the car, not be the passenger! It's all about ownership! Why don't you take a turn building sample meals and snacks? Fill in the following table, using some of your favorite foods:

Type of Meal	Fuel Choices	Portion Guide	# of Fuel Groups	Correct Portions
BREAKFAST				
LUNCH				
DINNER				
SNACK				

How did you do? Were your meals 3 to 4 fuel groups? Snacks 1 to 2? How did you estimate your portions (remember, baseball, ping pong ball, and palm of your hand!)?

Do you have to pre-plan your meals like this? No, but now you know you can if you need or want to do so!

Some of the examples above used fuel from the "Other" fuel group to complement the meal. It's time now to look at what foods fall into this "Other" group. The following table lists these foods for you; however, since these foods have lots of calories and few, if any, nutrients, react to these foods as you would react in any high-traffic area:

PROCEED WITH CAUTION!

THE "OTHER" FUEL GROUP	PORTION GUIDELINES FOR WEIGHT LOSS
ALL SUGARS • ALL cakes, cookies, frozen desserts, pies, including FAT-FREE VERSIONS • ALL candies, including chocolates • ALL sodas, excluding diet	**Proceed with CAUTION:** ½ baseball amount = 1 serving of sugars, such as cookies, pie, cake, ice cream 1-2 ping pong balls = 1 serving of most candy, chocolates

THE "OTHER" FUEL GROUP	PORTION GUIDELINES FOR WEIGHT LOSS
ALL FATS **SATURATED:** • Bacon (2 slices=1 ping pong ball) • Butter • Cream cheese • Coconut and products made with coconut or palm kernel • Mayonnaise and salad dressings made with mayonnaise	**Proceed with CAUTION:** (Fats are divided into two types: saturated and unsaturated. You will learn much more about these types in Week 4.) Up to 3 (*women*) or 4 (*men*) ping pong balls daily (1 ping pong ball=1 tablespoon).

	NOTE: If reduced-fat product is used, you may double the serving size.
• Sausage (1 patty/link = 1 ping pong ball) • Sour cream **UNSATURATED (preferred)*:** • ALL oils and oil-based dressings, except coconut and palm kernel oil • Avocados • Some margarines • Olives, black and green	
SPECIAL FATS: • ALL FRIED foods • ALL pastries (like doughnuts) • HIGH-FAT breads (like biscuits and croissants) • ALL cream-based casseroles	**LIMIT to NO MORE THAN 2** of these "special fats" per week. 1 serving = about 1 baseball (*women*) and 1 ½ baseballs (*men*)
THE "OTHER" FUEL GROUP	**PORTION GUIDELINES FOR WEIGHT LOSS**
ALL ALCOHOL: • Beer (12 ounces) • Light Beer (serving varies) • Liquor (1 ½ ounces) • Wine (5 ounces) Ounces listed indicate amount in one serving.	**Proceed with CAUTION:** Alcohols are concentrated carbohydrate calories that act more like fats after consumed. Count each serving of alcohol as one of your fat servings (**1 serving=1ping pong ball of fat)** *Moderation is considered:* 0 – 1 serving/day (*women*) 0 – 2 servings/day (*men*)

A CLOSER LOOK AT SUGARS

Let's talk about how to handle each of these "Other" fuels: sugars, fats, alcohol, separately, starting with **SUGARS**. In Week 4, you will learn a lot more about the two types of carbohydrates, grains (or starches) and sugars, and how the body uses them differently. In the meantime, you can proceed with caution and deal with your "sweet tooth" in several ways:

1) *You can choose dessert in place of your roll or serving of other starch/grain),* but be aware that you give up vitamins, minerals, fiber, and the type of carbohydrate energy that is "long lasting."

2) *You can choose to have dessert as an **extra** to your meal,* but be aware that it IS extra calories. Try to eat it within 30 minutes of your meal, to take advantage of the other fuel groups present. The fiber and protein from foods like meat and vegetables will slow down your body's response to the quick rush from sugar.

Regardless, keep a close eye on your hunger and fullness level. If you choose option #1, you will hopefully be quite full from the other fuels at your meal and consume only a small amount of dessert as a result. You CAN eat AGAIN, remember! If you choose option #2, remember that a large portion of dessert after a balanced meal can send the extra fuel spilling out of your gas tank into your fat stores. So why not savor the best two bites of any dessert-the first, and *last*, bite! Save the rest for later when your body is more capable of burning it. And who knows? You might even decide that those two bites satisfy your need for sweets, and your desire for the same dessert is gone by the time your next "fuel" break rolls around!

A CLOSER LOOK AT FATS

Now let's look at **FATS**, especially how to handle those special fats. Limit your added fats, like salad dressings and mayonnaise, to an *average* of no more than 3 (women) or 4 (men) ping pong ball amounts daily. On certain days, you may find that you have only one or two. Other days, you may discover that you had five or six before you realized it! But you averaged only three ping pong balls per day, so the amount of fat used will balance out in the end. Special fats, like creamy casseroles, cheesy combination-style foods such as enchiladas, or fried foods, are best limited to no more than two servings per week regardless whether you are male or female. Use your baseball guideline to keep the portion controlled. For example, are you offered a creamy chicken casserole with rice and vegetables at a potluck style event? Or maybe an enchilada covered in cheese sauce at the local Mexican restaurant? The amount of one baseball for women and around one and a half baseballs for men would be your limit for these special fat choices, and then fill up the rest of your plate with extra vegetables or fruits. What about French fries? Keep it to one baseball portion, which translates to a *small* order at most fast food places. Calories, and saturated fats, in commercial French fries add up fast!

A CLOSER LOOK AT ALCOHOL

Finally, take a look at **ALCOHOL**. Are you surprised that alcohol, made from grain itself, counts as a fat serving? Yes, it is a carbohydrate, although it has 7 calories per gram compared to sugar's 4 calories per gram. But, alcohol is broken down and stored in the body much more like a fat than a carbohydrate. Therefore a serving of alcohol, beer, wine, or liquor counts as one of your ping pong balls of added fat. So if you choose to have a glass of wine with dinner, that would be an ideal time to choose NOT to add the ping pong ball amount of butter on your whole grain roll! Since alcohol lowers your ability to resist overeating and stimulates your appetite, be cautious and consume a full glass of water between every serving of alcohol, just to stay on the safe side and keep you fuller in the process! The American Heart Association (AHA) considers a moderate intake of alcohol to be up to one serving daily for females and up to two servings daily for males. If you do not drink at all, the AHA does not encourage you to start.

These "Other" fuel group foods complement your meals or snacks and do not have to be avoided. They are certainly made to enjoy and enhance your foods…but the key is what you do **MORE OFTEN**

THAN NOT. Take a minute to notice how you feel and how your body responds to sugars, fats, or alcohol. Does the energy last? Does it increase your desire for even more food? Does it leave you feeling "heavy" and bloated, and just "over the top"? Was it worth it?

Sometimes, a dessert or a high-fat appetizer might be worth it, because it is a special occasion or just *because*. But it is important to know that your fuel choice was probably made because of the emotional benefits and not your body's actual physical hunger or need for sugar or fats. It may be temporarily worth the emotional effects, but often it may not be worth the longer lasting physical effects, such as the drop in energy, increase in cravings or the extra calories that have nowhere to go but storage.

When you know how to tell the difference between an emotional need and a physical need for a certain food, like that favorite dessert, you keep control of the direction your metabolism is heading. You can enjoy the side trip without the guilt that can keep you sidetracked. The difference in using these foods to complement instead of using these foods to fuel is what makes the difference in your metabolism. In other words, your goal is to choose healthy fuel *more often than not*. Keep an eye on your fuel gauge and your hunger and fullness levels. Soon you will become more in tune with your body and more aware of your reasons *for* your fuel choices and your reactions *to* your fuel choices.

Feeling overwhelmed? How will you remember to balance everything? Anything worthwhile takes an investment in time and energy. Don't try to "get it right" immediately! Here's what you need to do:

A)   **Simply EAT**
B)   **RECORD what you eat**
C)   **CHECK how you did**

You can choose to record your meals or snacks at the end of the day, but you might want to make a quick note on a piece of paper right after you eat and transfer it to your journal later. Regardless, at the end of the day, take a few minutes to check how you did. Did you eat a meal or snack every 4 hours? Did you have 3 to 4 fuel groups per meal? One to 2 per snack? You're making progress! Now, look at your portions. Your plate can be divided into 1/3 protein, 1/3 grain or starch, and the remaining 1/3 full of vegetables and fruit. Check it out-how many baseballs of grain or starch did you eat at a meal? Did you limit the protein at lunch and dinner to the size of your palm? Up to 3 (women) or 4 (men) ping pong balls of added fats daily? Do you see any place you could make changes? More fruit at breakfast? More vegetables at dinner? More turkey on your sandwich at lunch? Less grains everywhere? Simply *learn* and grow closer to your goal of wellness for a lifetime with every step!

Your **FOOD CHALLENGE** for Week 2: **Eat 3 to 4 fuel groups at meals, and 1 to 2 fuel groups at snacks**, using the portion guidelines. Record what you eat in your Maintenance Log.

"Rev It Up! has given me the food groups to choose from, and I was taught how to measure my food by sight without having to weigh or measure anything. It is a great program!"   Michelle

---

WARNING!

Please attempt to build your meals and snacks on your own. Remember, OWNERSHIP is important! But if you need to look at more examples, see the Appendix. A sample day, using grain choices for energy, is provided. For those who avoid grains from either misplaced fear of weight gain or misinformation, a sample day using only vegetable and fruit choices for energy is also included. The Rev It Up! guidelines are flexible and allow you the freedom to choose your own energy and protein sources depending on your preferences. Hopefully, this program will help clear any misconceptions about all the fuel groups over time.

Chapter 7

Headlights on Fluid:
Fill Up Your Water Tank

The key is turned in the ignition, you've been checking your water level, and now you are ready to move your car out of the garage. But if you took the challenge to double the amount of water you drink, up to 8 cups (64 ounces total) of water every day, you may be feeling that the only location you want to move is to the nearest restroom! Yes, you are probably making more frequent side trips to the restroom, but this side effect will not last long!

Your body will adjust to drinking more water by the end of the next few weeks, if not by the end of this week. Your trips to the restroom will begin to subside to once every 2 hours or less. When you get to the finish line of Rev It Up!, 8 cups of water will be your new daily standard!

If you have found yourself behind the challenge at the end of the day, you may have tried to "catch up" by drinking extra in the evening. This is not an effective strategy since you will find that your side trips to the restroom are interfering with a good night's sleep. Recommit yourself to the strategies from Chapter 4 and try to drink water throughout the daytime to avoid nighttime interference.

Just don't give up. Remind yourself that your body is mostly water, and almost everything that happens in your body, including metabolism, depends on a constant supply of adequate water. Water is important for your health and a healthy metabolism.

If this is the first time that you have tried to drink 8 cups of water daily, you may not want to hear that certain circumstances can increase the amount your body needs. You lose water through daily breathing and sweating, so any situation that makes you breathe faster and sweat heavier causes more water loss. Moving your body for exercise is certainly one of those situations! So it makes sense that your need for fluids is even greater when exercise is part of your lifestyle.

You have two choices. If you don't exercise, then your water needs will not increase. But you've learned that exercise gives a boost to your metabolism, so avoiding exercise is really not an option, right? So your other choice is to drink extra when you do exercise!

Do you remember that one of the key functions of water is to act like a radiator to cool your body off when your temperature begins to rise during exercise? What you may not realize is that you sweat about 2 to 4 cups of water for each hour of exercise. This is in addition to the normal amount of water you lose in an hour just from breathing and regular perspiration. If you do not replace this water, your body is not only unable to cool down appropriately but also risks dehydration.

Even mild dehydration can affect your energy level and lead to headaches, dizziness, cramps, even shortness of breath if allowed to continue. Making sure you drink extra water before, during, and after exercise is important to your health as well as your energy and performance. So here's how to fill your fluid level for exercise:

1.   Maintain your "daily 8" cups of water.
2.   Drink an extra ½ cup of water about 30 minutes BEFORE exercise.
3.   Drink an extra ½ cup of water DURING exercise.
4.   Drink an extra cup of water within 30 minutes AFTER exercise.

This equals about 2 cups of extra water on the days you exercise. If you are exercising outside in the heat, you may want to increase even more. Don't wait until you are thirsty to decide to drink. Thirst can be suppressed by exercise or just by habit! Drink enough to satisfy your thirst, and then a little more! You'll keep the radiator cool and your car (or body) performing at its best with just a little extra effort. It's worth it!

Your **FLUID CHALLENGE** for Week 2: **Drink EXTRA for exercise**. Check off the daily 8 cups you now drink and any extra cups for exercise at the top of the page of your Maintenance Log.

Chapter 8

Headlights on Fitness:
Check Your Gas Mileage

What kind of gas mileage are you getting with each mile traveled? Knowing the mileage that you can cover on each tank of gas may not be necessary for actually driving your car, but it is very helpful information. The efficiency of your gas mileage goes a long way in planning where and when you stop for fuel. And it works in similar ways for your body, too. In other words, are you working hard enough when you exercise to get the most mileage out of your fuel?

If you are new to exercise, or you just started exercising again, you may not feel that you are ready to talk about *working hard enough*. Just getting to the gym, or even putting on your walking shoes, takes planning and effort! Certainly committing to and beginning an exercise routine is a big step towards improving your fitness for a lifetime. But what if you are not new to exercise? What if you have been exercising for a long time but just don't see the results you thought you would? You faithfully walk on the treadmill or attend that same aerobics class, but you feel "stuck". You can remember feeling stronger the first few months, but now you see little change in your body. Is the effort worth it?

Maybe the problem is not in the effort to get to the gym but in your heart's effort during the time your body is exercising. Is your "gas mileage" efficient-in other words, is your heart really working hard enough to gradually but continually improve your fitness, but not too fast to be dangerous?

The best way to check your gas mileage (quality of performance) is to know your target heart rate range and monitor your workout's intensity. What is a target heart rate? It is the lowest and highest number of heartbeats per minute required to keep you in the aerobic (or oxygen burning) zone, which you learned about in Week 1. You can calculate your target heart rate range and then simply check your pulse during your exercise, or purchase and use a heart rate monitor, which reads your heart rate for you.

A recent study (University of Florida) used heart rate monitors to measure the intensity of the workouts of new exercisers. Although almost 50% rated their work level as moderate, their heart rate monitors showed that *only 15% were right!* Knowing your heart rate takes out the guesswork! Before you calculate your target heart rate, look at the following:

RESTING HEART RATE (RHR):

This is the number of heartbeats per minute when your body is at complete rest. Your heart itself is a muscle, and regular exercise makes stronger muscles. So it makes sense that regular exercise can decrease your resting heart rate since the stronger heart muscle does not have to work as hard to pump the same amount of blood.

Want to calculate your own resting heart rate?
Before you get out of bed in the morning, first thing after waking up when you are lying still and breathing quietly, find your pulse rate and count for 60 seconds. Repeat this for 2 more days and then average the results.

MAXIMUM HEART RATE (MHR):

This is the highest number of heartbeats per minute that your body can give. It can actually be tested only under medical supervision, or you can estimate the number with a simple formula using your age.

Want to calculate your own maximum heart rate?
Pick a formula below (male or female!), insert your age in the blank, and subtract from the first number. The result is your MHR.

(Male)   220 – (_____) = _____ MHR
(Female)   226 – (_____) = _____ MHR

TARGET HEART RATE RANGE (THR):

Again, this is your aerobic heart rate range-the minimum and maximum number of heartbeats per minute required to get the most out of your exercise time. Remember, aerobic means "using lots of oxygen". The lower end is about 65% of your maximum heart rate, and the upper end is about 85% of your maximum heart rate. Beyond 85%, you move into the "anaerobic" range, where your breaths become shorter and quicker and less oxygen is used as the intensity of the work increases. You can train for brief periods of time in this zone, but the majority of your exercise needs to be between 65 – 85% of your maximum heart rate.

Ready to calculate your own target heart rate?

Multiply your MHR by 0.65 and then by 0.85 to figure out your lowest and highest intensity heart rate range in your target zone:

(MHR _____)x .65 = _____ (lowest intensity THR)

(MHR _____)x .85 ⁻ _____ (highest intensity THR)

Divide the lowest and highest intensity THR numbers by 6 to determine what a 10-second heart rate count would be for you (that is an easier number to count when doing aerobic activity):

(Lowest intensity THR _____)÷6 = _____ (lowest 10 sec count)

(Highest intensity THR _____)÷6 = _____ (highest 10 sec count)

NOTE: The formula above is well accepted and designed for average adults who are sedentary or infrequent exercisers. A formula incorporating resting heart rate, which is more individualized and accurate for someone who exercises consistently, will be discussed in Week 6.

Now you can find your pulse on the inside of your wrist and count the number of beats for 10 seconds any time during exercise to know if you are working hard enough but not too hard! The best times to check your heart rate are (1) right after your warm-up to make sure you have entered the aerobic zone, (2) at least once during your exercise, and (3) immediately following exercise. You may want to check your heart rate one final time after the cool-down to make sure your heart rate is back to normal. The amount of time it takes for your heart rate to recover back to your pre-exercise rate is a great indicator of your fitness level. The quicker you recover, the better trained you are and/or the better rested you are. So keep an eye on how fast your heart rate recovers after working out to track improvements in your fitness level as the weeks go by.

Your heart rate range is the best way to check your level of work, but many things can lower or raise your heartbeat outside of exercise alone. Be aware that medications, like over-the-counter medicines for colds or allergies, can raise your resting heart rate. If your resting heart rate is falsely high, your target heart rate range will be affected as well.

Other things that raise or lower your heart rate include, but are not limited to: 1) caffeine from a morning coffee break, 2) outside temperatures--a hot day will increase your heart rate and a cold day will lower it, 3) illness--usually increases your heart rate, 4) use of your upper body during exercise--adding arm or upper body movements will increase your heart rate, and 5) lack of sleep, which can increase your heart rate range depending on how your energy level affects your workout. So use your target heart rate numbers as a guideline only! Pay attention to how your body feels. Always slow down or stop if you feel short of breath, dizzy, or faint.

Another way to pay attention to your target heart rate range is called "perceived exertion." Perceived exertion is simply how intense you perceive the activity to be based on how you feel. The following table will help you monitor your intensity if you don't use a heart rate monitor or the pulse counting method above. Heart rate monitors are relatively inexpensive when you count how many times you will use them but this table works just fine, too.

Exercise Intensity Scale

% of THR	How This Level Feels
Up to 65%	"I'm not even working; I'm very comfortable."
65 – 70%	"My heart's beating faster but I could do this a long time. I can even talk to my neighbor at this pace."
70 – 80%	"My heart and body are working hard. Small talk is all I can do now."
80 – 85%	"Okay, this is intense! Yes/No questions only, please!"
85 – 92%	"I can't talk now!"
Above 92%	"Don't even go there!"

Your **FITNESS CHALLENGE** for Week 2: **Check your heart rate once before, during and after exercise** on at least 2 of the 4 days. Record these numbers in your Maintenance Log. Adjust how hard you are working, depending on whether your heart rate is too low or too high.

A Look in the Rearview Mirror

Week 2: Move Your Car Out of the Garage!

Foundation: Eat breakfast within 1 to 1 ½ hours after rising, and do not wait longer than 4 hours between each meal or snack.

Food: Eat 3 to 4 fuel groups at meals, and 1 to 2 fuel groups at snacks.

Fluid: Drink extra for exercise.

Fitness: Check your heart rate (or perceived exertion) once before, during, and after exercise on at least two days

Now, record any changes you notice this week:

Date	Thoughts, Feelings, Body Changes?

Week 3:

Get in Gear

*"I feel I have learned to take
better care of my body, so my body
will take better care of me."*   T. T.

Chapter 9

Headlights on Foundation:
Follow the Speed Limits

As you continue to work on your meal alignment from Week 2, turn your headlights towards those "have to have them but they can be so annoying" SPEED LIMIT signs. On a busy street, a speed limit provides guidelines for how quickly you travel in order to control the traffic and maintain safety. A speed limit helps protect you from losing control of the car, which can result in an accident or collision. Likewise, during a busy day, a speed limit for meals and snacks provides guidelines for how quickly *or slowly* you eat in order to control your body's response to the fuel and maintain safety from a collision with your metabolism!

Did you know that it requires about 20 minutes before your stomach can communicate with your brain that it has received fuel from food and is satisfied? If you ignore the *speed limit*, you risk losing control of your body's ability to tell you when you are full. If you are not aware that your tank is full, you will probably continue to eat, right? But more fuel (or calories) than your body needs leads to more fuel storage than your body may want! Fuel is stored in your blood or muscles for more immediate, daily needs OR as body fat for long-term surplus. If your fuel tank overflows, and your muscles already have adequate fuel storage, the extra fuel will be made into more body fat. Although your body is being quite efficient when it adds more long-term storage, you may not be as appreciative of the long-term results.

Watching the speed limit or *slowing down* the meal and snack time so that your stomach has time to communicate with your brain that you are full can help prevent, or at least slow down, storage of extra body fat. When you are aware that you are full and satisfied with your meal or snack, you will stop eating before your body has to figure out what to do with the extra fuel it did not need in the first place.

So what are the minimum speed limits for completing a meal or snack?

TWENTY (20) minutes a meal!
....and TEN (10) minutes a snack!

You may be thinking, "Hey, I can finish a meal in 8 minutes flat, and a snack in seconds! To take 20 minutes for a meal and 10 for a snack – I just don't know if I can do that!" You're not alone. Most of us eat too fast, but slowing down can help you eat more realistic portions while enhancing the amount of enjoyment your food gives.

Do you have to literally eat for 20 minutes at mealtime? No, but commit to allowing a full 20 minutes for the meal "experience." Remain at the table, enjoy the company or the solitude, a chance to take a break from the speedway. Think about what foods you just enjoyed, and how they make you feel. Energized? Relaxed? Make a commitment to *not* return to the kitchen for a second serving until you have waited the full 20 minutes and re-checked how hungry you are then. By that point, your brain and stomach will have had time to communicate, and you may be surprised at their responses! The second serving does not look or sound as good as it did before, because you just aren't hungry anymore. Repeat those now-famous words-**"I CAN EAT AGAIN!"** Feel confident that your efforts to follow the speed limits helped you avoid a ticket for a metabolism disaster-eating too much when you are not really hungry. Way to go!

Your **FOUNDATION CHALLENGE** this week: Glance at the clock or your watch when you begin a meal or snack, and challenge yourself to make your eating experience last according to the speed limit sign: **20 minutes to enjoy a meal and 10 minutes to enjoy a snack**. The key is to slow down and let your stomach communicate to your brain that it is satisfied *before* you look for more fuel!

Chapter 10

Headlights on Food:
Paint Your Portions

You have taken a challenge to follow the speed limits. During that time, why don't you sit back a minute and check out your paint job? How "colorful" are your snacks and meals? Why is color important, anyway?

Do you realize that your grocery store, your pantry, and your plate can contain powerful defenses against disease? These defenses rest quietly and patiently in the produce section of the grocery store, but may never make it to your home, and, even more so, on your plate. These powerful, but often overlooked, superstars are vegetables and fruits-the COLOR in your snacks and meals!

The average American eats only 1 ½ servings of fruits or vegetables daily. Think back to your day: How many fruits or vegetables have you had today? Research has shown, over and over, that people who eat more fruits and vegetables, about five or more daily, have half the risk of cancer then those who eat less than 2 servings daily.

Fruits and vegetables, two of your energy fuel groups, continue to amaze scientists because of the depth of benefits they provide, many of which are still not fully understood. Why is everyone so amazed? First of all, these colorful foods provide fiber, which maintains a healthy intestinal track, helps lower blood cholesterol, and may play a significant role in preventing certain cancers. Secondly, these same unsuspecting foods contain a treasure of vitamins and minerals that are the *spark plugs* for your body. Bananas, citrus fruits, potatoes, and tomatoes all contain potassium, a mineral that regulates every heart beat. Did you know that folic acid, found in orange juice and dark green leafy vegetables, maintains healthy blood cells? And, of course, the famous "antioxidants" beta-carotene and Vitamin C are found in bright orange, yellow, red, and deep green fruits and vegetables, like kiwi, ruby red grapefruits, broccoli, sweet potatoes, and watermelon. Antioxidants help protect your cells from damage, boost your immune system, and reduce the risk of heart disease, cataracts, and some cancers. Just think of them as the superheroes of the body. But there's a catch! It all depends on where you get your antioxidants-from a vitamin and mineral supplement, or from food itself?

For years, every time you picked up a newspaper or turned on the television, another health problem or disease had been successfully attacked by antioxidants. Sales of antioxidant supplements went sky high until April 14, 1994. That's when researchers from Finland and the National Cancer Institute dropped the bomb: Not only did beta carotene supplements fail to reduce the risk of lung cancer, they might even *cause* harm. This shocking news resulted from a study of 29,000 Finnish male smokers, who were randomly chosen to be in one of four groups taking one of the following: a placebo, 33,000 IU of beta carotene supplement, 50 IU of Vitamin E supplement, or beta carotene and Vitamin E combination supplement. After 5 to 8 years, those taking the beta carotene had an 18 percent higher occurrence of lung cancer. What happened? The earlier studies that showed lower cancer rates among people who ate fruits and vegetables assumed that it was the beta carotene present in these foods that was the key. But these studies failed to realize that maybe it is not the beta carotene, pulled out and put in a supplement, which turned the cancer around. There must be something else in fruits and vegetables that work with the beta carotene to protect the body from cancer.

What do you do now?

First, reconsider taking a separate supplement for antioxidants alone, like beta carotene. Secondly, and most importantly, do not stop eating fresh fruits and vegetables! There is no reason to worry about the beta carotene in foods. People who eat more fruits and veggies, especially those rich in carotenes, have a lower risk of most cancers. So just taking a supplement containing the antioxidants is not the answer. But eating more fruits and vegetables may be!

The key to cancer prevention appears to be hidden in these colorful foods, and scientists are just beginning to discover what it is. The "secret" components are called phytochemicals-or chemicals that

FIGHT ("phyt") the evil diseases lurking to attack. Hundreds of phytochemicals exist now and continue to be discovered. These powerful chemicals act like antioxidants and slow down growth in the size of tumors and number of cancer cells. Some of the foods that have high numbers of phytochemicals are the same foods that provide you with vitamins, minerals, and fiber.   Broccoli, cauliflower, oranges, grapefruits, blueberries, red onions, cherries and red peppers are just a few great sources.

Look at your next meal or snack and ask yourself, "Is it mostly brown? White? Somewhere in-between?" Even a "healthy" meal like a turkey sandwich on wheat, with pretzels, is brown and colorless, lacking the balance of fruits and vegetables that not only add color but also add fiber, vitamins, minerals, and phytochemicals for fewer calories overall. "Painting" your sandwich with green leafy lettuce and a sliced tomato, and substituting crunchy green snap peas or baby carrots for the pretzels, brightens up your plate and your health!

Try one of the following tips to begin "painting your portions":

1.   Choose a different color to concentrate on each day. For instance, Monday can be RED, and even though you are not limited to just RED colors, you can have fun looking for ways to eat more red: strawberries, raspberries, red grapes, red apples, watermelon, cherries, tomatoes, red peppers, red onions, beets. You get the picture-PAINT IT RED!

2.   Keep convenient packages of vegetables and fruits available at all times- small snack size bags of raw snow peas or carrot sticks for munching, fresh fruit cups from the grocery store for snacking, cherry tomatoes to toss on your salad, ready-to-eat salad greens to stuff in your sandwiches.

3.   Frozen fruits and vegetables always provide a quick back-up, especially for someone on the go who does not cook often.

4.   Freeze chunks of banana or washed grapes, and enjoy as a snack or "dessert." The ice cream-like texture and temperature is a refreshing change, especially in the summertime.

5.   Experiment with different cooking techniques. Instead of simply steaming broccoli, try roasting it in a little olive oil, or shredding it for salads.

6.   Try a new vegetable or fruit that you have never tried before, like star fruit, or kale.

7.   Keep dried fruit, like raisins, dried raspberries or dried apricots, in your car for a quick snack when you are on the road. Avoid the high-sugar types of dried fruits, like banana slices, papaya or pineapple.

Your **FOOD CHALLENGE** for Week 3: **Paint your portions by adding five or more colors every day** in any combination of fruits and vegetables. 100% fruit juice can count, but limit it to 1 serving (4 to 6 ounces) per day. And don't cheat yourself-a large entrée-size salad can certainly count for at least 3 servings of color. So this challenge may not be as difficult as you think. Just keep your eyes open for reds, oranges, yellows, purples, blues, greens, and anything in-between! Highlight or circle the daily "colors" consumed in your Maintenance Log.

What About Vitamin and Mineral Supplements?

Ideally, if you eat balanced meals that include fruits, vegetables, whole grains, lean meats, and low fat dairy products, you do not need to take an additional supplement. But realistically? Most people probably don't. As you learn the Rev It Up! principles, you will begin eating more balanced, but in the meantime, consider taking a multivitamin/mineral supplement that provides 100% of the recommended daily allowances and has the USP mark on the label. And women, please take a calcium supplement with Vitamin D daily if you do not consume 3 dairy servings or high-calcium foods daily.

Chapter 11

Headlights on Fluid:
Match Up!

You began Week 1 by checking your water level, and you met the challenge to drink 8 cups of water daily. Week 2 continued the challenge by adding extra water for exercise. How are you doing so far? Are you ready for challenge #3? At this point, trying to meet your water challenge may have naturally decreased the amount of any other beverage consumed. In that case, the challenge this week may be easy. So what's your challenge now?

MATCH UP for QUALITY!

Much debate surrounds the question, "Which fluids count?" According to the Dietary Reference Intakes released in February 2004 by the Food and Nutrition Board, any fluid that hydrates "counts" towards your daily fluid needs. Does current research back the long thought principle that coffee dehydrates? Surprisingly, no it doesn't. What about the safety of diet drinks? If the Food and Drug Administration (FDA) approves the safety, can you consume all of your daily fluids from this kind of fluid? Current research does not negate the hydrating effects of any beverage containing coffee or artificial sweeteners.   Therefore, if you are to meet the Dietary Reference Intake guidelines, all of these fluids can count.

But if you want to take the Rev It Up! challenge to match up for quality, you will need to take a second, closer look. If essentially all fluids can count towards your daily needs, it begs the question, "But is that fluid the best choice for my body?" Just because it counts doesn't mean it is the ideal. Rev It Up is all about quality-quality in your fuel choices and quality in your fluid choices. Fluids with caffeine and beverages with artificial sweeteners, even an occasional alcoholic beverage, have a place in anyone's daily fuel plan, but these beverages need to be consumed in moderation if you want to give your body the best-quality fluid with which to run its engine!

Your Fluid Challenge for this week? In addition to your daily 8, match any amount of these other beverages you consume (caffeine, artificially sweetened, or alcoholic) with equal amounts of additional "match-up fluids". Don't worry-you can count fluids like tomato juice, vegetable juice, and low-fat milk, too. For example, if you have a cup of coffee in the morning, simply match this by filling up your cup with an equal amount of water to drink. Or, if you already consume low-fat milk with breakfast in addition to your coffee, then you have matched up your fluids already! (NOTE: You do not have to match up plain decaffeinated coffee or tea if no more than 1 tsp of added sugar, sugar substitute, and/or creamer is included.)

Now it's time to turn your headlights to focus on more detailed information about caffeinated, artificially sweetened, and alcoholic beverages:

CAFFEINE DRINKS:

Many studies over the years list caffeine as a potential diuretic, which works to release stored water from your cells. However, newer studies have indicated that caffeine may or may not act as a diuretic; that does not seem to translate into actual dehydration for the body. Caffeine may not act as a dehydrator even if it does act as a diuretic in your body. But are caffeine-containing fluids the best choice you can make? Can you meet all of your fluid needs drinking coffee or other caffeine drinks? What amount is considered "moderate" for caffeine intake? Rev It Up! is all about taking your health to the next level of wellness. What you do "more often than not" is what makes a difference. Moderation is the key!

So what is considered moderation for caffeine intake? About 300 milligrams (mg) or less, no more than two or three caffeine drinks daily. If you drink more than 300 mg, you may want to consider reducing the total amount you consume. *A note about soft drinks: As a general rule of thumb, the darker the color of the soft drink, the more caffeine it has. But, as you know by now, there is ALWAYS an exception! Root beer has no caffeine, but popular yellow- and orange-colored sodas may have equal or more caffeine than a dark colored cola!*

Check out the table that follows to view the top caffeine culprits and the # of milligrams per serving:

TYPE OF BEVERAGE	MILLIGRAMS OF CAFFEINE
COFFEE:	
Brewed, 8 ounces (1 cup)	50-150 mg (avg of 100 mg)
Instant, 8 ounces	30-120 mg (avg of 75 mg)
Sweetened mix, 8 ounces	40-80 mg (avg of 60 mg)
TEA:	
Brewed, 8 ounces (1 cup)	20-100 mg (avg of 60 mg)
Instant, 8 ounces	30-70 mg (avg of 50 mg)
SOFT DRINKS:	
Mountain Dew, 12 ounces	54 mg
Colas, 12 ounces	36-46 mg (avg of 41 mg)
Diet colas, 12 ounces	35-46 mg (avg of 41 mg)
OTHER:	
Milk chocolate, 1 ounce	6 mg
Semi-sweet chocolate, 1 ounce	14-35 mg
Chocolate milk, 8 ounces	20-25 mg
Excedrin, 1 tablet	75 mg
Cold medicine, 1 dose	30 mg

To help you determine how much caffeine you really drink, complete the table below. First, list the number of cups you drink of each beverage. Second, multiply the number of cups for each beverage by the specific number of milligrams of caffeine for that beverage, and record the total in the last column. **EXAMPLE:** If you drink 3 cups of brewed coffee daily, your total number of milligrams of caffeine from the coffee would be 300 mg (3 x 100 mg per cup = 300 mg). Now it's your turn:

TYPE OF BEVERAGE W/ CAFFEINE	NUMBER OF CUPS	AVERAGE # OF MG OF CAFFEINE	TOTAL # OF MG PER BEVERAGE
Coffee, brewed		100 mg	
Coffee, instant		75 mg	
Coffee, sweetened mix		60 mg	
Tea, brewed		60 mg	

Tea, instant		50 mg	
Mello Yello, Mt. Dew or Sundrop		54 mg	
Diet Mello Yello, Mt. Dew, Sundrop		54 mg	
Soft drink, dark-colored		41 mg	
Diet soft drink, dark-colored		41 mg	

Now, add the total number of milligrams of caffeine per beverage (column #4) to see the "grand total" amount of caffeine you consume daily._____

If you drink more than 300 milligrams of caffeine daily, consider reducing the amount of caffeine by about 25% for the first 3 or 4 days. But reduce your caffeine very gradually! Caffeine is addictive, so your body may experience some withdrawal symptoms, like headaches, shakiness, and irritability, if you reduce it too quickly. If you have ever had a "caffeine headache", you *know* how your body reacts if you drop your caffeine level too fast! Once you have adjusted to the first reduction, decide if you want to continue reducing even more. Whether you decide to stay at a 1 or 2 cup level, or eliminate it altogether, your body wins!

TO SUMMARIZE: For every cup of caffeine-containing fluids you consume, make sure you consume an appropriate "match up" fluid sometime during the day, such as tomato or vegetable juice, low-fat milk or an additional 8-ounce cup of water. And if you regularly consume more than 300 mg of caffeine, consider reducing the overall amount of caffeine you drink every day.

ARTIFICIALLY SWEETENED DRINKS:

Now let's move on to another popular drink: a "diet" or artificially-sweetened beverage, with or without caffeine. According to the Food and Drug Administration (FDA), it is safe and acceptable to consume foods and beverages sweetened with any of the current artificial sweeteners seen in the marketplace: aspartame, saccharin, acesulfame potassium, neotame, sucralose, and stevia. However, the reports on side effects from artificial sweeteners remain somewhat controversial. Some individuals report that artificial sweeteners like aspartame or sucralose not only stimulate their appetite but may also encourage water retention. It is important to pay attention to how your body responds to these drinks and consider the amount you are currently consuming.

Let's check out the daily acceptable amount of aspartame, one of the most popular types of artificial sweetener. FDA has established 25 milligrams per pound of body weight as acceptable. So if you are 150 pounds, that would mean that your acceptable daily limit is 3750 mg/day (150# x 25 mg per #). Want to calculate your acceptable daily limit? Put your current weight in the first blank and multiply by 25 mg:

(_____ #) x 25 mg (per #) = _____ mg per day

Wow! That is a lot, regardless of how much you weigh! How much is in foods? One packet of aspartame contains 35 milligrams (mg). Diet hot cocoa and diet gelatin each contain about 90 mg. And a diet soda, 12 ounces, contains about 170-195 mg (about five packets of aspartame).

It is doubtful that you consume anywhere near the upper limit of FDA's guidelines for a safe daily amount. However, that does not necessarily mean that more is better, either. One or two diet drinks can fit easily in your day, but repeated and excessive use of any artificially sweetened product replaces the opportunity to choose the best quality for your body. The long-term effects of repeated and excessive intake of artificial sweeteners aren't fully understood yet, even if their use is considered safe. Side effects reported over the years since artificial sweeteners were introduced range from an increase in appetite and sugar cravings to headaches and nausea. Because of these side effects, even if limited to a very small group of people, consider diet drinks as one of the beverages on the Match Up list.

TO SUMMARIZE: Try to limit your intake to no more than 2 daily servings of food or drink that contain artificial sweetener, and match up what you consume with an equal amount of other appropriate fluids (tomato or vegetable juice, low-fat milk, or extra water).

ALCOHOLIC DRINKS:

You have discovered that alcohol is a concentrated carbohydrate but is stored in the body much more like fat than sugar once it is consumed. That is why you count a serving of an alcoholic beverage as one of your ping pong balls of fat (See Chapter 6 for a quick review). But regardless of how it is stored in the body, alcohol also needs to be in the "match up" fluid category because it dehydrates. So for every serving of alcohol (12 ounce beer or light beer, 5 ounce glass of wine, or 1 ½ ounce serving of liquor), match up by consuming an extra 8 ounce glass of water. An added benefit? The water between servings will help subdue the effect of alcohol on your appetite and cravings, too.

WHAT ABOUT THOSE NEW
FITNESS AND FLAVORED WATERS?

You may be saying to yourself, "But I just don't like plain water! What about all those cool new specialty waters? Can I drink those instead?" These products deserve a closer look:

Fitness Waters: These waters are typically lightly flavored, sweetened with a blend of natural and artificial sweeteners and include small amounts of vitamins and/or minerals to help replace fluid losses in an active person. It can be a first step, but the use of artificial sweeteners has other considerations (as you know now!).

Vitamin Waters: These waters are usually sweetened with sugars and contain significant amounts of vitamins and herbs. Check the label – some of these contain as much sugar in 8 ounces as a typical can of regular soda! And the use of herbs can be a concern, especially if you are on medications.

Flavored Waters: These waters are usually calorie-free alternatives, flavored entirely with artificial sweeteners. Similar to a diet soda, without the carbonation.

Oxygen Waters: Just plain water "infused with extra oxygen". Some claim they have more than 10 times the oxygen content of regular tap water-and therefore improve energy, athletic performance, recovery time and brain skills. That's quite a promise! But the American Council on Exercise along with the University of Wisconsin at LaCrosse recently tested these claims and found that "oxygenated water is no more beneficial than regular tap water because there is no physiologic mechanism to get that oxygen in the blood stream where it can be used."

Caffeinated Waters: Water that contains as much caffeine as an 8-ounce serving of coffee-and usually free of sugar, calories, preservatives, and carbonation. But do we REALLY need more caffeine choices?

Lots of choices, lots of options. How can you decide? Think Rev It Up! and think fluid quality!

Are you drinking enough quality fluids?

So how do you know if you are drinking enough to meet your fluid needs with the highest quality choices possible? Ask yourself the following questions:

1.   *Are you thirsty?* Thirst usually controls how much fluid you drink. But it can also be a delayed response and therefore not as reliable. For example, when you exercise and sweat, you lose lots of water but exercise itself can blunt your thirst trigger for a period of time. And small children as well as older adults have a thirst system that is not as sensitive and often find themselves dehydrated. Don't always wait for thirst alone to tell you that more water is needed!

2.   *Is your urine clear?* If you are becoming dehydrated, your urine may be darker because the kidneys end up

concentrating the fluids when less is available. If your body has enough water to go around, urine usually remains clear and diluted. However, there are two exceptions to this rule.

Exception #1: If you are taking a multivitamin supplement and it is providing more of the water-soluble vitamins (the B vitamins, and Vitamin C) than your body needs, your urine will be more yellow or maybe even orange. For example, if you have plenty of Vitamin C in your blood and body tissues, your body will simply release the extra through "water" in your urine. This extra darkens the color of your urine, just like dehydration can.

Exception #2: If you drink a lot of caffeine-containing beverages, your urine can appear clear and diluted. However, the clear color may not be from adequate hydration but from the fact that caffeine dilutes the concentration of the water present.

Can you drink TOO many fluids, especially water?

You've asked if you are drinking too little water. Can you drink too much? Anything can be done in excess. However, water intoxication, drinking way too much water, is rare in the average population. If you have kidney disease or high blood pressure, especially if you are on medications and treatments to control these, your water intake needs to be moderated by your physician.

People who struggle with compulsive addictive behaviors such as an eating disorder can also drink too much if using water to avoid eating foods yet are already at an unhealthy low body weight. Endurance athletes who run for long distances and do not replace the sodium and potassium that is lost in their sweat can be at risk if they drink plain water without adequate electrolytes. So consuming too much water can certainly be harmful, but it is not common. If you are going to the restroom every 2 hours or so, you are drinking enough but not too much. If you are going more frequently than this, you may want to look at the amount of caffeine, for example, and decrease those beverages instead of automatically decreasing your water intake. They are probably more of the culprit than your water intake itself. Remember, your body is good at getting rid of what it does not need, but it cannot get more water unless you give it!

"I never thought I'd be able to give up my Diet Mt. Dew, but now I find myself wanting water instead!"   Jan

Your **FLUID CHALLENGE** for Week 3: Circle each caffeinated, artificially sweetened, or alcoholic beverage you consume daily in your Maintenance Log, and challenge yourself to **match up amounts of these "other" drinks** with one of the higher quality fluids (water, tomato or vegetable juice, or low-fat milk).

Chapter 12

Headlights on Fitness:
Pump for Power

You have been moving your body and working on your aerobic fitness...now you're ready to shift into gear and experience Pump Power! Aerobic, or cardiovascular, exercise burns more calories and uses more oxygen, but strength training builds the muscles that heat up your body and increases how fast you burn calories at ANY time, even while sitting! Strength training not only increases muscle mass but also increases the muscle's activity level, or the speed at which the body "makes up and breaks down" protein within your muscle tissue. In addition, strength training also strengthens your bones, which helps reduce your risk of developing osteoporosis. That's reason enough!

Do You Have to Bulk Up?

No! And in fact, if you are a woman, your body is not capable of producing the bulk that can result from strength training, or weight lifting, in men. Your body is not designed that way! Regardless of whether you are a man or a woman, you do not need to "bulk up" to start "melting" your metabolism. Even a little more muscle gained means a little more calories burned when resting. And that leads to better control over your weight! So how do you increase the amount of muscle you have? By pumping for power, or engaging in strength training.

How Much Time Do I Need to Spend?

To pump for power, your goal is to lift weights or use strength training machines or natural body weight exercises two days a week. The goal? <u>One to three sets</u> each of eight to ten resistance exercises to build strength and increase muscle mass. Keep in mind you should try to train A) big muscles before small ones and B) core [central trunk or torso] muscles in addition to upper and lower body muscles.

Your stomach (abdomen) and back muscles serve as the body's *stabilizers* and provide *balance* for your entire body. Your abdominal muscles are actually three sheets of muscle fiber that crisscross completely around you like an old-fashioned girdle, holding in organs and helping hold your entire body upright. If you do not have core strength in these sheets of muscles, you increase the chances of injury when you move weights away from your body. Improved abdominal strength can also "translate into better performance from your body during daily activities" according to the American Council on Exercise (ACE) personal trainer manual. And that will improve quality of life.

Regardless of which muscle group you are working, try to work up to 8 to 12 repetitions per set of each exercise, with a goal of using enough weight that can be lifted at least eight but no more than twelve times. How do you do this? Constantly challenge yourself to add a little more weight, or 1 more repetition, every week or two as you train for strength. If you always lift the same amount of weight the same number of times, you will not get stronger after a period of time. When you are able to do the specific exercise more than 12 times, it is time to add more weight to your routine. And to challenge your muscles even more, try a different exercise for the same muscle group every month or two (More information on these concepts coming in Chapter 18).

Do not feel that you have to add more days, however. Your rest days are very important, since strength training actually tears your muscle tissue, and the new strength and tissue gains you are trying to achieve result from the repair of these tissue tears during rest. In fact, it may be harmful to perform strength exercises for the same muscle group on two consecutive days. Rest at least 48 hours before strength training those SAME muscles again!

Do You Burn Calories Even AFTER the Activity?

Your metabolism can stay revved up after you do any kind of exercise, but the actual number of additional calories burned after exercise varies widely. It depends on the type of workout, and how hard and how long you worked.   Many studies have shown that strength training may have a longer "after-burn" of calories than aerobic exercise. One reason may be that this type of exercise raises the level of a hormone called epinephrine, which stirs up metabolic rate. Another reason may be that your body uses up more energy to repair the damage done to your muscles by weight lifting. Regardless of why, exercise like strength training is important for a meltdown of your old metabolism and a jumpstart to a newer one!.

Your **FITNESS CHALLENGE** for Week 3: Make an appointment with yourself to go to the gym, or stay at home and use hand held weights or natural body weight and **pump for power (strength train) 2 days a week**.   It need not take more than 30 minutes, depending on how many repetitions and sets are done. Your schedule may not permit-and your goals need not include-more than four hours of exercise time per week. No problem! Simply combine your aerobic activity and strength training on two of the four days. For example, spend 20 or so minutes (including a 5-minute warm-up and cool-down) doing your aerobic activity, like walking or running on a treadmill. Then spend the rest of your time, about 30 minutes, strength training. Save 5 minutes afterwards to complete your stretches. And you are done!

To help keep track, record the total amount of time you participate in exercise, specifically in pump power, in your Maintenance Log. Be sure to make a note of any increase in repetitions or weight, as you progress. And watch your metabolism start shifting!

Is Strength Training a New Concept for You?

Many people, especially women, do not feel comfortable with strength training. You may be one of those individuals! Again, think *small* and *practical*. Put a simple, practical pattern into place and as your routine slowly becomes habit, you will find yourself more at ease with the use of weights to build and strengthen your muscles. An "At-Home Strength Training Starter Program" follows to help you get started.

At-Home Strength Training Starter Program

Although many people make the time and effort to do aerobic exercise, strength training can be more intimidating and challenging, especially if you are not familiar with a gym or the use of weight equipment. Because you may not be a member of a fitness center and unfamiliar with strength building exercises, the following program provides an at-home, simple strength training guide to help get you started. This program can also be followed when you are traveling or are limited in space or time.

WHAT YOU NEED:
A set of 3# hand held weights (dumbbells)
A set of 5# hand held weights (dumbbells)
A set of 10# hand held weights (dumbbells)

As you progress, you can increase your weights by holding either both the 3 and 5# weights in each hand for an 8# dumbbell OR both the 5 and 10# weights for a 15# dumbbell. Eventually you may want to invest in additional hand held weights, up to a 20# set.

WHAT TO DO:
1.   Perform 1 to 3 sets of each exercise.
2.   Complete 8 to 12 repetitions
3.   Do each repetition for 6 seconds, 3 seconds up and 3 down
4.   Use a weight that can be lifted at least 8 times but no more than 12.
5.   REST at least one day in between strength training

WHERE TO BEGIN:
Start with your lower body (hips, legs and butt muscles), follow with your upper body (chest, upper back, and arms) and finish with your "core" muscles (abdominals and lower back). The following exercises are in this order for you already:

SQUATS: Start by holding a 3 to 5# dumbbell in each hand. Stand with feet a little more than shoulder width apart, holding your abdomen tight and keeping your chin and chest lifted, shoulders open (not rounded forward). Lower your body, without lifting your heels, until your thighs are almost parallel to the floor. Remember to keep the weight in your heels (you should be able to wiggle your toes in your shoes). Hold for 3 seconds and then return to your starting position over the next 3 seconds. Remember to keep your hips above your knees and do not arch your back. Beginners may want to try this without weights and place a chair behind them so that they go down with their buttocks and barely touch the chair before returning to the start position. You may also want to grasp a bar placed over your shoulders and behind your head (a broom or mop will do) to keep your chest lifted. Repeat this exercise 8 to 12 times for 1 to 3 sets. As you become stronger, you may increase the amount of weight that you hold in your hands.

PUSH UPS: Start on your hands and knees, with your hands slightly wider than your chest. Keep your lower legs on the floor, but walk your hands slightly forward, keeping your shoulders, hips, and knees in a straight line. Lower your chest over a 3 second count towards the floor, then push back up to your starting position over the next 3 seconds. Repeat this exercise 8 to 12 times for 1 to 3 sets. As you become stronger, you can change your position by keeping your knees on the floor but lifting your lower legs. Push up as before, over a 6 second count. As you get stronger, you can position yourself in the third, or hardest, position, which requires lifting your knees and lower legs, keeping only your hands and balls of your feet connected to the floor. Your hands should be slightly wider than your chest and your feet about shoulder width apart. Repeat the 3 second count as you lower your body towards the floor. Remember to keep those abdominal muscles pulled in. Regardless of the position used, beginning to advanced, keep your back slightly arched, and don't allow your back to drop below your shoulders.

BENT-OVER DUMBBELL ROWS: While standing on the left side of a bench or chair, rest the right leg (the one closest to the bench or chair) by bending at the knee and placing the lower leg on the bench. Slightly flex the opposite left leg at the knee, keep your spine neutral, and bend at your waist to rest your right hand on the bench or chair seat. Hold a 5-10 pound dumbbell in the hand farthest away from the bench. Extend this arm toward the floor, with the palm of the weight-bearing hand facing towards your side. Pull the dumbbell straight up toward your mid-back, keeping elbow close to your side. Pause; return arm to extended position. Repeat this movement 8 to

12 times, alternating arms for a total of 1 to 3 sets. As you become stronger, you can increase the amount of weight you hold in your hand.

BICEP CURLS: Stand with your feet shoulder width apart. Hold 3-5 pound dumbbells in each hand with your palms facing toward your sides. Keep your elbows at your side and curl the dumbbell upwards over 3 seconds, rotating your palms up towards your shoulders. Then lower the dumbbells back to your starting position over the next 3 seconds. Repeat this exercise 8 to 12 times for 1 to 3 sets. As you become stronger, increase your weights.

TRICEP KICK-BACKS: Stand with your feet shoulder width apart. Hold 3-5 pound dumbbells in both hands with elbows at your side and your palms facing each other. Bend your arms at the elbow so that your forearms are parallel to the floor. With your elbows at your sides, extend or "kick back" your arms over 3 seconds, turning your palms upwards towards the ceiling to isolate the triceps muscles. Slowly return to your bent-arm starting position over the next 3 seconds. Repeat this exercise 8 to 12 times for 1 to 3 sets. As you become stronger, increase your weights. (You may also wish to do single arm kickbacks).

ABDOMINAL CRUNCHES: Lie down on your back with your knees bent and feet flat on the floor. Cross your arms in front of your chest (easier) or place your hands behind your head (harder), and tighten your abdominal muscles. Raise your shoulders off the ground over a 3 second period, keeping the small of your back on the floor at all times. Keep your neck relaxed, using your arms to support your head and not to lift your upper body. Think about your eyes focusing on the ceiling and imagine a baseball under your chin so that you don't bring your chin into your chest. Slowly lower your shoulders back (but not all the way down) towards the floor over the next 3 seconds. Repeat this exercise for 1 to 3 sets at 25 repetitions per set. As you become stronger, you may increase the number of repetitions and/or sets. For variation, as you raise your shoulders off the ground, twist your right shoulder towards the opposite knee to work your oblique (side) abdominal muscles. Alternate by using the left shoulder and twist towards the opposite knee. Repeat 1 to 3 sets of 25 repetitions each.

LOW BACK: Lying face down with hips pressed into floor and abdominal muscles contracted, lift right arm and left leg. Pause and return to the floor. Repeat on the opposite side. Make the exercise more difficult by lifting your arms and legs at the same time, and hold for longer counts during each contraction. Be careful not to over extend your arms and legs-this is a small movement. Stop this exercise (as with any exercise) if you feel pain.

A Look in the Rearview Mirror

Week 3: Get In Gear

Foundation: Follow the speed limits: 20 minutes to enjoy the meal experience, 10 minutes to enjoy the snack experience.

Food: Paint your portions by adding five or more colors every day in any combination of fruits and vegetables.

Fluid: Match up caffeinated, artificially sweetened, and alcoholic beverages with an equal amount of one of the "match up" fluids (low-fat milk, tomato or vegetable juice, water).

Fitness: Pump for power (strength training) 2 days/week.

Now, record any changes you notice this week:

Date	Thoughts, Feelings, Body Changes?

Week 4:

Tune Up!

"I can't begin to tell anyone how Rev It Up! has changed my life. It is very easy principles being applied. Today I am 40 pounds lighter, my portion control is much better and I am much more conscious of what I put into my mouth. I knew the basic concepts of losing weight and keeping it off but just the word exercise made my head ache. But now, I went from a waist size of 38 to 32 and pant size from nearly 20 to a 14. If it was not for this program, I would probably still be at that 202 or heavier. My blood pressure has dropped, my cholesterol level is better, and I am much more energetic." Kathy

Chapter 13

Headlights on Foundation: Recheck Your Fuel Gauge

By now, you are well on your way to building a new foundation for a revved up metabolism! You have been concentrating on your fuel gauge, or hunger/fullness levels, before and after each meal or snack. You followed this with meal alignment, the "what" and the "when". Next, you began watching your speed limits for your meals and snacks. It's time to see how much progress you have made! Let's look back since you started Rev It Up!, how many changes have you made? Check off any and all of the following:

- Are you eating breakfast every day (or almost every day)?
- Drinking your daily 8 cups of water?
- Doing an aerobic activity regularly?
- Choosing 3 – 4 fuel groups to build a meal, 1 – 2 to build a snack?
- Trying to eat within 4 hours of the previous meal or snack?
- Eating protein at every meal (dairy or animal/plant protein)?
- Limiting your added fats to 3 ping pong balls daily (4 for men)?
- Limiting special fats, like creamy casseroles and fries, to twice weekly?
- Drinking more water when you exercise?
- Pumping for power by strength training twice a week?
- Concentrating on eating five or more "colors", or fruit and vegetable servings?
- Watching your speed limits by slowing down at meal times?

If you said "yes" to at least two of the above, you are making a significant difference in your health already. Now turn your headlights specifically on your fuel gauge, your hunger (H) and fullness (F) cycle, since this is one of the most important signals that your body uses to communicate with your brain. If you have been recording in your Maintenance Log, look over the numbers you wrote in the "H" and "F" columns, and ask yourself the following:

- Do I wake up hungrier now than before I started this program?
- Do I realize that I am hungry before 4 hours pass between my last meal or snack and the next?
- Can I distinguish more of a variation now between my levels of hunger and fullness?
- Do I notice a positive change in my energy level throughout the day?
- Do I notice that my cravings for sugars and fats are more controlled?

If you are able to answer "yes" to any one of these questions, you are seeing proof-positive signs of a metabolism that is turned on, backed out of the garage, and hopefully in 1st or 2nd gear by now. Congratulations!

Your **FOUNDATION CHALLENGE** for Week 4: **Plan a victory lap!** Choose a reward for your hard work-one that doesn't center around food-and celebrate *you* and your success so far. Record all of the changes you have made in the first month's box on the Victory Lap page (Page 249), and make sure you choose a reward for your hard work. And don't forget to actually make the reward happen for you… soon!

Chapter 14

Headlights on Food (Part 1):
Check the Carb Quality

As part of your Week 4 tune up, it's time to turn your headlights on the *quality* of your fuel choices. This chapter concentrates on the quality of your carbohydrate fuel and the following chapter takes a closer look at the quality of your fat fuel. Carbohydrates and fats are getting lots of media attention now and, frankly, the information can be conflicting and confusing. Carbohydrates, the most important fuel source for your body's muscles and brain, have taken on a heavy burden in recent years as the main reason America continues to gain weight. But a low-carbohydrate approach is heavy on protein and often full of fat. Is this the answer to America's obesity problem?

The high-protein diet was actually one of the very first fad diets introduced in America *over 30 years ago*. Can a high-protein, low carbohydrate diet produce weight loss? Sure! But at what cost to you? If body weight is a combination of mostly water, and other vital components like muscle, organs, bone, and, yes, fat, what exactly are you losing when you lose weight? Are the immediate benefits really worth the possible long-term health consequences?

An extreme approach often leads to an extreme backlash. The result of the first round of high-protein diets was the fat-free craze – almost every food from salad dressings to brownies were made into a fat-free version. Was this the answer? Absolutely not! Fat-free usually means extra sugar. Without protein, and fats, the sugar content increases, the satisfaction factor decreases, and subsequently the total amount of calories eaten continue to increase. Americans began eating less fat than they ever have, but gaining weight!

Both the fat-free craze and the high-protein diet are extremes that significantly decrease at least *one entire food group*…a *big warning flag* itself! And both can neglect vegetables and fruits-the natural powerhouses of nutrition. Fruits and vegetables are low in calories but high in health promoting fiber, vitamins, minerals, water and phytochemicals-the cancer fighters and immune boosters. High protein diets usually eliminate most of these foods because they are carbohydrates-assumed to be the enemy of weight loss. The fat-free craze, high in simple carbohydrates, also limits these simply because it becomes easier to grab fat-free cookies for a snack than a fruit that may have to be washed and peeled first. So America finds itself eating more, and gaining more weight, so it's back to looking for the next quick fix. Let's stop this crazy, unhealthy cycle!

Take a good look at how the body uses fuel. During digestion, carbohydrates are broken down into glucose, the simplest form of energy required by your cells. Glucose is carried in the blood to be used by the brain, nervous system and, subsequently, muscles for energy.

Every muscle contraction requires glucose, and your brain itself can only be fueled by glucose-about 400 calories daily for the brain alone! When carbohydrates break down into glucose, the length of time it takes varies depending on how much fiber, fat and protein is present. For example, your body works a lot harder to break down lentils into glucose than it does to convert simple sugar fuel, like jelly beans, into glucose.

Your body stores glucose in its muscles and liver, and can store up to 2000 calories at any one time. When you eat, you refuel these glucose stores, and your body uses it between meals to keep it functioning properly. If you exercise between meals, your body is really quick to reach for those glucose stores to fuel the activity. Your meal or snack that follows helps replenish the stores again for the next round.

Are you aware that when your body stores glucose in your muscles and liver, your body adds extra water, in a 3:1 ratio, in the storage process? So stored glucose also means extra fluids stored in your muscles and liver. That's good, because your body *is* mostly water (about 65% +), and water is vital to *every* single metabolism process that occurs-from muscle contractions for a bicep curl to burning stored body fat.

So what happens when a person significantly restricts the body's most important fuel source, glucose? For the first 3 days, your body ignores the protein or fat that might have been eaten and looks for whatever stored glucose it can find in the muscles and liver. Guess what happens next? As glucose is released to be used by your brain or a muscle, so is water! In a few days, your glucose energy stores are fairly depleted, and you get on the bathroom scale, and WOW! Weight loss! Really? Actually, mostly *water* loss – not body fat loss. *The average female can lose only about 1 to 1 ½ pounds of body fat per week, and the average male can lose only about 2 to 2 ½ pounds per week.* So any weight loss greater than these amounts within a week's time is not fat. What's left? Water, and muscle, and even bone, over time.

Once your stores of glucose are used up, your body begins trying to adapt to its circumstances in an effort to maintain life. So, it begins forcing itself to use the protein you are eating as fuel from which to make new glucose. It can convert a piece of chicken into glucose if it has to, but at greater effort and less efficiently than it would whole wheat bread. Your body can also just as easily eat its own muscle if fuel is not readily available, and, in fact, it will do so under the strain of a high-protein diet over a period of time. And, yes, fat stores are used, too-but again not as predominately as you'd like to believe.

The process of breaking down protein and fats, the predominant fuels in steak, eggs or cheese, to glucose can lead to a condition called ketoacidosis. Any medical professional will tell you that if a hospital patient went into ketoacidosis, it is considered a state of alert-and a sign of starvation. For example, if a cancer patient tested positive for ketones, a registered dietitian would be called in quickly to help change the food intake level and type to prevent, or stop, this condition. And a high level of ketones is also a warning sign for which a physician looks when testing for diabetes. It is a sign that something in the body is not working as it should, and the body has compromised to survive. Finally, keto**acid**osis, with *acid* being the key word here, increases the body's risk of kidney stones. And, more importantly, ketoacidosis increases the risk of bone loss from the body and decreases the body's ability to recover by forming new bone. How can ketoacidosis, and a high-protein diet, be a good thing now?

Weight loss may continue on a high-protein diet, but realize that it is not just pounds lost from fat. Water loss is a constant problem because protein itself, when it is digested, forms ammonia (a quick chemistry lesson!), ammonia forms urea, and urea will make (you guessed it) urine. So the more protein eaten, the more urine made, and the more water loss. Your poor kidneys are doing double duty! And eventually weight loss may simply continue because you are tired of all that meat and cheese and you just begin eating less of it. Less calories, of course, leads to weight loss, too.

Boredom sets in -- the choices are pretty limited if you avoid most all of the grains, fruits and vegetables suggested. Maybe you break down and have a piece of bread, or a cookie you have been craving. What happens? Well, your body is so thrilled to have the real, usable form of carbohydrate again that it breaks it down readily and returns some glucose to the muscle stores for later use. But remember, glucose is stored with water. Uh oh! What does the scale do? It goes *up* -- seemingly overnight, bread has made you feel "fat" again. No, bread doesn't make you fat like that, but eating a carbohydrate like bread *did* re-hydrate your dried-up muscles-and the scale is weighing in that extra fluid.

But the weight gain itself can be too hard to handle, and the temptation is to avoid all carbohydrates yet again. But avoiding carbohydrates is avoiding your body's most important energy source! The problem is not carbohydrates themselves, but the **quality of the carbohydrate fuel** you choose. Both simple sugars (like jellybeans) and grains or starches (like oatmeal and 100% whole-wheat bread) are carbohydrates that are broken down into glucose; however, how *fast* this process takes place is the key to running out of energy or fueling smart. Smart carbohydrate fuel provides lasting glucose energy that keeps your brain powered up and your muscles fueled.

Carbohydrate like simple sugar found in most candies, cookies and colas breaks down into glucose energy in a very short period of time –less than 30 minutes. Energy is available quickly, but is used up quickly as well. This usually results in a drop in energy level that can not only affect your muscle and brain power but also lead to cravings for another sugar "high" within 1-2 hours. And if your fuel tank itself is pretty full already, all of the quick energy suddenly available has nowhere to turn but to your fat stores to be used later.

On the other hand, high-quality (complex) carbohydrates like whole grains, fresh fruits and vegetables take longer to break down completely into glucose -- since this type of carbohydrate has long chains of starch and more fiber to "work through". Also, add lean protein and a little fat to the same meal, and the process will be slowed down even more, allowing a gradual release of fuel into your body over a longer period of time. So, at a meal that includes 3 to 4 fuel groups, even the simplest carbohydrates like white rice, or a dessert like sherbet, will be released more slowly because of the protein and/or fat present in the other foods at that meal.

Therefore, a balanced meal has a built in buffer - the protein and fat fuel-because they help slow the rate of energy released, used and stored from carbohydrates. But a snack can be more difficult. Will your snack choice give your body low- or high-quality energy? *It all depends on the type of carbohydrate you choose, and if protein and/or fat is included.*

For example, a high-quality snack is an apple, sliced, with natural peanut butter. This combination gives you carbohydrate energy from the fruit, and protein and fat from the peanut butter. If you substitute 100% whole-wheat crackers for the apple slices, you have another good option. But what if you only have saltine or club-type crackers available? These common crackers are white-flour based, processed carbohydrates. The more "processed" a carbohydrate (or in other words, the higher the amount of white flour), the quicker it is broken down into sugars, or glucose-since the manufacturer has done the work for you, and little if any fiber is present. That's where the addition of peanut butter helps! Spreading natural peanut butter on even your "white flour" crackers will slow down the rate in which the crackers are broken down into glucose energy. A slower rate of breakdown means a more stable blood sugar level-avoiding the quick sugar drop that zaps your energy and increases your cravings.

What about graham crackers? They are also broken down fairly quickly, but adding dairy protein like a glass of 1% milk will slow the process down. Likewise, vanilla or lemon flavored yogurt has some added sugar, but the protein from the yogurt itself will help slow down the release of those sugars and encourage a more gradual rise and fall in your energy level. You can use the artificially sweetened yogurts, but you may receive more satisfaction from choosing a yogurt that is not artificially sweetened but still has less sugar than your typical fruit brands. Yogurts that have less sugar include many organic brands, Greek style brands, vanilla or lemon flavored brands and the "fruit on the bottom" brands, since you can control how much sweetened fruit syrup you stir in.

The following list gives you more suggestions for SMART SNACKS for one or two fuel groups. The key is to look for more whole grains and less sweetened, "instant", or "white-flour based" products. Remember: the more processed a carbohydrate, the quicker it is broken down into sugars, or glucose. Pay attention to how your fuel gauge responds. If you are hungry again within an hour, you probably chose a lower-quality fuel that "burned out" quickly, or did not eat any source of protein or fat with it. Learn to snack smart, and choose high-quality fuel that keeps your energy level running smoothly!

Your **FOOD CHALLENGE** (Part 1) for Week 4: Choose a snack combination that will improve the **quality of your carbohydrate fuel**. Continue to record what you eat in your Maintenance Log.

"I love eating the Rev It Up! way. Less amounts of meats, more fruits and vegetables, better choices for grains, more low- fat milk and yogurt. The afternoon snack is wonderful. As long as I eat every 3 to 4 hours, I feel more energized and more in charge of me."   Joyce

---

Are you still confused on what exactly determines whether a carbohydrate is a "whole grain"? See Question #3 in the "Most Frequently Asked Questions" section of the Appendix.

Smart Snack Suggestions

The following list provides suggestions for smart, high-quality fuel for snacks. The "1 Fuel Group" snacks are more ideal for mid morning-to give you a little boost between breakfast and lunch. The "2 Fuel Group" snacks are ideal for the afternoon, when you have a long stretch between two meals. The added protein or dairy fuel will help the energy from the grain or fruit last longer. Experiment with different choices, and notice how your body responds.

1 Fuel Group Snacks
Any fresh fruit
Dried, unsweetened fruit like raisins or apricots
Carrot sticks or fresh snow peas
Low-fat yogurt or cottage cheese
Mozzarella cheese stick
A "baseball size" amount of pretzels or low fat chips**
Graham crackers, about 1 large rectangle**

2 Fuel Group Snacks
Low-fat yogurt with sliced almonds
Fresh fruit or vegetables with low-fat cottage cheese
Graham crackers and natural peanut butter
Reduced-fat (2%) cheese and whole-wheat crackers
A "mini" whole grain pita pocket and 1 to 2 lean turkey slices
An energy/protein bar (look for about 200 calories, 10+ gms protein)
Apple slices and a mozzarella cheese stick
A banana with natural peanut butter
A mix of whole grain cereal with walnut pieces

**_Proceed with Caution_ with choices like these, since they have a higher percentage of white flour, with added sugar. When eaten alone, expect the energy to last a shorter period of time than fuel choice with more fiber, protein, fat.

***See Question #13 in the "Most Frequently Asked Questions" section of the Appendix for guidelines on appropriate energy bars.

Chapter 15

Headlights on Food (Part 2): Check the Fat Quality

Of all the fuel choices you have, which one do you think can have the most powerful long-term impact on your weight and health? If you guessed fats, you're right! Sugars certainly have an impact and can provide a quick rush of calories that overflow the capacity of your gas tank easily; however, fats provide the biggest calorie load in the smallest amount and can add up much quicker than you might realize. It's time to turn on your headlights and take a look at the quantity and quality of the fat fuel in your meals and snacks; in other words, raise that hood and check your oil!

Take a moment to think back to your car. Gas is the fuel for your engine, but it cannot do its work alone. Motor oil works hand in hand to make sure the engine can use the gas efficiently. Oil lubricates the motor, and the quality of the oil used determines how well and how long it will do its job before losing its effectiveness. Oil not only lubricates but also picks up "trash" that is left over from the day's work. This "trash" directly interferes with the oil's ability to lubricate and keep the motor running smoothly for a longer period of time. You do not need nearly as much oil as you do gas, and an oil change will last longer than a tank of gas. But even if the quantity is small, its job is big.

Now compare motor oil to the fats in your foods. In a similar way, the fats that you eat are necessary to lubricate your body's motor and keep it running smoothly. However, different types of fats exist, just like different grades or quality of oils. And some oils are simply full of "trash" that interferes with your body's performance.

Take a moment to check your oil. In other words, let's check the amount and the grade, or *type,* of fat in your daily meals and snacks. Your body does not need nearly as much oil, or fat, compared to foods needed from the five fuel groups, but the right kind of fat is the key to keeping your body performing well!

What does fat in your daily meals and snacks do for your body? Look at this list of functions and see if you are not impressed at the work it can accomplish:

- Fats provide structure for every cell in your body.
- Fats provide linoleic acid, an essential fatty acid that must be obtained from food sources.
- Fats provide transportation for all the fat-soluble vitamins, Vitamin A, D, E, and K. Vitamin A is necessary for healthy skin and eyes, Vitamin D for healthy bones, Vitamin E for a healthy immune system, and Vitamin K for efficient blood clotting. If no fat is available from our foods, these key vitamins do not have any means of transportation to do their job!
- Fats increase satiety from a meal or a snack (in other words, you feel fuller longer), since they contain 9 calories per gram. Proteins and carbohydrates provide only 4 calories per gram. Therefore, adding a small amount of fat can provide a large amount of energy, or calories! This can HELP you if you know it will be at least 4 hours before you are able to eat again.
- Fats, as well as proteins, help stabilize blood sugars, and buffer or slow down the digestion and absorption of carbohydrates. Therefore, the energy you receive from carbohydrates you eat will last longer if that food choice is eaten with a fat and/or a protein.

Pretty amazing, isn't it? You can see the importance of fats, but different grades or types of fats do exist. The two types of fats are **SATURATED** and **UNSATURATED**.

What is the difference in these? A tablespoon of either saturated or unsaturated fat contains the same number of calories. For example, a tablespoon of butter (a saturated fat) equals the same number of calories (about 100!) as a tablespoon of olive oil (an unsaturated fat). But saturated fats actually raise your cholesterol levels and contribute to heart disease, unlike unsaturated fats. Let's take an even closer look at these two types of fats, so you can choose the best grade or quality of oil for your body's motor.

SATURATED FATS

Saturated fat equals <u>animal fat</u>; that's easy to remember. But, there is always an exception to the rule, especially when you are talking about nutrition. (Don't you love it?) Saturated fats from animal foods like meat and cheese are easy to see, but saturated fats from plant foods are not as easy to identify but do exist. These plant food exceptions include coconut (hence, coconut oil), palm kernel oil, vegetable shortening, and margarines that contain *hydrogenated* fat. *Hydrogenated,* or *hydrogenation,* is a key word that indicates saturated fat. Anytime you see this word on a food label, you know that it contains more saturated fat. Soon, all labels will be required to indicate how much saturated fat from hydrogenated ingredients is present. In the meantime, an easy rule-of-thumb that you can use to estimate how much is present is to check out the order of the ingredients on the label itself. The further down the list, generally the less amount of hydrogenated fat used. So what exactly is hydrogenation? It is a chemical process that takes *unsaturated* oil like corn oil and changes it to a semi-solid or solid fat, hence, *saturated.* Another word for this type of fat is *trans fat.*

If hydrogenation makes a fat saturated, and saturated fat is the culprit behind higher cholesterol levels, why is it still used by food manufacturers? It makes a food that normally would not stay fresh be able to last a long time. In other words, it makes that same food shelf stable. Oil can become rancid, changing the smell and taste and quality of the food in which it is used. Hydrogenation prevents this. This is good news to vending machine suppliers! The products in that vending machine will remain fresh for a long time. That is why a food like a quick-stop cream filled sponge cake can sit in that vending machine for months (years?) and taste the same. *If the fat in that food can resist change for that long -- how long can it resist change, or stay solid, in your heart arteries?* Makes you wonder!

Here's a list of saturated fats from animal foods and from plant foods:

SATURATED FATS FROM ANIMAL FOODS	SATURATED FATS FROM PLANT FOODS
Red Meats (Beef, Lamb, Pork)* Dark meat chicken and turkey* Chicken or turkey skin Egg yolks Whole milk and whole-milk cheeses Butter and cream Processed meats, like hot dogs, bacon and sausage *Saturation depends on cut of meat (Ex: prime rib is higher-fat cut; sirloin is lower-fat cut)*	Coconut and coconut oil Palm or palm kernel oil Margarine (with hydrogenated oil as the first or second ingredient)** Vegetable shortening** Products made with hydrogenated oil (such as many vending machine snacks and sweets)** Fried foods cooked in shortening** **These foods contain trans fats, which elevate blood cholesterol.*

Is this list telling you not to ever have these fats? No. Red meats, like beef, lamb and pork, contain high-quality protein, and are rich sources of vitamins and minerals like Vitamin B12, zinc, and iron to name a few. Egg yolks are also great protein sources, full of iron, Vitamin E, and lecithin. The American Heart Association recommends lean red meats up to four times a week, and egg yolks up to 4 times a week. Recent studies have even indicated that egg yolks could be eaten more often than 4 times a week within a balanced diet because the cholesterol in egg yolks did not seem to promote an increase in saturated fats in the study subjects who ate an egg every day. A choice like beef or egg deserves a place on your plate, but the choices to consider most carefully are the saturated fats from certain plant foods and the hydrogenated fats, or trans fats.

To make sure you understand what a trans fat is, let's compare butter and margarine. Butter is from an animal and contains saturated fat. Notice how hard butter is when you remove it from the refrigerator? It takes quite a while to soften! Margarine, on the other hand, is made from oil, an unsaturated fat, which has been made semi-solid or partially hydrogenated through a chemical process. It now remains hard or solid at room temperature from the presence of trans fats, although not quite as hard as butter. Some researchers argue that trans fats can increase the bad cholesterol level in your body as much as a food high in saturated animal fats. But unlike saturated animal fats, trans fats, or hydrogenated oils, can also *decrease* the good cholesterol (explanation of "bad" and "good" cholesterol is coming up!). And we need as much of the "good" cholesterol as possible to protect us against heart disease.

So do you never eat a Twinkie again? Maybe, maybe not – but at least know what you are eating. What if you have to choose between a vending machine snack or going longer than four hours before eating again? Your metabolism will appreciate a snack and having something between meals will help prevent overeating at the next meal. Just try to make the healthiest choice available. Nowadays, many food manufacturing companies are beginning to take notice and produce more products that have less, if any, trans fats. Even vending machines sometimes offer healthier fat alternatives, like low-fat pretzels or heart-healthy nuts. But if a healthier alternative does not exist, an occasional Twinkie is not going to raise your trans fats significantly. If you do not eat from vending machines often and limit processed foods overall, your level of trans fats is probably not a problem.

How do you deal with the other saturated fats, the ones from animal foods? Helpful hints include using lean cuts of red meats, removing the skin of the chicken or turkey, limiting high-fat breakfast meats and substituting lower-fat versions, and moderating the number of egg yolks you have each week. What if you are at your favorite restaurant, and they serve you fresh homemade bread with tiny butter pats (you know, the ones that are shaped like flowers or stamped with the restaurant logo)? It is not the time to ask for a tub of diet margarine, right? You may wish to use that butter on that warm roll. Enjoy the taste and aroma as it melts-but limit to one, and make it last! Sure, you had saturated fat, but within moderation. Not a problem!

UNSATURATED FATS (in other words, SMART FATS!)

On the opposite side, unsaturated fats are usually *liquid* at room temperature and found in plant foods. Unsaturated fats help lower the "bad" cholesterol and reduce your risk of heart disease. Different types exist:

POLYUNSATURATED FATS	MONOUNSATURATED FATS
Corn oil	Canola oil
Safflower oil	Olive oil
Sunflower oil	Peanut oil
Soybean oil	Nuts and seeds, such as the
Fatty fish*, such as the	following: peanuts, almonds,
following:	pecans, walnuts*, pistachios,
Salmon, tuna, herring, sardines,	sesame seeds
mackerel, rainbow trout, halibut,	Nut butters, like peanut butter
Atlantic bluefish, eel, and lake	Avocados
trout	Olives, black and green

Did you know that a fatty fish like salmon, and even walnuts, are high in polyunsaturated fats, specifically omega 3 fatty acids, which protect against heart disease? Omega 3 fatty acids help lower levels of blood fats, reduce blood clotting, help make irregular heart beats less likely, and often increase the production of "good" cholesterol. The American Heart Association has added the recommendation to eat fish, preferably fatty fish, at least twice a week. Concerned about the safety of eating cold-water fish due to information you've heard about mercury levels in the water? The FDA has acknowledged that it is safe to eat fatty fish oils in amounts up to 3 grams of omega 3 fatty acids daily. One serving (3 ½ ounces) of salmon contains about 1 gram of omega 3 fatty acids, so even a daily serving of fish meets the safety guidelines. If you are still uncomfortable, or just don't go for that fishy smell, add walnuts to your meals or snacks daily. They are also a good source of omega 3's.

Okay, you are now aware of the types of fats, saturated (including trans fats), and unsaturated (including fatty fish). Have you noticed the terms "good" cholesterol and "bad" cholesterol have been associated with the different types of fat? Saturated fats increase the bad cholesterol, and trans fats even lower the good cholesterol. What exactly IS cholesterol, and which ones are *good* or *bad*?

CHOLESTEROL

Cholesterol is a waxy-like substance that is found only in animal tissue. Cholesterol is made in the liver by the body, which is the reason why you will only find it in something that has a liver! (A cow, a pig and a chicken all have livers…but a corn stalk does not! Hence, fats in foods from these animals will have cholesterol but corn oil will not.) Cholesterol is very important to your body, because it plays a role in making all of the body's steroids, such as bile salts (which help digest fats), Vitamin D (which helps build strong bones), and your reproductive hormones (you know what those do!). It also gives physical structure to every cell. Your body makes cholesterol in the liver and works to balance the amount it makes with the amount you eat. So, reducing the cholesterol intake from your meals and snacks would probably cause little harm to the body because it can usually make its own. If you eat less cholesterol, your body is designed to make more to meet the demands. Likewise, if you eat more, your body, in most cases, can make less to keep the balance.

The body does have the ability to balance cholesterol, but this ability can be greatly affected by what you eat as well as your family history. The American Heart Association warns that one of the significant risk factors for heart disease is a high level of blood cholesterol. A diet continually high in cholesterol can lead to higher levels of cholesterol in the blood. So it is important to limit the amount of saturated and trans fats in your diet because these fats trigger your body to produce more cholesterol.

Once it's produced, just how does cholesterol get from the liver to the other parts of the body? It takes a ride through the blood stream! This is not as simple as it may sound, because cholesterol and blood are a lot like oil and water…they do not mix well! Your amazing body has a special system of transportation designed to carry cholesterol in the body to where it's needed. It does this in the liver by mixing fats with protein and making different types of "transportation vehicles" called lipoproteins ("lipids", which is another word for fats, plus "protein"). Since blood itself is a protein, it can now mix with fat in the form of a lipoprotein so that cholesterol can be carried throughout your body.

One main type of lipoprotein is the LDL, which stands for low-density lipoprotein. The LDL contains about 60-80% cholesterol, and it really loves to travel and deliver its cholesterol package to the cell walls of the heart arteries. Saturated fats, including trans fats, trigger the production of this type of lipoprotein, the LDLs. Therefore, this lipoprotein is known as the *bad* cholesterol. What can you do to lower the LDLs? *Eat less saturated and trans fat!*

The other main type of lipoprotein is the HDL, which stands for high-density lipoprotein. The HDL contains more protein and less cholesterol (only 20%) than the other lipoproteins. HDLs love to travel to the cell walls of the heart arteries and *remove* the cholesterol deposited by the LDLs. Then the HDLs deliver this cholesterol back to the liver for eventual removal from the body through the intestines. HDLs actually protect against heart disease, so they are known as the *good* cholesterol.

If HDLs are so good for you, what can you eat to make more of them? Sorry, food intake has little effect and no particular food will significantly increase the level of HDLs in your body. But, *exercise will*! That is yet another reason you benefit from the aerobic exercise and strength training you do on a consistent basis.

Who thought checking the oil would be this complicated? Well, let's make it as simple as possible. Here are some common challenges and suggested strategies to improve the grade or quality of oil that goes into your body:

 Continue to moderate or limit the amount of total fat you are eating daily by limiting your fats to no more than 3 "ping pong ball" portions for women, 4 for men, per day. Now, individualize your specific "Check the Oil" challenge and choose your road map:

CHECK THE OIL CHALLENGE #1:
Do you eat a lot of fried foods?
- Eliminate fried foods to no more than twice a week.
- Experiment with oil- and vinegar-based marinades.
- Grill, bake or roast instead of frying.

CHECK THE OIL CHALLENGE #2:

Do you eat a lot of red meat (beef, pork or lamb)?

- Choose lean cuts of red meats, like tenderloin, round or sirloin.
- Limit red meats to no more than four times a week.
- Moderate and balance the number of egg yolks you consume a week, either alone or within a casserole type recipe. You can often substitute egg substitute or egg whites in a recipe without losing the quality or consistency.

CHECK THE OIL CHALLENGE #3:

Do you eat enough omega 3 fatty acids?

- Increase your fish intake on a weekly basis by trying to eat fish, especially cold water fish, twice a week. Add it once a week for the first 2 weeks, and then increase to twice a week. By the end of this program, you will have made fish a regular part of your week!
- Order grilled fish in a restaurant if you do not like to prepare it at home, or take advantage of the precooked fish at your local grocery store.
- Add walnut pieces (at least one ping pong ball amount daily) to your breakfast cereals, home made trail mixes, yogurt or as a salad garnish.

CHECK THE OIL CHALLENGE #4:

Do you eat a lot of higher-fat dairy products?

- Substitute 1% or skim milk products for 2% or whole milk products, like milk, cottage cheese and yogurt.
- Substitute 2% cheeses for whole-milk cheeses, either block, sliced or grated versions. Fat-free cheeses are not necessary. They do not taste or melt like 2% or regular cheeses and can alter a recipe result.

Your **FOOD CHALLENGE (Part 2)** for Week 4: Plan your personal road map by identifying one of the "check the oil" challenges that you face most frequently. Then select one or more steps to concentrate on this week to **improve the quality of your fat fuel.** Record what you eat in your Maintenance Log, noting any improvements in your fat quality as the week progresses.

MY PERSONAL "CHECK THE OIL" CHALLENGE IS:

_____
_____
_____
_____
_____

THE STEP(S) I WILL TAKE TO IMPROVE THE QUALITY OF FAT FUEL ARE:

_____
_____
_____
_____
_____

"Great news! My official weight loss was 17 pounds in 3 months. My overall cholesterol when down from 265 to 202, and my LDL (bad guys!) went down from 169 to 119. My triglycerides went down from 170 to 115. My overall ratio decreased from 4.3 to 3.4-GREAT, huh?" Doris

Chapter 16

Headlights on Fitness:
Check for Safety and F.U.N.

Ready to tune up your fitness program and check for safety? How about checking for F.U.N.? Safety is critical when it comes to your exercise form and body alignment. If the wheels on your car are out of alignment, it can cause extensive (and expensive!) damage. Likewise, if your form is out of alignment, it may cause damage to your body's ligaments and joints. And when it comes to enjoying safe exercise, keeping the F.U.N. is just as important. Let's start with the safety check:

SAFETY CHECK

BREATHING (All exercises):
1. Pay attention to your breathing, and NEVER hold your breath.
2. Stay relaxed and inhale during the down phase of the movement.
3. Stay relaxed and exhale during the up phase or exertion of the movement.

UPPER BODY MOVEMENTS:
1. Avoid swinging your arms-only lift weight that you can take through the movement without momentum.
2. Keep your shoulders and neck relaxed.

LOWER BODY MOVEMENTS:
1. Avoid extending your knees past your toes.
2. Keep your hips above or parallel to your knees.
3. Again, don't swing or use momentum.

ABDOMINAL MOVEMENTS:
1. Avoid lifting your lower back off the floor.
2. Support your neck with your arms without pulling your head and shoulders forward.
3. Keep an imaginary tennis ball under your chin to keep your head in the correct position.

Anything you need to change? Make a mental note or even jot down a reminder on a post-it note and stick it on your treadmill at home, or in your tennis shoes if you work out at a gym or walk around your neighborhood. That way you won't forget when you get ready to exercise again. And make sure you perform a safety check regularly to keep things in line.

The safety check has been covered, so time to move on to the F.U.N. part. Take a few minutes and "play with" your fitness goals right now, and see if you need a F.U.N. strategy to rev things up again!

Make Fitness F.U.N.

F = FLEX your schedule
U = UNDERSTAND your challenges
N = NIX the negatives

F is for FLEX, not your muscles but your schedule! The best way to fit a workout into your life is to schedule it as you would any other appointment. Try blocking off the same times every week, but be realistic. If you know that you are NOT a morning person, there is no need to set that alarm for an early hour and then feel guilty when you hit the snooze button every 5 minutes! Likewise, if you know that the end of the day always includes some kind of interference that prevents you from getting to the gym, schedule your fitness appointment before work or during your lunch hour. And when an emergency happens-at work OR home-and you simply cannot keep your commitment to exercise, handle it as you would any other important appointment. Reschedule, as quickly as possible-and let go of any guilt for doing so when your circumstances have prevented it. If someone you know has to reschedule an appointment with you because of an injury, sickness or a last-minute emergency, you understand and are flexible. Why not offer the same courtesy to yourself?

Flexibility in your schedule is important, but so is flexibility in the *type* of exercise you do! Plan variety into your activities to not only keep the engine warm and your car moving but also simply keep your interest! If you do the same activity over and over, your body becomes very efficient doing the same moves repeatedly and begins burning fewer calories to do the same amount of work. Adding variety each week helps prevent the body from "getting used to it" and maximizes the benefit you receive for your efforts. It also is just a lot more enjoyable!

U is for UNDERSTAND your challenges! Life is full of different seasons - a season for education, a season for work challenges, a season for travel, maybe a season for raising children or taking care of an elderly family member. What specific challenge are you facing in this season of life?

- Young children at home
  - Understand the limitations on your time.
  - Swap "babysitting time" with a neighbor to allow you to get to the gym.
  - Purchase an at-home exercise video, or complete the strength training starter program, when your children are napping or busy.
  - Find a gym that has reputable childcare and arrange your day to fit activity in during the time it is available.
- Overtime hours at work
  - Consider exercise a "must" for stress release instead of a way to burn calories, and you might be less likely to miss your exercise appointment.
  - Split up your exercise time into smaller sessions until your work schedule is relieved.
    - Walk 20 minutes in the early morning.
    - Stop by the gym on the way home for a quick 20-minute workout to round out a 40-minute session.
    - Look for ways to add activity to your every day routines, such as parking your car further away from the office door and taking stairs instead of elevators.

- o   Compromise by trying to exercise only 1 out of the 5 workdays, but make exercise a priority on both *weekend* days until your work schedule changes.
- o   Schedule the days you will NOT exercise to release you from guilt about "missing a day"-view it as a day of rest for which you planned.

Whether the challenge lies in the workplace or family commitments, these strategies can help you work around the challenge without neglecting your fitness.

N is for NIX the negatives! The more often you hear something, the more you start believing it. Do you hear yourself say negative statements like "I knew I couldn't stay committed", "I always quit!", "It works for you but it's impossible for me", or "I never can find the time"? You'll eventually start believing it, if you don't already. Try to nix the negatives in its tracks. Be prepared to battle back with positive punches-"I have had a difficult week but I'm starting fresh today", "I will make it work for me, even if I have to make several changes along the way to find the right routine", "I deserve to move and exercise-it makes me feel better!" or "One day at a time is all I have to do!" If you have a choice to be around a friend with a negative attitude or a positive attitude, which one are you most likely to choose? A positive attitude attracts, a negative attitude repels. Begin saying positive statements, and you'll notice how much more you *enjoy* being with yourself!

How about looking for an exercise partner that will keep you accountable while encouraging your progress? As important as finding a good mechanic or body repair shop that you can trust to do honest, reliable service on your car, you need someone you can trust to support and encourage you as you travel through life's traffic. A friend with whom you exercise can help you see your own progress when discouragement blindsides you. That same partner can motivate you to keep going that last 10 minutes to meet your goal! And, honestly, an exercise partner simply makes fitness more fun!

Maybe you have an exercise partner already, and you try to encourage yourself with affirmations. Things are going smoothly....until an illness or injury hits you! This is a negative that is out of your direct control, and it happens to everyone, elite athlete or recreational exerciser. Do not let it defeat your program. If you are sick, stop exercise until you are 24 hours past the last sign of your sickness, then start back cautiously until your strength has built back up. If you are injured, stop exercise with that body part until the pain goes away. Remember, an injury is not the same as a little muscle soreness from having a great workout. If you are a little sore the next day or two, but are able to carry out all of your daily activities without any problems, know that you are working hard and progress is happening. If the pain has not gone within 2 to 3 days, see a physician.

Both situations present a good time to schedule "NO exercise" in your appointment book, to help release the guilt and remind yourself that rest is important for your injury to heal. Your body will not begin losing significant fitness benefits from lack of activity until about two weeks have passed, and most illnesses and injuries do not exceed that length of time, right? You will need to return to your exercise program cautiously and conservatively, but your body will be right back where you left it within a week or so!

Your **FITNESS CHALLENGE** for Week 4: Perform a safety check by following the form and function guidelines during your next exercise session, noting any areas that need improvement. Secondly, look at the F.U.N. in your current exercise routine, and choose one strategy to put more flexibility, understanding, or positive reinforcement into your weekly exercise routine. **Record any safety changes and F.U.N. strategies in your Maintenance Log.**

A Look in the Rearview Mirror

Week 4: Tune Up

Foundation: Record at least three changes you have made on the Victory Lap chart (page 249) since Week 1, and reward yourself!

Food (Part 1): Choose at least three different snacks that will improve the quality of your carbohydrate fuel at your afternoon snack break.

Food (Part 2): Identify one of the "check the oil" challenges that you face and choose one step to improve the quality of your fat fuel.

Fitness: Improve one specific area under safety check and one under the F.U.N. strategies this week.

Now, record any changes you notice this week:

Date	Thoughts, Feelings, Body Changes?

PHASE TWO:
Let's Accelerate!

Week 5: Plan Your Pit Stops

Week 6: Charge Your Battery

Week 7: Clean the Rearview Mirror

Week 8: Deal with Detours

Week 5:

Plan Your Pit Stops

"People don't believe the weight battle I've had in the past (my whole life!) People always ask me how I remain thin in the restaurant business (I now own 2 Cheeburger Cheeburger restaurants in Louisiana and it is CRAZY!), and I tell them about Rev It Up!. Although my weight has fluctuated a little, I remain very close to the weight I was when I finished the program (over 2 years ago). I'm actually there now! I also wander off of the program occasionally (tired, stressed, eating at the restaurant every day, etc.) but ALWAYS come back to Rev It Up! and jump back in!"   Rebecca

Chapter 17

Plan Your Pit Stops:
Follow the Traffic Lights

You have spent a lot of time putting down a new foundation and meeting the challenges for all four "F's", including food, fluid, and fitness. You have taken the driver's seat and are revving up your metabolism-taking control-and noticing the difference. Now, the time has come to accelerate your focus-and begin fine-tuning your engine. Let's start Week 5 by turning our headlights on Food for an accelerated look at eating out-or, in Rev It Up! terms, PIT STOPS!

A *pit stop* for routine service or to refuel the engine is a common part of maintenance for any vehicle. Sometimes a pit stop may be required more frequently depending on the amount of driving or wear and tear on the vehicle. How does this translate to you and your metabolism? For Rev It Up! purposes, a *"Pit Stop" includes food you pick up, take out, eat out or that you purchase prepackaged.* Pit stops take you out of the controlled atmosphere of your home and put you at the mercy of someone else's menu or preparation. These stops may be even more frequent if you have a fast-paced schedule or are often on the road.

Did you know that the average person eats out at least one out of every three meals? Fast food restaurants with quick drive through windows make a pit stop easy. With "quick stop" food marts available on almost every corner, even a snack can be purchased in a matter of minutes. But choosing smart fuel or getting a quick paint job (fruits or vegetables!) can be very hard to do when your choices are high-fat foods that typically do not include color or whole grains.

What are some key strategies to take with you at any pit stop - fast food, quick stops or a sit-down restaurant? Learn the Traffic Lights to follow for your Pit Stops.

RED LIGHTS FOR PIT STOPS

1.   Don't go hungry! Watch your body's fuel gauge, and keep an eye on that clock. If you know you will be eating out for the next meal, make sure you plan for a snack in between meals if your body's fuel tank will have to wait longer than 4 hours. Making a pit stop BEFORE you reach a hunger level of 1 or 2 (you know, the "give me anything I can get my hands on…and quick!" levels!) will help control your cravings for fats or sugars. When you are able to think clearly and check the menu, you are more likely to select healthier food.

2.   Don't skip meals or neglect snacks! What's the problem with skipping a meal or snack, or two, to save up your calories to go splurge at one of your favorite restaurants? What may seem to make sense to you will not make sense to your body and its hunger and fullness cycle. Remember that your fuel tank holds about 4 hours of fuel at any given time, and if the tank is way beyond empty, you will most likely overeat. And when you overeat, any extra fuel that your body cannot use will need to be stored. Your body will be primed, ready and waiting to store the extra fuel as fat to prepare itself for the next time the pit stop is long overdue! So please, don't save up calories by skipping meals or snacks.

3.   Don't fill up on fast "fillers"! What sits on your table, tempting you to fill up before your meal even arrives? The bread or chip basket! It's hard to resist the warm smell of fresh baked bread or crispy chips. And a roll or a handful of chips can certainly be included as part of your grain portion. But too often, one baseball becomes 2 baseballs, maybe 3…even 4! And when the meal arrives, you are not physically hungry anymore but often eat most or all of your meal anyway because you are paying for it, or feel guilty and defeated and therefore assume "why not?" To stop filling up before the meal, choose one of the following strategies:

a.   Ask the wait staff to skip the bread or chip basket.
b.   Ask the wait staff to remove the bread or chip basket after
        you have selected a small amount.
c.   Ask the wait staff to bring the bread or chip basket to the
        table with your entrée to prevent filling up too early.

Okay, you are probably seeing enough "red" right now. Time to check out the green lights!

GREEN LIGHTS FOR PIT STOPS

1.   Do save your ping pong balls! Don't save calories by skipping meals through the day, but you CAN save your fat servings (remember those three ping pong ball size portions?) for a meal at your favorite restaurant. Go ahead and eat balanced, but low- to no-fat, meals and snack on your regular schedule throughout the day. Save up most or all your ping pong ball amount of added fats for the restaurant meal. Your fat servings may all come at once, but your metabolism will not be slower and your cravings will be more controlled because you have eaten regularly throughout the day.

2.   Do plan your splurges! When you arrive at a restaurant, decide on a "splurge" item and include it in your meal. Maybe your splurge is a dessert that you can share with the entire table. Or maybe you decide to share an extravagant entrée with a friend, and balance it by ordering a salad and a side order of vegetables. Assume that these special items will be cooked with fat for extra flavor; therefore, compromise in other areas that you can control. Ask for condiments like salad dressings "on the side" and skip the added butter on the bread. Limiting the added fats that you can control helps balance the special items that already have fat as part of the preparation. And if you continue to use the baseball guidelines to control your grain choices, the palm of your hand to control your protein, and look for ways to eat as much color as possible, you can still come out ahead AND enjoy yourself, too!

3.   Do expand your expectations! You probably enjoy eating out for not only the food but also the atmosphere, the company with whom you are dining, and the night off from having to prepare a meal yourself. Expand your expectations of eating out to include the whole experience, and maybe the meal itself will take on a smaller role. This in turn can result in more attention to the event itself and less attention to finishing your plate.

4.   Do drink your water! Restaurant or fast food meals typically contain more sodium (salt), used in the preparation, so drinking your water is an important strategy to help balance the higher sodium content. In addition, water is especially important if you consume alcohol at your meal. Alcohol will not only dehydrate you but also lower your resistance to food temptations and possibly increase your appetite at the same time. Remember to match up any alcohol you drink with an equal amount of additional water. This helps dilute the effect of the alcohol and ensures your body stays hydrated.

5.   Do remember "I can EAT AGAIN!" Once you eat your baseball amounts of grain, lots of color, and your palm sized portion of protein, ask the restaurant staff to bring a take-home box. Remember, you *can* eat it all, but listen to your fuel gauge when it tells you it's full, and eat the rest *later*!

Notice more green lights than red lights? Good! Eating out will remain a big part of our culture and can be incorporated into a healthy, well lifestyle with just a little more effort and planning. *Concentrate on the positive strategies and remember to take your Rev It Up! principles with you whenever you order a meal outside your home.* Don't leave home without them!

To help you make decisions about what fuel to order, take a look at the following list. It provides a guide to help you choose healthy options at a sit-down restaurant. The list is not comprehensive, but highlights common lower-fat options found in most restaurants.

Healthy Restaurant Fuel Choices

Appetizers:
Select items like tomato juice, broth-based hot or cold soups, or fresh fruit for a colorful start. Or choose shrimp cocktail, steamed mussels or an appetizer like pot stickers for more protein. Many restaurants will serve an appetizer portion of most entrées, which, along with a salad, can serve as your entire meal.

Salads:
Any mixed green salad is a great addition, and the deeper the green of the lettuces used, the better! Watch out for high-fat additions like

bacon, grated cheese, and croutons. And always request salad dressings on the side, so that you can control the amount used.

Entrées:
Lean cuts of beef or pork, roasted or grilled are great options. Also, roasted or grilled chicken, turkey or Cornish hen, with the skin removed, are excellent protein choices. And remember that broiled or grilled fish can help you meet your "check the oil" challenge to eat more omega 3 fatty acids. (NOTE: Many restaurants, particularly steakhouses, baste their beef, pork, poultry, and fish entrées with butter or oil. Ask if this is done, and if so, request that the chef eliminate this step.) Other options include pasta entrées with tomato-based sauces or even vegetable pizza, with a thin or traditional style (not thick) crust.

Sides:
Any grilled, roasted, baked, boiled or steamed vegetable side dish helps add color to your meal. But avoid vegetables that are in a cream sauce (like creamed spinach or spinach dip), fried (like fried okra or potatoes) or in a casserole (like broccoli casserole). Grain type side dishes are always available, but note how they are prepared. A grain, like rice or risotto, is most often cooked in a cream or butter base. And many restaurants pour melted butter over their plain steamed vegetables, as well. So always ask how it is prepared if you do not know already, and keep an eye on portion control if the dish is made with added fats.

Desserts:
The lower-fat desserts are sorbet, sherbets and fruit-based choices. However, dessert is often a splurge, so you may opt to order a full-fat version but split it with several friends and/or take home the rest to share later.

Now you have a road map for sit-down restaurants. What about fast food options? Lately most if not all fast food restaurants have worked to bring at least a few healthy options for entrées and side items. The menu items can change, and some are regionally selective, but the following table will give you a head start on making healthy Rev It Up! choices for fast food pit stops:

Healthy Fast Food Fuel Choices

FAST FOOD	HEALTHY CHOICES	PORTION GUIDE 1 ppb = 1 ping pong ball (for fat serving)
Arby's	Roasted chicken sandwich, w/o mayo, side salad, *low-fat dressing Regular roast beef sandwich w/ side salad, low-fat dressing (***use 1 ppb amount for all dressings**) Grilled chicken salad, low-fat dressing*	1 baseball of grain, palm size animal protein, 1 vegetable, 1 dairy protein (if cheese), 1 ppb fat* 1 baseball of grain, palm size animal protein, 1 vegetable, 1 ppb fat* palm size animal protein, 1 vegetable, 1 fruit, 1 ppb fat*
Burger King	Grilled chicken Whopper, w/ all the trimmings EXCEPT mayo, side salad w/ low-fat dressing* Grilled chicken salad, w/ low-fat dressing*, and fruit side (if available)	1 ½ baseballs of grain, palm size animal protein, 1 vegetable, 1 ppb fat* palm size animal protein, 2 vegetables, (1 fruit), 1 ppb fat*
Chick-Fil-A	Grilled chicken deluxe sandwich, w/ small carrot raisin salad or fresh fruit Grilled or spicy chicken wrap, with low-fat dressing*	1 baseball of grain, palm size animal protein, vegetable and fruit combo 1 ½ baseball of grain, palm size animal protein, 1 vegetable, 1 ppb fat*

Chick-Fil-A (continued)	Grilled chicken salad w/ low-fat dressing*, carrot raisin or fruit salad	Palm size animal protein, 2 vegetables, 1 fruit, 1 ppb fat*

KFC	BBQ chicken sandwich, side of green beans* (fat added in cooking)	1 baseball of grain, palm size animal protein, 1 vegetable, 1 ppb fat
	Grilled chicken breast (no skin) w/ mashed potatoes (no gravy), green beans*	1 baseball of grain, palm size animal protein, 1 vegetable, 1 ppb fat*
McDonald's	Grilled chicken sandwich, w/o mayo (ask for extra lettuce & tomato), apples	1 baseball of grain, palm size animal protein,1 vegetable, 1 fruit
	Grilled chicken salad, without bacon, w/ low-fat dressing*, apple slices	palm size animal protein, 1 dairy protein, 2 vegetables, 1 ppb fat*
	Grilled chicken snack wrap, no sauce, apple slices	1 baseball of grain, ½ palm size animal and dairy protein (combo), 1 fruit
Subway	Any of the "6 grams of fat or less" sandwich options, loaded with fresh veggies (6" size); vinegar optional, apple slices or raisins	2 baseballs of grain, palm size animal protein, 2 vegetable, (1 dairy protein if cheese included), fruit

Taco Bell	Two soft chicken tacos	1 ½ baseballs of grain, palm size animal protein, 1 vegetable, 1 dairy protein
	Taco salad without the hard shell, with salsa as dressing	1 baseball grain (beans), palm size animal protein, 2 vegetables, 1 dairy protein
Wendy's	Baked potato (no butter / sour cream), stuffed with chili, and garden salad w/ low-fat dressing*	2 baseballs of grain, palm size animal/ plant protein (chili), 2 vegetables, 1 ppb fat*
	Bowl of chili, garden salad, w/ low-fat dressing*	1 baseball of grain, palm size animal/ plant protein (in chili), 2 vegetables, 1 ppb fat*
	Grilled chicken sandwich (no sauce), garden salad w/ low-fat dressing*	1 baseball of grain, palm size animal protein, 2 vegetable, 1 ppb fat*
	Mandarin chicken salad (w/ almonds, noodles*, oranges), w/ ½ pack oriental sesame dressing*	1 baseball grain, palm size animal/ plant protein, 2 vegetables, 1/2 fruit, 1 ½ ppb fat*

Although this list is not comprehensive, hopefully it will help you make a more informed decision about where and what to eat. The portion guidelines are specifically based on the food items listed in the middle column compared to the calorie calculations provided by each restaurant; therefore, the portions listed may or may not meet your individual goal so adjust accordingly. If you do choose to have the traditional fast food meal of a hamburger and French fries, just try not to "super size" and listen to your body's fuel gauge for fullness. Remember that *balance is the key* and one high-fat meal will not slow down your progress. It is what you do *more often than not* that will make the long term difference and promote a revved up metabolism.

Healthy pit stops can help you stay on track. But what about those times when you are hungry but unable to stop at a restaurant or even drive through for fast food? Two of the most common situations are when you are <u>driving</u> or when you are <u>flying</u>.

The strategies that follow will help you prepare for the next time you might be on a long trip in the car or an airplane, heading towards an empty fuel gauge but unable to stop to refuel.

REV IT UP WHEN YOU ARE DRIVING:

1.   Carry a small cooler with an ice pack inside and include foods such as fresh fruit, baby carrots, drinkable low-fat yogurt, and string cheese.

2.   Stash some high-energy treats in the glove compartment, such as energy bars (Choose the flavors that will not melt! See Question #13 in "Most Frequently Asked Questions" in the Appendix for more information on energy bars). Other options include dried fruits like raisins, single serving whole grain cereal boxes, small snack bags of nuts and pretzels, or nuts and cereal mix (home made is preferable).

3.   Take the smart approach at a gas station pit stop-purchase a water bottle and a healthier snack option like raisins, pretzels, or a cereal bar. Having a hard time resisting a candy bar? Choose a miniature "feel good" treat like a peppermint patty or several chocolate kisses instead. Savor the treat on the road by seeing how long you can make the chocolate last. You may find that a little bit can go a long way in satisfaction if you slow down enough to really enjoy it.

Staying on track with your fuel stops while driving is easier than when flying, but you can use the following guidelines to help you:

REV IT UP WHEN YOU ARE FLYING:

1.   Carry snacks with you in your briefcase or purse, such as dried fruit, home made trail mix in a throwaway container (try oat cereal with raisins and almond slices), or natural peanut butter crackers. And don't forget to purchase a water bottle right before stepping on the plane.

2.   Drink extra water at every opportunity. This is the perfect time to match up those fluids, since airplane travel automatically limits the availability of water and takes more water out of your body naturally.

3.   Check to see if your flight provides meals or snacks. Don't get caught in a time change and miss the opportunity to purchase a meal to carry with you if the flight does not provide it. Healthy options are available now in most terminal restaurants, and if all else fails, simply get a slice of cheese pizza to take on the plane (a bit messier, but it works in a pinch). Since color options are few and far between, try to plan and pack individual snack size bags of raw carrots, or individual boxes of dried fruit.

4.   Do the best you can! Don't worry if you get caught in the rush of traveling and forget to pack snacks or somehow miss a meal. Simply do what you can with what you have…and get right back on track when you arrive. Start by purchasing a water bottle and small bag of nuts once your plane lands, and enjoy these while waiting for your luggage. If your fuel gauge is running on empty, this snack will carry you through the taxi or bus ride to your next stop.

NOTE: *Now that you are in the Acceleration phase of Rev It Up!, you no longer have four separate challenges for Foundation, Food, Fluid, and Fitness. Your weekly challenge will concentrate on only ONE of the Four "F's", and will be found on the "Look in the Rearview Mirror" page after each chapter.*

A Look in the Rearview Mirror

Week 5: Plan Your Pit Stops

Your **ACCELERATION Challenge** for Week 5: Choose healthy options when you make a pit stop this week. Remember, pit stops include restaurant meals, fast food, and take-out foods.

Now, record any changes you notice this week:

Date	Thoughts, Feelings, Body Changes?

Week 6:

Charge Your Battery

"I have found two benefits from the exercise part of the program: 1) You lose inches, and 2) You get more compliments! I have a dress that I wore to my nephew's wedding. I haven't really lost any weight since I wore it last August, but it was pretty form fitting. I wore it yesterday to Easter services and it is now loose-so I guess that as much as I do not like the gym work, it's good for me!

Today I also saw an eye doctor that I had not seen before, so he doesn't know what I used to look like, and he asked me if I played tennis, because I looked really fit! The other cool part was that I had decided to get new frame- the ones I had are outdated and are bigger than the current style-but in addition to that they are now much too big looking for my much thinner face!"   Beth

Chapter 18

Battery Charge
Using Aerobic Exercise

Whether a fitness plan was something new to you or you were already working out when you started Rev It Up!, over the past weeks you have started taking your body to the next level. Hopefully you are seeing the benefits of a stronger heart and stronger muscles in everyday life.

When you first started your exercise plan, or as you increased the amount and type of exercise you were already doing, this new level produced initial results that you could see and feel. You may still be seeing steady benefits, and your body does not need a battery charge just yet. But, you will inevitably hit a fitness plateau sometime in the future as your body adjusts to its new routine. In fact, you may already have noticed that the benefits you first obtained seem to have lessened over time. And you are getting discouraged. If you are, what can you do to stop this plateau from happening? Learn how to *charge your battery* using both types of fitness to make the most of your efforts over the long haul.

Have you ever experienced the frustration of trying to start your car, but discover no response? Your battery is dead! The only way to correct the problem is to charge it up again. Likewise, if you feel your exercise is lacking energy or not getting the results now that you noticed when you first started, charge your battery!

BATTERY CHARGE USING AEROBIC EXERCISE

A battery charge, using aerobic exercise, requires changing the intensity of your aerobic workout. At what level of intensity will you receive the most benefit from your exercise? In other words, how do you keep your battery charged for the most efficient performance? Three strategies to try are as follows:

Strategy #1: Exercise at a steady rate but a HIGHER intensity level during the entire workout.
Strategy #2: Alternate higher bursts of intense activity with periods of recovery during the same workout.
Strategy #3: Use correct form while you exercise on equipment like a treadmill, stair climber or an elliptical trainer.

STRATEGY #1:

Exercise at a STEADY rate but HIGHER INTENSITY level

During any type of physical activity, your body gets its fuel from both fat and stored carbohydrate, called glycogen, found in your muscles and your liver. If you exercise at a lower intensity, say, 65% of your target heart rate, your body prefers to use more of its fat stores and less of its glycogen stores. If you exercise at a higher intensity, say 80 to 85% of your target heart rate, your body draws more energy from your glycogen, or carbohydrate, stores instead of your fat stores. Does this mean that lower-intensity exercise is better? Not necessarily! The key is not the type of fuel you burn but the amount that you burn that charges your battery most efficiently. Let's look at an example:

Scenario A: *45 minutes* of exercise time, *lower* intensity

Joe works out for 45 minutes at 65% of his target heart rate and burns a total of 350 calories. About 50% of the total calories burned are fat, so Joe burned about 175 calories from his fat stores in 45 minutes.

Scenario B: *Same amount* of exercise time, but *moderate* intensity

Joe works out for 45 minutes at about 75% of his target heart rate and burns a total of 500 calories. About 40% of his total calories burned are fat, so Joe burned about 200 calories from his fat stores. Increasing the intensity resulted in more calories burned from his fat stores than working out at a lower intensity, even in the same amount of time.

Scenario C: *Less* exercise time, but *highest* intensity

Joe works out for 30 minutes only, but at about 80 to 85% of his target heart rate and burns a total of 500 calories. About 35% of his total calories burned are fat, so Joe burned about 175 calories from his fat stores. Increasing the intensity even more resulted in the same number of calories burned from his fat stores as did the lowest intensity workout but in *less* time!

Did you notice what happened? Compare the first and second scenarios. When Joe worked out for the *same* amount of time, but at different intensity levels (harder), he not only burned *more* calories but also a little more body *fat*, even though the total % of calories burned from fat was less. Compare this to the third scenario, when Joe actually worked out *less* time but at the highest intensity level. He burned more calories and the same amount of fat as in the first scenario but in only 30 minutes, saving 15 minutes. This can come in handy when your own exercise time is limited. So learn from Joe and take advantage of a battery charge by increasing the intensity of your workout within your target heart rate range.

Just in case you do not remember your target heart rate (THR) range, look back in Chapter 8 on page 89. You can continue to use that formula, or you can incorporate your resting heart rate (RHR) into the formula that follows. This formula, called the Karvonen Method, is more individualized and accurate, especially for someone who has been exercising regularly for awhile. But the key is to know your resting heart rate. Once you have your RHR, you subtract that number from a standard maximum heart rate for males or females, then you add the RHR number back into the equation after multiplying by the intensity level. Work this out step by step:

KARVONEN TARGET HEART RATE FORMULA:

Determine your average resting heart rate (RHR) by taking your pulse rate (hold the count for 60 seconds) immediately upon waking, before rising from bed. Record, and repeat this for three days. Determine your average RHR by multiplying the three days' numbers together and dividing by three; RHR = _____

For males:

(220 – RHR_____)x 65% + RHR = _____ (Lowest THR)

(220 – RHR_____)x 85% + RHR = _____ (Highest THR)

For females:

(226 – RHR_____)x 65% + RHR = _____ (Lowest THR)

(226 – RHR_____)x 85% + RHR = _____ (Highest THR)

You can now divide these two final numbers by 6 to determine what a 10 second heart rate count is for you:

Lowest THR _____) ÷ 6 = _____ (lowest 10 sec count)
Highest THR_____) ÷ 6 = _____ (highest 10 sec count)

STRATEGY #2:
ALTERNATE higher bursts of activity
with periods of recovery

Do you want to try another approach to increase intensity? Alternate bursts of intense activity *several times* during the same workout instead of just staying at the same intensity level, albeit higher, during the entire workout. This concept is known as **interval training**.

For example, increase your intensity on the treadmill to the upper limit of your target heart rate zone (80 to 85%, or the "I can't talk now!" zone) after about 5 to 10 minutes of warming up your muscles and hold this highest intensity for 1 to 2 minutes. Then reduce the intensity back to 65% of your target heart rate and recover 2 to 4 minutes. Repeat this *burst and recovery* pattern (in which you have a 1:2 ratio for the amount of time at the intense level and the amount of recovery time, respectively) during the entire exercise time, allowing for about a 10-minute cool-down before stopping exercise. If your health history allows, you can take this concept one step further and increase your intensity above your target heart rate zone (85% to 90%). Hold this level for 15 to 30 seconds, followed by about 2 minutes of recovery, allowing your heart rate to return to 65%, the lower intensity target heart rate zone.

Another way to incorporate interval training is varying the aerobic machines during the same workout period. For example, after warming up, work 10 minutes on the treadmill, then immediately switch to the elliptical trainer for the next 15 minutes, followed by a final 10 minutes on a stationary cycle. Return to the treadmill for your 5-minute cool-down. Changing machines changes the muscles worked, and your body stays more "alert" in the process.

Is there a beneficial difference between interval training or simply increasing intensity at a steady rate? Both certainly rev up your metabolism, and both will encourage your body to continue to burn calories at a higher rate for a period of time after the exercise is over. But the interval training gives you the longest after-burn effect and trains your body to recover more quickly. Even if your burst and recovery pattern is irregular or at different durations of time, you will see your body benefit. For example, you may choose to maintain high intensity for 3 or 4 minutes and recover for the same amount of time, or your bursts may be as short as 60 seconds. Get creative. Burst when you feel like it and slow down when your body tells you, even if the time periods don't fit a pattern. You WILL see a difference!

STRATEGY #3:
Use CORRECT FORM while exercising

If you enjoy exercising on the treadmill, stair climber or elliptical machine, here is a hint that will help you get the most out of your workout time...*let go of the handles!* Research has proven that holding the handrails of an exercise machine while you work out reduces your heart rate and the amount of oxygen consumed. Your body will not burn the amount of calories that it should burn if you hold on, unless the equipment itself is designed to include movable arm handles for an upper *and* lower body workout.

You may not feel secure increasing the speed or the elevation without holding onto the handrails at the same time. But part of the challenge itself is the balance required to do the activity. You may need to decrease the speed at which you normally work when you first let go. And make sure you do not increase the speed or elevation too quickly-only small increments at a time. Too high a speed or pace will probably force you to hold on, and holding on at high speeds can lead to serious back or knee injuries because it requires you to rotate your hips to an incorrect angle. *Just make sure that you do not increase the speed or elevation too quickly-only small increments at a time.*

On that same thought, keep your head aligned with your spine, keep your shoulders relaxed and hold in your stomach muscles to maintain correct form. Once you have adjusted to letting go, readjusted your speed and feel comfortable again, challenge your body by maintaining that speed but gradually adding elevation or resistance in small increments. The next week, maintain your speed and elevation and add a little more time or distance, like an extra ¼ mile. Regardless of what change you make, you are charging your body's battery and improving your balance at the same time.

Chapter 19

Battery Charge
Using Strength Training

Charging your battery by aerobic exercise depends on the level of intensity of your workout. What about charging your battery using strength training? The key is to develop both muscle strength and muscle endurance. You can develop both of these, strength and endurance, by using the following principles to charge your battery for strength training:

Strategy #1: Overload your muscles using resistance, frequency and duration for each movement.

Strategy #2: Change the amount of rest between exercise.

Strategy #3: Switch movements for the same muscle group.

STRATEGY #1:

OVERLOAD your muscles

Overload in strength training is a good thing. It happens when the resistance (amount of weight), the frequency (how many times it happens) or the duration (how long it continues) increases. You can do this by changing the amount of weight (resistance), changing the number of sets of each exercise (frequency) or changing the amount of time it takes to do the exercise (duration). Using bicep curls as an example, let's look at ways that you can put this principle to work for you:

RESISTANCE: Let's say that you can comfortably lift a 5 pound dumbbell for 3 sets of 12 repetitions each (that's 36 times!). It is now time to charge your battery and one way to do this is to add resistance. Increase the amount of weight to an 8 pound dumbbell. However, when you increase the weight load, you need to automatically decrease the number of times you lift it at first. Work your way back up as you gain strength.

FREQUENCY: As you progress, you can add one or two repetitions for each set over a period of weeks until you can comfortably lift 3 sets of 12 repetitions.

DURATION: Adding repetitions naturally adds to the time each set will take, increasing the duration of the exercise. Another way to extend the duration is do the repetition even slower-try four counts up and four counts down. Once you can complete 3 sets of 12 repetitions, for a longer duration, it is time to overload again.

STRATEGY #2:

CHANGE the amount of REST between exercises

In your current routine, you may complete your 3 sets of bicep exercises, rest between each set, and start your triceps exercises. Instead, why don't you perform 1 set of bicep curls, follow this with 1 set of tricep kick-backs, follow by repeating the bicep curls, then complete another set of tricep kick-backs? Continue until you have completed three sets of each, and then rest. You can alternate an exercise for the bicep with a movement for the tricep because you are working complementary or opposite muscle groups. This routine takes the greatest advantage of your time and challenges your muscles to be stronger and endure longer.

STRATEGY #3:

SWITCH MOVEMENTS for the same muscle group

Pump up the intensity of your workout by doing the same exercise, but in a more challenging way. For example, if you have been doing sit-ups or abdominal curls with your hands resting behind your head, try to rev it up by extending your arms further behind your head when you do this exercise. Be careful to keep your shoulders as relaxed as possible, and keep the lower back pressed to the floor. You will probably need to decrease the number of repetitions in the beginning and work your way back up.

Another example uses push ups. If you have been doing this exercise with your knees and lower legs on the floor, try a more challenging position. Do them with only your knees on the floor and your lower legs lifted. Or extend your legs with only your feet and hands supporting your body. Keep your back straight and lift your body using only your chest and arm strength. This is the hardest way, but you can build your strength by reducing the number of sets and repetitions in the beginning, and work up to the full count again.

Or try doing your bicep curls and tricep kick-backs while sitting on a flex ball. The motions are the same, but your body has to ask your abdominal muscles to help balance you on the flex ball. The more muscles you are working at any given moment, the more benefit you receive. You are strengthening your core at the same time you are building upper body strength. It's a win-win situation!

Time to *take some action*! With any change in exercise, a record of your progress can be very encouraging and reminds you how you are improving your fitness week by week. Take a minute and complete the following:

Record any current exercises that are easy for you:

Aerobic exercise: _____

_____   _____

Strength training exercise: _____

_____

Next, choose one of the strategies below to charge your fitness battery for each type of exercise:

Increase the intensity of your aerobic workout by:

1.   Increasing your heart rate within your target range and holding this new level for the duration of the activity.

2.   Alternating bursts of intensity with periods of recovery by repeatedly increasing your heart rate to 85% of your target range for 1 to 2 minutes followed by recovering your heart rate back to 65% for 2 to 4 minutes.

3.   Letting go of the handrails (probably will need to reduce the intensity at first!) to challenge not only your heart but also your balance.

Increase the intensity of your strength training by:

1.   Overloading your muscles during your workout.

2.   Changing the amount of rest between your exercises

3.   Switching movements for the same muscle group.

Now, finish the following sentence, filling in one or more of these strategies: *I will charge my fitness battery using each type of exercise in the following new way:*

Aerobic exercise: _____

_____

Strength training: _____

_____

Finally, do it THIS WEEK!

A Look in the Rearview Mirror

Week 6: Charge Your Battery

Your **ACCELERATION Challenge** for Week 6: Charge your battery by choosing one strategy to increase the intensity of your aerobic activity on 2 of the 4 days and/or one strategy to increase the intensity of your strength training on 1 of the 2 days. Highlight the days that you use these strategies in your Maintenance Log.

Now, record any changes you notice this week:

Date	Thoughts, Feelings, Body Changes?

Week 7:

Clean the Rearview Mirror

"The most beneficial part of Rev It Up! has been feeling good about myself and healthy in my own body. Knowing that being healthy at this point in my life is more important than being skinny."   Sandy

"It has been one year since I started Rev It Up!. To date I have lost around 35 pounds and 30 inches. Can't really do the size thing, because I have changed size ranges-no more "W's" at the end of the size I wear! I was on the beach last week in a bathing suit and just a cover-up and was not self-conscious about the way I looked. Thanks again for teaching me how to do this!"   Elizabeth

Chapter 20

Clean Your Mirror
to Improve Your View

Pit stops, battery charges….can you hear your engine accelerating as a result of your new choices? The changes you have focused on these last two weeks have been external choices-what you actually order from a restaurant menu, or what combination of aerobic machines you choose at the gym. You've been looking on the outside-it's time to stop and turn your headlights inward. Are your thoughts about yourself matching up with the changes you are making on the outside?

Picture this: You enter the doors of your gym for a workout, feeling proud of yourself that you have made time to exercise. As you walk towards a treadmill, you begin noticing the gentleman lifting heavy weights, the lady running on another treadmill nearby, and the aerobic instructor heading to class. Your biceps do not look like that guy, your pace cannot even keep up with your neighbor's, and the aerobics instructor must not have an ounce of fat on her legs! All of a sudden, you do not feel so proud of yourself, decide to shorten your workout time and head home.

What happened? Your body image has entered the picture, and it's not a reflection you like. How you see your body and how you think others see your body greatly affects how you feel about yourself. And how you feel about your body cannot be separated from how you treat that very same body…the fuel you give it and the activity you ask it to do.

A positive body image does not necessarily mean that you love everything about your body and have no need or desire to make any changes. It *does* mean that you have a healthy self identity, can appreciate the positive things that your body can do, and can enjoy life for the moment instead of waiting until you reach a certain weight.

Do you struggle with a negative body image? "Look in the mirror" and see how you answer the following:

Yes No   Body Image Test

___ ___ • Your mood can change immediately if someone comments on your clothes, your looks, or your body.

___ ___ • You catch a glimpse of yourself in the mirror and only notice what you do not like about your body.

___ ___ • You refuse to accept a compliment from someone, and often negate the remark or criticize yourself in some way.

___ ___ • You frequently ask your family or friends if you look okay.

___ ___ • You believe that if you can just lose a certain number of pounds or wear a certain size that you will feel better about yourself.

___ ___ • You frequently criticize other people's bodies or clothing, or looks.

___ ___ • You frequently make excuses to avoid a social event because you feel fat or do not like your appearance.

___ ___ • You punish yourself by not allowing yourself to eat certain foods because they are "bad."

___ ___ • You exercise only to burn calories in an effort to try to lose weight or burn off excess calories you consumed in a previous meal.

___ ___ • You fixate on a certain body part you do not like rather than concentrate on your body or appearance as a whole.

Enter the total of your 'Yes' and 'No' answers:
Yes _____   **No** _____
If you answered yes to five or more, your negative body image has strong influences over your level of health and wellness.

So what can you do? Where do you start to make a change from a negative to a positive body image? Check the mirror and notice what you see. Does it reflect the *real you* or is the image distorted? It's time to *clean your mirror* to improve your reflection.

When you drive your car, you depend on your mirror to see behind you, in order to drive safely and with purpose. You also need your mirror to be clean, not cloudy or broken. Only a mirror free of dirt or broken glass can give the driver a true reflection of the situation. And regardless of the condition of the mirror, you cannot look in your mirror constantly and continue to move forward. You must look away from the mirror to concentrate on the road ahead. In fact, most of your driving requires a steady look ahead with just an occasional glimpse in the mirror's reflection.

Likewise, your body's image is the reflection you see in your mirror. The mirror often reflects what is in your past, behind you, and includes images that have been developed throughout your life. These images are influenced by things you have heard, read, and seen. Over time, dirt may have accumulated and it affects how clearly you can see what is really happening. Or your body image might even be broken from years of abuse or neglect. Do you spend more time looking back in the mirror's reflection, unaware that it's broken or dirty and distorts the picture you see?

To move forward, you need to clean and repair your mirror, or body image, *and stay focused on the road before you instead of the path behind you.* This can take a lot of time and patience, but the rewards of a clear reflection help guarantee more security and confidence as you keep your eyes on the road ahead. So let's see what it takes to clean your mirror. In other words, change your body image.

First, believe that your body is capable of change. Remind yourself about all the things you have changed already like drinking more water, eating more colors, listening to your hunger cues, or eating every four hours. Next, believe that change happens one small step at a time. No need to feel that change must happen overnight to be successful. It's a process that takes time. Finally, believe that your body image does not have to be limited to body weight changes only. Body image changes include how we relate to other people, how much we allow our thoughts about our body to affect our moods, and how we interact socially.

True change cannot be rooted in external changes that work only as a temporary Band-aid to cover up the problem, but must be rooted from the inside out. To be successful in body image change, you need to *own* your own body and its ability to change. Begin implementing and maintaining these changes as an ongoing lifestyle, not without setbacks but always without judgment.

Are you ready to clean your mirror, and begin seeing a new reflection? Try one of the following strategies:

Clean Your Mirror for a New Reflection

1.   *Think about someone you admire and respect.* Describe the characteristics of this person that you most admire:

_____

_____

_____

Don't be surprised if appearance is *not* one of the top priorities that you list when describing characteristics you respect!

2.   *List 5 physical strengths about your body as a whole.* For example, "my legs are strong…" or "my smile is engaging…"

_____

_____

_____

3.   *Make a list of positive statements about your body that emphasize the way you want to think about yourself.* For example, "my body deserves to be nurtured by food"…or… "I can enjoy a day at the pool regardless of my swimsuit size."

_____

_____

_____

Repeat this list to yourself at least once in the morning and once in the evening. You do not have to feel or believe any of these positive statements as you say them, but you do need to repeat them. Just like hearing a song on the radio repetitively until you notice that one day you know every word without even trying-and that same song runs through your head all the time-new words, positive statements, that you repeat frequently can begin covering up the old reflections of your body and replacing it with a more nurturing one.

4.   *Avoid magazines, television shows, or movies that make you feel bad about yourself* or only present the impossible as a role model.

5.   Make an effort to *avoid criticizing other people* about their weight, clothes, or looks. If you comment on that person, limit it to positive comments about who they are or something they do, not how they look.

6.   Look around when you are in a grocery store or in a department store and *notice that everyday people in your life come in ALL shapes and sizes.* Their bodies are more realistic than the models in the magazines.

7.   Commit yourself to *view exercise as an opportunity to enjoy the movement of your body a*nd enjoy the experience itself. Notice how your body breathes, how your muscles work, and how your stress level decreases after you cool down.

8.   *Begin eliminating your good/bad food list.* All foods have a place in your life, but become aware of how different foods affect your energy and your overall wellness. If you crave a gourmet chocolate chip cookie, you will not be satisfied by substituting a fat-free

alternative. But if that chocolate chip cookie is on your "bad" list, then you automatically become a "bad person" by eating it. Get rid of the moral judgments surrounding food! You are so much more than what you eat! To remove the craving, it may be best to simply indulge in one of those cookies, but eliminate other distractions, sit, and slowly enjoy every bite. And then just *move on*! Your craving will be satisfied without having to eat more calories from other alternatives that are not what you really wanted in the first place.

9.   Notice what words you use to describe yourself and *do not allow yourself to select negative descriptions about your size or shape.* If you catch yourself criticizing your appearance, follow that with a positive comment about your body or looks or even your efforts to make a difference in how you view yourself.

10.   Whenever you are tempted to concentrate on only one body part that you do not like, *remind yourself to look at the whole picture.* Remember that you do not compartmentalize other people that you respect and admire; so do yourself the same favor.

Hopefully this list of strategies for cleaning your mirror provides a starting place for a new body image. Regardless, realize that old dirt and cracks are hard to remove, so be patient and kind to yourself as you create a new reflection. You won't look in the mirror the same way again!

A Look in the Rearview Mirror

Week 7: Clean the Rearview Mirror

Your **ACCELERATION Challenge** for Week 7: Write down at least two positive statements and/or physical strengths about your own body, and display this list in a location that is privately accessible to you. Read this list at least twice a day, preferably in the morning after rising and in the evening before going to sleep.

Now, record any changes you notice this week:

Date	Thoughts, Feelings, Body Changes?

Week 8:

Deal With Detours

"Most definitely Rev It Up! has been a positive influence on my life. It taught me self-control and the means to achieve the body and health I wanted. Even when I 'mess up' with my eating, I know that it doesn't mean I've failed. I just get over it and begin again." Becky

Chapter 21

Four Detours that
Block Your Road

Last week was not easy. Cleaning those mirrors can be very exhausting, especially if they have years of dirt and grime. Your efforts will pay off-don't give up-because a clear view in your rearview mirror will guarantee less stress and more focus as you travel. In the meantime, since your headlights are already focused internally, let's take a good, hard look at the detours in your life.

Imagine this scenario: You are driving along, your tank has plenty of gas, and your car is running great. You have planned your time well, and traffic is minimal. You expect to reach your destination with a few minutes to spare. But what you *don't* expect is waiting for you right around the next corner...a DETOUR SIGN!

Often when you think things are running smoothly, you'll reach a fork in the road, pointing the way to a detour on an alternative road that may or may not be familiar to you. Detours can take you out of the way of your destination, but if you remain calm and patient, and stay alert, you will find your way back. You might lose some time, but *you do not have to lose your way.*

What detours do you run across most often on your road to a revved up metabolism? Is it the Detour of **SPECIAL EVENTS**, the Detour of **SIGHTS, SOUNDS, AND SMELLS**, the Detour of **PEOPLE PRESSURES**, or the Detour of **EMOTIONS**? Take a closer look at each one, and let's find new directions to follow to get us back on track.

The DETOUR of SPECIAL EVENTS

Are you able to follow your hunger and fullness cues, and choose smart fuel choices, UNLESS:

- You are on vacation?
- It's a holiday?

- You are at the movies?
- You are attending a sports event?
- It's your birthday party?
- It's your friend's birthday party?
- For that matter, it's the second cousin of your friend's former neighbor's birthday party?
- Basically, it's ANY PARTY?

Certainly special occasions like your birthday, Thanksgiving, or other holidays are times to celebrate, and a celebration usually includes an abundance of foods. Likewise, a vacation from work or routines can trigger a vacation from healthy food choices and exercise as well. In fact, a movie or a baseball game may even qualify for a "mini" special event or vacation. Do movie theaters trigger the need for a super-sized soda and large buttered popcorn, even if you have just eaten a meal? Does a sporting event, like a baseball game, trigger the desire for a foot-long hot dog and order of curly fries? Every time? Regardless of whether you are hungry or not? Does a vacation on the beach go hand in hand with several trips down that famous seafood buffet line-to try everything even if you feel more stuffed than the flounder entrée you just ate?

If you answered "yes" to two or more of these questions, a special event detour may force you to take an unexpected left or right turn more often than you realize.

The DETOUR of SIGHTS, SOUNDS, and SMELLS:

Ahhhh, the aroma of fresh baked cinnamon rolls...the crunch of potato chips resounding from your office's break room...the sight of brownie á la mode on a nearby restaurant table...the smell of barbecue on a hot summer day...even the sight of an advertisement in a magazine for Mrs. Field's chocolate chip cookies. Do these sights, sounds, and smells trigger an automatic "I must have these...now!" response, regardless of whether you are really hungry *or* whether it is time to refuel your tank or not?

It is not just coincidence that your local grocery store greets you with its bakery's smells and sights. And the big pictures of all the fast food combos at the drive-through window are not printed just to fill up space. These are designed to take advantage of your sight, sound and smell triggers...and hopefully trigger a bigger sale, and, therefore, a bigger profit!

Enjoying the sights, sounds, and smells of great food is part of the eating experience. However, if these things cause you to lose your direction often, and eat *just because*, you may want to look closer at this detour.

STRATEGIES for DETOURS 1 and 2

These first two detours, SPECIAL EVENTS and SIGHTS, SOUNDS AND SMELLS, often overlap each other; therefore, the strategies for dealing with these are similar. Stay alert, and you'll be more aware and on the lookout for the frequent warning signs of an upcoming detour. Then try the following strategies:

1. First of all, know which trigger causes you the most difficulty.
2. Be on the lookout for early warning signs.
3. Don't arrive hungry-keep an eye on your body's fuel gauge to make sure you aren't in the middle of a detour when your gas tank is empty.
4. Plan ahead and know your options.
5. Have an escape plan.

Here are some "escape plans" to consider:

A)   **AT THE MOVIES:** If you must indulge in movie popcorn whenever you go to a movie theater, try the following:

- Send someone else to purchase the smallest size so that you are not tempted to order "super size, with extra butter please!"

- Plan to share your popcorn with a friend or family.

- Try to eat a few kernels at a time, instead of grabbing and eating a handful each time you reach into the bag. (This one sounds so simple but can be so hard! Make it a game to see how long you can make the kernels last-going for the length of the entire movie!)

B)   **AT THANKSGIVING DINNER WITH GRANDMA:**   If you look forward to grandmother's famous sweet potato casserole at Thanksgiving, plan ahead. Don't miss the chance to have some, but stay in alignment with your meal and snack portions. Look at what is being offered to eat. Foods like hard rolls or buttered corn can be had at any time, but grandmother's casserole is a family holiday tradition. Choose it over the "nothing special" options, and savor each bite to maximize your enjoyment without over fueling your tank. You can skip the calories from the roll and the corn-grandmother's recipe is worth it!

C)   **AT THE ANNUAL HOLIDAY PARTY**: In this situation, your escape plan begins with a survey-*survey the buffet!* Look over all of the foods offered *before* putting the first bite in your mouth or on your plate. Have fried shrimp every year, but you've never tasted the stuffed crab? Eat brownies countless of times, but you rarely have an opportunity to enjoy your co-worker's famous chocolate candy? Choose two or three items that are "must have's", and fill up the rest of your plate with fresh fruit, crisp veggies, lots of color. Then move away from the buffet table, sit down, and savor every bite of those select items, nibbling on fruit and veggies to fill in the gap. You have made special choices, so you won't feel deprived, and you've survived a buffet without stuffing yourself! You made it through the detour's twists and turns and are on the road again.

D)   **AT THE MALL**: If you are in a situation where the sight of food is just too hard to ignore, consider purchasing it but plan to take it with you to enjoy later. For example, you are window-shopping in the local mall and smell fresh cinnamon rolls from the vendor nearby. You *must* have one!

- Purchase one, but ask to have it packaged to go and get away from the environment of the immediate sights and smells.
- Wait a few minutes, maybe by distracting yourself within another store. When you are not in the trigger's territory, you will have a chance to think more clearly. "Am I really hungry now? When did I last fuel my body?"

Be satisfied with the fact that you *own* that food item now. But make a decision based on your body's needs instead of your trigger's temptation. Don't forget the "I can eat again!" power. Save the treat for when you are really hungry and your fuel gauge is low. You might even find out that the cinnamon roll doesn't look or taste as appealing when it has been allowed to cool and harden. You don't know for sure, but it's worth a try. Now time to move on to another common problem...

The DETOUR of PEOPLE PRESSURES:

Do you have a friend or a family member who seems to always encourage you to eat "just another bite" or "try at least one?" What about the family member who trained you as a child to eat every last morsel of food on your plate because of the starving children in another country? Granted, children are starving all over the world, but eating everything on your plate probably did not help them in any way at that moment. But you still hear the voice of that relative each time you sit down to a meal.

What about someone who not only persuades you to eat even when you are not hungry but also acts hurt if you do not eat as much as they do? Or maybe your distant cousin, a great cook, claims that you must not like her food when you say no to the second helping at your annual family reunion. This detour is difficult, because your decision to eat or not to eat involves food AND relationships!

Your strategy is to identify the pressure. Once you have identified the people who create the pressure, you can better plan how to handle them. The following strategies are divided into a Relationship Option and a Reaction Option. Consider putting at least one of these into action:

STRATEGY for DETOUR 3
RELATIONSHIP OPTION:

Sometimes the situation will lead to the chance to talk to the people in your life who pressure you. Try to:

1.   Spend some time thinking about your friends and family, and distinguish who supports you and who pressures you.

2.   After you share your new understanding about your metabolism and your commitment to listen to your body with the person who pressures you, ask for his or her support of your new way of eating.

3.   Engage the person who pressures you as a Rev It Up! partner and challenge him or her to start listening to the body's own fuel gauge and see what happens!

REACTION OPTION:

Sometimes you are not able to discuss the situation with the people in your life due to the lack of opportunity or simply not feeling confident enough to do so. If this is the situation, concentrate on changing your reaction:

1.   Recommit yourself to listen to your body instead of listening to the person's pressure to eat when you are not hungry.

2.   Reconsider the results of your actions. Although you may feel subconscious pressure from the childhood memory of being told to "always clean your plate," doing so does not directly help anyone else who may need food. If you do not want to waste anything, simply put the leftovers in the refrigerator for a later time. And if that is not an option, decide whether the food left will be wasted on the plate or will be used as wasted energy in your body and stored as fat.

3.   Take a second piece on a take home plate if your friend or family member will be hurt if you do not have a second helping. Express your anticipation of enjoying it again at a later time.

4.   Remove yourself from the environment or from the people who pressure you before the situation even begins.

5.   Plan another event with your friend or family that does not center on food to help escape from "people pressure" to eat while still enjoying the company of the other person.

People pressure can certainly be intense and hard to deal with, but the most difficult detour remains.

The Detour of EMOTIONS

Special events, sights and smells, and people pressure may not cause you any detour delays. But, if you are feeling lonely or bored, upset or nervous, depressed or tense, or maybe even happy or relaxed, detours occur every time you turn the corner! Emotional triggers are not as easy to avoid because they can be unpredictable. It's a lot easier to avoid walking by the bakery at the grocery store than it is to control your feelings of boredom or depression. Is this detour inevitable? Probably, yes. Is it impossible to change your reactions to this detour? No!

Sometimes it seems that all of a sudden you find yourself halfway through the bag of chips before you even realize it. At first glance, it looks like you just went from feeling depressed to eating too much. But what may not be visible at first glance is *the chain of events* that occurred in between the "feeling" and the "consequence." For example, if you (1) have a bad day at work and are feeling depressed, (2) you find that you drive home (3) instead of going by the gym or (4) stopping to visit a friend. Once you walk through the front door, (5) you may not stop to change clothes or (6) read the mail but (7) walk directly into the kitchen. Once in the kitchen, (8) you may not take the time to look in the fruit bin to see what is there. (9) You open the pantry and (10) grab what is quickly available. You have a choice to open the bag, pull out a handful, close the bag, and return it to the pantry *before* you sit and eat your chips. However, (11) you take the bag with you, (12) sit on the couch, and (13) eat from the bag itself, without noticing how much has been eaten until you realize half the bag is empty. Thirteen links to the chain-all leading to one disastrous detour.

This is a *chain of events*, and with any chain, *it is only as strong as its weakest link.* Turn this scenario around, and look at what you can choose to do: (1) Knowing that you are depressed, (2) you decide to not even go home (3) until you go by the gym to walk, since exercise can help relieve depression. (4) Even if you do not feel like walking, you decide to at least avoid going home to a quiet house but (5) visit a friend (6) or go run some errands. (7) Once you arrive home, (8) you take time to change clothes before you enter the kitchen. (9) As you enter the kitchen, (10) you think about what you are really hungry for and (11) look for all the options available. (12) If you decide that you just HAVE to have chips, (13) you open the bag, and (14) remove your portion, then (15) return the bag back to the pantry. (16) You take your chips with you to the table, and (17) eat them slowly so that you do not miss even one bite of enjoyment from them! (18) Before you decide to get a second serving, you commit to remain where you are for about 15 minutes to allow your stomach time to realize that it has eaten. You may decide you still want more at this time, but at least you have taken steps to prevent a mindless response to an emotional detour. And you are much more aware of the effort required to go back for a second helping, which buys you more time to think through the consequences and whether you really are physically, or just emotionally, hungry.

It is obviously easier to avoid a major detour by breaking the chain early on in the sequence of events. The closer you are to the final turn into the detour, the harder it is to break the cycle of events; in other words, breaking the chain at #7 is easier than at #12, and breaking the chain at #3 is even better!

Look back at the times you know that you have eaten from an emotion and try to "put your car into reverse" and see the real chain of events that occurred. For example, were you too tired to go to the gym and exercise last week? Grabbed candy at work every time you passed the desk? Record the first behavior, or "chain link," and the last behavior, or "chain link," below:

First Chain Link (first behavior): _____

_____

_____

_____

_____

Last Chain Link (last behavior): _____

_____

_____

_____

_____

Spend some time thinking about that first and last behavior. What can you do differently between these two to break that emotional chain? Write different options to this scenario: _____

_____

_____

_____

Did you learn something about yourself in the process? You can break this chain by finding a way out of the detour--and the quicker you can change your pattern of behavior the easier it is to break its grip on you and your behaviors.

STRATEGY for DETOUR 4

To help you break an emotional chain of events, try these strategies:

1.   Stay alert to an emotional set-up. If you have had a bad day at work, expect that your emotions may try to convince you to take a detour. Awareness is over half of the battle!

2.   Keep your meals and snacks aligned in not only timing but also quality. Don't neglect that afternoon snack, and make sure you include protein fuel. This will ensure that any trigger to eat is not rooted in a physical craving from going too long between meals and snacks.

3.   Try to provide an alternative to eating as a way to feel better once you are aware of which emotions are triggers. What activities do you enjoy that relax or revive you? Do you like to listen to music? Do you enjoy going to a movie? Meeting a friend at the park for a walk? Taking a group exercise class? Enjoying a bubble bath or extra long shower? Think about an alternative that you can put in to action so that eating to feel better is not your only option.

4.   Keep a separate journal just for how you feel. Sometimes writing your thoughts on paper allows you to shorten the detour and control how you respond. Putting food in or writing it out-which choice will you make?

No matter what your triggers may be, every detour is a chance to learn more about yourself and how you handle bumps in the road. Each detour can make you stronger because you have a chance to learn how to keep control of your car as you face new, unexpected challenges.

A Look in the Rearview Mirror

Week 8: Dealing with Detours

Your **ACCELERATION Challenge** for Week 8: Note the specific detour that is most difficult for you. Review the strategies given for that detour and choose one to begin using this week. Write about your opportunities to use the new strategy in your Maintenance Log.

Now, record any changes you notice this week:

Date	Thoughts, Feelings, Body Changes?

The Rest of Your Life:

Your Maintenance Plan

"To this day, five years since starting Rev It Up!, I still try to eat every three to four hours and drink at least 64 ounces of water daily. More important to me, though, is the term I learned, 'more often than not.' It comes to play so many times for me. When I "fall off the wagon" and feel like I have failed myself by "cheating," I remember those words and that it is not the end of the world. I remember that I am still doing what is best for my health and my body 'more often than not' and that helps me to regain control again."   Rebecca

"As a result of Rev It Up!, I feel better, have lost weight and inches, and have a new outlook on food and eating."   Samuel

Chapter 22

Your Maintenance Plan

You did it! You have made it through 8 weeks of Rev It Up! challenges, and hopefully your body is feeling the benefits. Hard to believe, but it's now time to get serious about your long term maintenance plan. The newness of your healthy routines will wear off, just like the smell of a new car. But don't let your dedication begin to rust!

What do you do to keep your body's metabolism running smoothly and performing at its best? You perform routine checks to make sure everything is running smoothly-just like routine maintenance for your car. Doesn't sound exciting, but it is the key to a long life for a car; likewise, it is the key to a permanent lifestyle change for your body and your metabolism.

Where do you begin? First and most importantly, don't wait until you have a problem. Prevent a problem from happening in the first place by following the basic care guidelines from this Driver's Manual, your Rev It Up! principles:

1. Listen to your body's hunger and fullness cues.
2. Drink your daily eight cups of water, extra for exercise, and match up additional fluids.
3. Align your meal and snack timing and content-plan ahead!
4. Take time to do aerobic exercise and strength training each week--increase intensity for continued results.
5. Follow the speed limits to eat at a reasonable pace.
6. Tune up by choosing quality carbohydrate and fat fuel.
7. Paint your car with 5 colors every day.
8. Charge your battery by increasing exercise intensity periodically.
9. Plan your pit stops carefully.
10. Clean your mirror to avoid distractions and stay focused.

11.   Prepare for detours with a strategic plan to get you back on track quickly.
12.   Evaluate your daily performance in your Maintenance Log.

You may be saying, "I know the list of things to do but how do I keep the momentum I have now? What maintenance plan can I follow to keep seeing results?" Think through the Four F's-FOUNDATION, FOOD, FLUID, and FITNESS. Which area has been the easiest for you? Which has been the most difficult? Some of the challenges are harder than others, but successful maintenance requires an action plan for all 4 areas. Don't neglect the challenges that are easy for you, but plan to spend more time on the areas where you encounter the most "potholes." The key to a maintenance plan that really works is: *think specific, be sure to think practical, and think small!* Many small victories lead to one big win!

Your FOUNDATION Goal and Maintenance Plan

Let's go through an example for each of the four F's, beginning with FOUNDATION. The Foundation challenges that you have faced include: 1) record hunger and fullness levels, 2) do not wait longer than 4 hours between meals and/or snacks, 3) experience a meal for 20 minutes and a snack for 10, 4) review your progress on a monthly basis and plan a reward for your efforts, 5) improve your body image by concentrating on positive traits and thoughts, and 6) increase awareness of the traps that create a detour for you (sights, sounds, smells; special events; people; emotions), and follow an escape plan to avoid them. So, for example, a FOUNDATION Goal such as "I'll eat more slowly at all meals" is good, but is not specific enough to help you take practical steps to make it a habit. A better strategy that's both practical and specific follows: "I will practice slowing down at dinner on three different days this week." The action steps are:

1.   Select Monday, Wednesday, and Friday dinner as practice meals.
2.   Highlight these days and meals on your calendar or day planner.

3.   Before beginning your meal, notice the clock.
4.   Eat, and linger, at the table until 20 minutes have passed.
5.   Answer these questions in your Maintenance Log during this time: "How full am I? Did this experience give less or more enjoyment?"

Now it's your turn:

My FOUNDATION Goal: _____

_____

_____

_____

The steps I will take (remember-think specific, practical, and small):
1.   _____

_____

2.   _____

_____

3.   _____

_____

4.   _____

_____

Your FOOD Goal and Maintenance Plan

One "F" down, three more to go! Let's move to FOOD. The FOOD challenges that you have faced include: 1) eating breakfast within 1 ½ hours of rising, 2) eating 3 to 4 fuel groups for a meal, 1 to 2 for a snack, and following portion guidelines, 3) eating five or more fruits and vegetables daily, 4) choosing high-quality carbohydrates like whole grains, 5) limiting your intake of saturated fats, fried foods, and high-fat condiments, and 6) choosing healthy selections when eating out. So, for example, a FOOD Goal such as "I'll eat more fruits and vegetables" is too broad and does not provide specific, real-life steps to measure your success. How will you know if you are really making progress in this area? "I'll eat more fruit each week" is a little better, but "I'll eat fruit for a morning snack on Monday through Thursday" is even better. Think *specific, practical, and small* when you think about your Maintenance Plan:

1.   Take a separate "produce run" every Sunday to purchase fresh fruits and vegetables for the week.
2.   Select fresh cut fruit and grapes for work snacks.
3.   Divide the fresh fruit into 4 individual containers on Sunday night.
4.   Bring one container to work on Monday through Thursday.
5.   Put a daily note by your keys to remind you to take your fruit snack.

Okay, it's your turn again!

My FOOD Goal: _____

_____

_____

_____

The steps I will take (specific, practical and small!):
1.   _____

_____

2._____

_____

3.   _____

_____

4.   _____

_____

Your FLUID Goal and Maintenance Plan

Is your Maintenance Plan making more sense now? Hopefully, yes! Now, take a moment to review your FLUID challenges, which include: 1) drink your daily eight cups of water, 2) drink extra for exercise, and 3) match up caffeine, artificially sweetened and alcoholic beverages with an equal amount of extra "match up" fluids (water, low-fat milk, tomato or vegetable juice). Now, for example, a FLUID Goal of "I'll drink more water" is too broad. But "I will drink 16 ounces of water as I drive to and from work Monday through Friday" is specific, practical, and small-step oriented. The action plan may look something like this:

1. Fill up your clean bottle with water the night before.
2. Put a note by your keys to remind you to take it with you when you drive.
3. Commit to drinking half of the water on the way to work.
4. If feasible, bring your water bottle inside and refrigerate.
5. Finish off your water bottle on the way home from work.
6. Wash and repeat!

Your turn, again!

My FLUID Goal: _____

_____

_____

_____

The steps I will take (you know the rules by now!):

1. _____

2. _____

3. _____

4. _____

Your FITNESS Goal and Maintenance Plan

The final F is often the most difficult: FITNESS! 1) Are you finding time to fit in four aerobic sessions a week, if weight loss is your goal? 2) Have you put pump power into action by doing two strength training sessions each week? 3) Do you make an effort to vary the intensity of your aerobic workouts on at least two of the four days? 4) Your strength training on at least one of the two days? Have you found a routine that works for you, either at home or in a local gym? If you stick with an exercise routine for about 20 weeks, or 5 months, it is very likely that you will exercise the rest of your life. But making fitness a priority in your weekly schedule can be so difficult.

Sometimes life just gets in the way, doesn't it? What obstacles have you encountered along the way?

One common obstacle involves **lack of commitment**. Do you feel that exercise gets shuffled to the bottom of your priority list once the day gets going? Too many demands which take too much of your time? Lack of commitment, for whatever reason, is a difficult bridge to cross. Or maybe your obstacle has been **lack of support**. Your desire to make new healthy habits may not be getting a lot of support from the home front. Maybe the problem is simply not having an exercise partner? If no one is expecting you at the gym, then no one will know if you don't show up, right? A third obstacle you may face is **lack of any variety**. The "same old, same old" gets boring, over time! And when your progress slows down, it's easy to be tempted to slow down your efforts, too. Last but not least, you may have just simply **lost your perspective** on *why* you exercise. The focus on health has been replaced with a focus on weight loss only. When the weight loss doesn't seem to match your efforts, do you feel depressed? Mad? Discouraged? Losing your focus narrows the path of success and can even block it completely. Ask yourself:

1. Which of the four obstacles (lack of time, support, variety, or positive attitude) are you dealing with today?

_____

_____

2. What type of activity, either aerobic or strength training, is most affected by this obstacle? _____

_____

Now that you have looked at which obstacle is your biggest challenge, create a new road map with a FITNESS Goal and Maintenance Plan. For example, your FITNESS goal could be "I will walk right after work on Tuesdays and Thursdays." List the small, practical steps that you will take to make this action plan work for you:

- Talk to your family about your new commitment.
- Write your workout appointment on your calendar for Tuesday and Thursday.

- Choose a route from your office, the gym, or your neighborhood.
- Change into your workout clothes BEFORE leaving work.
- Go to your planned location, and START WALKING!

My FITNESS Goal: _____

_____

_____

My Action Plan:
1.   _____

      _____

2.   _____

      _____

3.   _____

      _____

4.   _____

      _____

Have you realized yet that you have just completed your first *personalized* maintenance plan? You are now in charge of your continued progress, and you are *ready* and *able* to meet the challenges. As you work through this next week, remind yourself of just how far you have traveled. It is time to revisit Page 249 and take another Victory Lap! Record a list of the changes that you have seen in your body and in your relationship with food and exercise during the second month. And, of course, plan a reward-and give it to yourself-*this* week.

And finally…you can and should be proud of yourself. Even if you only managed to maintain one or two of the challenges, your metabolism is not the same today as it was when you started. Every small change makes a difference. If you have seen your body change an old habit (such as not drinking enough water) into a new healthier habit (drinking at least 8 cups of water daily), you have proven to yourself that your body is *capable* of change. The changes you have seen are a direct result of your hard work, and you can *own* these changes with confidence. Keep an eye on the road ahead, but don't miss the scenery that surrounds you-the accomplishments you and your body have made so far-as you enjoy the rest of the journey.

See you at the Finish Line!

What about the rest of your life?

Big question, isn't it? Rev It Up! is "a new way of living…a better way of feeling!" It is carefully designed to give you the steady encouragement and real-life guidelines that you need to actually own and maintain your new lifestyle. But being an owner means taking responsibility.

The principles for weight loss presented in Rev It Up! can be continued until you reach your desired weight range. Weight loss does not usually follow a steady, consistent pattern-you will experience ups and downs, and occasionally even hit a plateau that seems to linger longer than you'd like. When this happens, revisit the strategies presented throughout the program, especially Chapter 6, Balance Your Meals and Snacks, and Chapters 18 and 19, Charge Your Battery. Maybe your portions have gradually increased, or your body has adjusted to your exercise routines and needs a jump start to shake things up again. Read the "Most Frequently Asked Questions" section in the Appendix, especially Questions #1 through #4. These specifically deal with breaking weight plateaus and provide you simple strategies to get you back on track.

Once you have reached your goal range, you can experiment with fuel choices and portions-but depend on your hunger and fullness responses to those choices to help you make your decisions. Remember to relax-and enjoy the fact that you have reached your goal. Your body is not going to turn on you overnight and return back to where it started. Your metabolism is different, and your lifestyle proves that. What you do "more often than not" allows for occasional splurges-and your body is more capable of handling those splurges now. And take confidence that you will not want to return to your old habits, anyway.

Many, many individuals who lose weight, regardless of the specific program they follow, are successful in keeping it off-and you can be, too. Researchers have taken time to look at the common traits that these individuals have, regardless of what program they followed to lose the weight. In fact, the similarities between how they lost the weight are minimal (although diet and exercise changes are both required), but the similarities between how they are *keeping it off* are remarkably consistent. The keys are:

1. Keeping a daily journal for self assessment and monitoring.
2. Eating breakfast, consistently.
3. Having group support in place; family or friends that actively encourage them.
4. Regular physical activity, a consistent exercise program, and a commitment to simply live more actively-walk instead of drive, steps instead of elevators, etc.

These four habits are maintaining their weight loss, for the long haul. And you have these habits already in place, so the key is keeping them there!

Stay in touch. Go to the Web site, www.revitupfitness.com, and read Nutrition Tips that will help keep you on track. Become a friend on the Rev It Up! Fan page on Facebook, and chat with Tammy and other Rev It Up! alumni. Ask questions, share successes, and simply encourage each other on-line. Enjoy hearing from others who are revving it up…and enjoy *your* new way of living!

"It is amazing that total strangers are willing to reach out and help another total stranger get back on the pathway to healthier living. If I totally forgot everything I learned in Rev It Up! (which I haven't), just the support that I received in the last three days from other alumni of the program is worth every penny and then some! Due to the encouragement I received from just one person, I truly feel that I have made some headway this week and that definitely gives me the incentive to push on."   T.J.

Your Maintenance Log

Welcome to one of the most important parts of your journey-your Maintenance Log. Using these logs, you can quickly and clearly see areas in which you may need to work harder. But *more* importantly, you can see where you are succeeding, and what habits or patterns are changing for the better. It's a visible picture of how far you have come!

You will notice four goal boxes, one for each "F": Foundation, Food, Fluid, and Fitness. Use these boxes to highlight specific challenges on which you are working. These challenges are listed on the "Look in the Rearview Mirror" page at the end of each week. But you are not limited to these guidelines. Be as creative as you would like, and write down any helpful hints in your goal boxes that help you stay on track.

Set a goal to record *at least three days each week-two weekdays and one weekend day* (since we all know weekend eating can be very different from the rest of the week!). Follow these tips each time:

1. Record what and when you eat and drink, noting hunger (H) levels before you eat and fullness (F) levels after you eat.

2. Check off each cup of water you drink.

3. Write down any movement (aerobic activity) you complete, checking if you warm up, cool down, and stretch.

4. Write down any strength training you complete. Record the specific weight and number of repetitions for different exercises if desired. Watch your strength improve!

5. Take time to look back on your progress and compare notes. You may be amazed at how many changes you are making when you actually stop and look.

Consistent records reveal specific patterns unique to you and your lifestyle. So much can be learned with just five minutes of routine maintenance every day, so Rev It Up! and go for it!

Maintenance Log S M T W T F S

Water

Date: _____

GOALS

AEROBIC

Activity: _____
Time: _____ HR: _____

Warm up ☐ Cool Down ☐ Stretch ☐

STRENGTH

Exercise	Lbs.	Rep Sets		
		1	2	3

Foundation

Food

Fluid

Fitness

FOOD/BEVERAGE

H	Time	F
AM		
PM		

Maintenance Log   S M T W T F S

Water

Date: _____

GOALS

Foundation

Food

Fluid

Fitness

AEROBIC

Activity: _____
Time: _____   HR: _____

Warm up ☐   Cool Down ☐   Stretch ☐

STRENGTH

Exercise	Lbs.	Rep Sets		
		1	2	3

FOOD/BEVERAGE

H	Time	F
AM		
PM		

Maintenance Log S M T W T F S

Date: _____

Water

FOOD/BEVERAGE

H	Time	F
	AM	
	PM	

GOALS

Foundation

Food

Fluid

Fitness

AEROBIC

Activity: _____
Time: _____ HR: _____

Warm up ☐ Cool Down ☐ Stretch ☐

STRENGTH

Exercise	Lbs.	Rep	Sets		
			1	2	3

Maintenance Log   S M T W T F S

Date: _____

Water

GOALS

Foundation

Food

Fluid

Fitness

AEROBIC

Activity: _____
Time: _____   HR: _____

Warm up ☐   Cool Down ☐   Stretch ☐

STRENGTH

Exercise	Lbs.	Rep Sets		
		1	2	3

FOOD/BEVERAGE

H	Time		F
	AM		
	PM		

Maintenance Log   S M T W T F S

Date: _____

Water

FOOD/BEVERAGE

GOALS

AEROBIC

H | Time
AM

PM

F

Foundation

Food

Fluid

Fitness

Activity: _____
Time: _____   HR: _____

Warm up ☐ Cool Down ☐ Stretch ☐

STRENGTH

Exercise   Lbs.   Rep Sets
                          1   2   3

Maintenance Log   S M T W T F S

Date: _____

Water

FOOD/BEVERAGE

H	Time	F
	AM	
	PM	

GOALS

Foundation

Food

Fluid

Fitness

AEROBIC

Activity: _____
Time: _____   HR: _____

Warm up ☐   Cool Down ☐   Stretch ☐

STRENGTH

Exercise	Lbs.	Rep Sets
		1 2 3

Maintenance Log   S M T W T F S

Date: _____

Water

AEROBIC

Activity: _____
Time: _____   HR: _____

Warm up [ ]   Cool Down [ ]   Stretch [ ]

STRENGTH

Exercise	Lbs.	Rep Sets		
		1	2	3

GOALS

Foundation

Food

Fluid

Fitness

FOOD/BEVERAGE

H	Time	F
	AM	
	PM	

Maintenance Log   S M T W T F S

Date: _____

Water

FOOD/BEVERAGE

H	Time	F
	AM	
	PM	

GOALS

Foundation

Food

Fluid

Fitness

AEROBIC

Activity: _____

Time: _____   HR: _____

Warm up ☐   Cool Down ☐   Stretch ☐

STRENGTH

Exercise	Lbs.	Rep Sets		
		1	2	3

Maintenance Log   S M T W T F S

Date:

Water

GOALS

Foundation

Food

Fluid

Fitness

AEROBIC

Activity: _____
Time: _____   HR: _____

Warm up ☐   Cool Down ☐   Stretch ☐

STRENGTH

Exercise	Lbs.	Rep Sets		
		1	2	3

FOOD/BEVERAGE

H	Time	F
	AM	
	PM	

Maintenance Log   S M T W T F S

Date:

Water

FOOD/BEVERAGE

H	Time	F
AM		
PM		

GOALS

Foundation

Food

Fluid

Fitness

AEROBIC

Activity: _____
Time: _____   HR: _____

Warm up ☐   Cool Down ☐   Stretch ☐

STRENGTH

Exercise	Lbs.	Rep Sets 1 2 3

Maintenance Log   S M T W T F S

Date: _____

Water

FOOD/BEVERAGE

H	Time	F
AM		
PM		

GOALS

Foundation

Food

Fluid

Fitness

AEROBIC

Activity: _____
Time: _____   HR: _____

Warm up ☐   Cool Down ☐   Stretch ☐

STRENGTH

Exercise	Lbs.	Rep Sets		
		1	2	3

Maintenance Log   S M T W T F S

Date: _____

Water

FOOD/BEVERAGE

H	Time	F
AM		
PM		

GOALS

Foundation

Food

Fluid

Fitness

AEROBIC

Activity: _____

Time: _____   HR: _____

Warm up ☐   Cool Down ☐   Stretch ☐

STRENGTH

Exercise	Lbs.	Rep Sets 1	2	3

Maintenance Log   S M T W T F S

Date: _____

Water

AEROBIC

Activity: _____
Time: _____   HR: _____

Warm up ☐   Cool Down ☐ Stretch ☐

STRENGTH

Exercise	Lbs.	Rep Sets		
		1	2	3

GOALS

Foundation

Food

Fluid

Fitness

FOOD/BEVERAGE

H	Time	F
	AM	
	PM	

Maintenance Log   S M T W T F S

Date: _____

Water

FOOD/BEVERAGE

H	Time	F
AM		
PM		

GOALS

Foundation

Food

Fluid

Fitness

AEROBIC

Activity: _____
Time: _____   HR: _____

Warm up ☐   Cool Down ☐   Stretch ☐

STRENGTH

Exercise	Lbs.	Rep Sets		
		1	2	3

Maintenance Log   S M T W T F S

Date: _____

Water

FOOD/BEVERAGE

H	Time	F
	AM	
	PM	

GOALS

Foundation

Food

Fluid

Fitness

AEROBIC

Activity: _____
Time: _____   HR: _____

Warm up ☐   Cool Down ☐   Stretch ☐

STRENGTH

Exercise	Lbs.	Rep Sets		
		1	2	3

Maintenance Log   S M T W T F S

Date: _____

Water

FOOD/BEVERAGE

H Time
AM

PM

F

GOALS

Foundation

Food

Fluid

Fitness

AEROBIC

Activity: _____
Time: _____   HR: _____

Warm up ☐   Cool Down ☐   Stretch ☐

STRENGTH

Exercise   Lbs.   Rep Sets
1   2   3

Maintenance Log   S M T W T F S

Date: _____

Water

FOOD/BEVERAGE

H	Time	F
AM		
PM		

GOALS

Foundation

Food

Fluid

Fitness

AEROBIC

Activity: _____
Time: _____   HR: _____

☐ Warm up   ☐ Cool Down   ☐ Stretch

STRENGTH

Exercise	Lbs.	Rep Sets 1	2	3

Maintenance Log   S M T W T F S

Date: _____

Water

GOALS

Foundation

Food

Fluid

Fitness

FOOD/BEVERAGE

H	Time	F
AM		
PM		

AEROBIC

Activity: _____
Time: _____   HR: _____

Warm up ☐   Cool Down ☐   Stretch ☐

STRENGTH

Exercise	Lbs.	Rep Sets 1	2	3

Maintenance Log   S M T W T F S

Water

Date: _____

FOOD/BEVERAGE

H	Time	F
	AM	
	PM	

GOALS

Foundation

Food

Fluid

Fitness

AEROBIC

Activity: _____
Time: _____   HR: _____

Warm up ☐ Cool Down ☐ Stretch ☐

STRENGTH

Exercise	Lbs.	Rep Sets		
		1	2	3

Maintenance Log   S M T W T F S

Date: _____

Water

FOOD/BEVERAGE

H	Time		F
	AM		
	PM		

GOALS

AEROBIC

Activity: _____
Time: _____   HR: _____

Warm up ☐   Cool Down ☐   Stretch ☐

STRENGTH

Exercise	Lbs.	Rep Sets		
		1	2	3

Foundation

Food

Fluid

Fitness

Maintenance Log   S M T W T F S

Date: _____

Water

FOOD/BEVERAGE

H | Time

AM

PM

F

GOALS

Foundation

Food

Fluid

Fitness

AEROBIC

Activity: _____

Time: _____   HR: _____

Warm up ☐   Cool Down ☐   Stretch ☐

STRENGTH

Exercise   Lbs.   Rep Sets   1   2   3

Maintenance Log   S M T W T F S

Water

Date: _____

GOALS

AEROBIC

Activity: _____
Time: _____   HR: _____

Warm up ☐ Cool Down ☐ Stretch ☐

STRENGTH

Exercise	Lbs.	Rep Sets 1 2 3

Foundation

Food

Fluid

Fitness

FOOD/BEVERAGE

H	Time	F
	AM	
	PM	

Maintenance Log   S M T W T F S

Date: _____

Water

FOOD/BEVERAGE

H	Time	F
AM		
PM		

GOALS

Foundation

Food

Fluid

Fitness

AEROBIC

Activity: _____
Time: _____   HR: _____

Warm up ☐   Cool Down ☐   Stretch ☐

STRENGTH

Exercise	Lbs.	Rep Sets		
		1	2	3

Maintenance Log   S M T W T F S

Date: _____

Water

GOALS

Foundation

Food

Fluid

Fitness

AEROBIC

Activity: _____
Time: _____   HR: _____

Warm up ☐   Cool Down ☐   Stretch ☐

STRENGTH

Exercise   Lbs.   Rep Sets
1   2   3

FOOD/BEVERAGE

H | Time   F
AM

PM

Maintenance Log   S M T W T F S

Water

Date: _____

GOALS

Foundation

Food

Fluid

Fitness

FOOD/BEVERAGE

H	Time	F
AM		
PM		

AEROBIC

Activity: _____
Time: _____   HR: _____

Warm up [ ]   Cool Down [ ]   Stretch [ ]

STRENGTH

Exercise	Lbs.	Rep Sets 1	2	3

Maintenance Log　S M T W T F S

Date: _____

Water

FOOD/BEVERAGE

H	Time	F
AM		
PM		

GOALS

Foundation

Food

Fluid

Fitness

AEROBIC

Activity: _____
Time: _____　HR: _____

Warm up ☐　Cool Down ☐　Stretch ☐

STRENGTH

Rep Sets

Exercise	Lbs.	1	2	3

Maintenance Log   S M T W T F S

Water

Date:

FOOD/BEVERAGE

H	Time		F
	AM		
	PM		

GOALS

Foundation

Food

Fluid

Fitness

AEROBIC

Activity: _____
Time: _____   HR: _____

Warm up [ ] Cool Down [ ] Stretch [ ]

STRENGTH

Exercise	Lbs.	Rep Sets		
		1	2	3

Maintenance Log   S M T W T F S

Water

Date: _____

GOALS

AEROBIC

Activity: _____
Time: _____   HR: _____

Warm up ☐   Cool Down ☐   Stretch ☐

STRENGTH

Exercise	Lbs.	Rep Sets		
		1	2	3

Foundation

Food

Fluid

Fitness

FOOD/BEVERAGE

H	Time	F
AM		
PM		

Maintenance Log   S M T W T F S

Water

Date:

AEROBIC

Activity: _____
Time: _____   HR: _____

Warm up [ ] Cool Down [ ] Stretch [ ]

STRENGTH

Exercise	Lbs.	Rep Sets		
		1	2	3

GOALS

Foundation

Food

Fluid

Fitness

FOOD/BEVERAGE

| H | Time | F |
| AM | | |

PM

Maintenance Log   S M T W T F S

Date: _____

Water

FOOD/BEVERAGE

H	Time	F
AM		
PM		

GOALS

Foundation

Food

Fluid

Fitness

AEROBIC

Activity: _____
Time: _____   HR: _____

Warm up ☐   Cool Down ☐   Stretch ☐

STRENGTH

Exercise	Lbs.	Rep Sets		
		1	2	3

Maintenance Log   S M T W T F S

Date: _____

Water

FOOD/BEVERAGE

H	Time	F
	AM	
	PM	

GOALS

Foundation

Food

Fluid

Fitness

AEROBIC

Activity: _____
Time: _____   HR: _____

Warm up [ ]   Cool Down [ ]   Stretch [ ]

STRENGTH

Exercise	Lbs.	Rep Sets		
		1	2	3

Maintenance Log   S M T W T F S

Water

Date:

FOOD/BEVERAGE

H	Time	F
	AM	
	PM	

GOALS

Foundation

Food

Fluid

Fitness

AEROBIC

Activity: _____

Time: _____   HR: _____

Warm up ☐   Cool Down ☐   Stretch ☐

STRENGTH

Exercise	Lbs.	Rep Sets 1 2 3

Maintenance Log   S M T W T F S

Water

Date:

FOOD/BEVERAGE

H | Time
AM

PM

F

GOALS

Foundation

Food

Fluid

Fitness

AEROBIC

Activity: _____
Time: _____   HR: _____

Warm up [ ] Cool Down [ ] Stretch [ ]

STRENGTH

Exercise   Lbs.   Rep Sets
                      1   2   3

Victory Laps

What exactly is a victory lap? If you have ever seen a NASCAR driver celebrate after winning a big race, you know what a victory lap is! It's taking time to enjoy the moment, celebrate your win, and be proud of your accomplishments. It's as much a part of the race as the wave of the flag at the starting line!

The following table gives you an opportunity to record your own Rev It Up! victory laps. Each block represents a month. Write down the month in the left column, and list any and all of your victories during those four weeks. In the right column, plan and record how you are rewarding yourself. Repeat this exercise for each month, and enjoy celebrating your efforts. No one deserves it more!

My Victory Lap for the Month of _____	My Reward:

APPENDIX

Most Frequently Asked Questions

QUESTION #1: *I think I am "stuck"! I've lost weight, but now the scale is staying the same even though I don't think I'm doing anything different. What can I do to break this plateau?*

ANSWER: First of all, if you have a history of many attempts at weight loss, and have tried various programs with different measures of success, your body may be more resistance with each attempt. This is more common if your weight loss occurred too quickly. Your body's ability to lose weight may have slowed down, even if you can see positive changes in other ways, such as more energy and fewer cravings. Nevertheless, it is hard not to be frustrated about slow, or no, weight loss.

Secondly, over time, it is often easy to overestimate portions and/or amounts of added or hidden fats that creep into your daily foods. Since fats pack a lot of calories in a small amount, they can often be the contributor to slowed weight loss or a plateau. So try the following as your emergency plan to break your plateau and begin losing weight again: 1) Reduce your portion of grains (or "brown" carbohydrates) at the dinner meal by half. This is the meal that will most affect your weight since it is at the end of the day, when your body is slowing down naturally and burning fewer calories in preparation for bedtime. Or you can decide to completely eliminate grains at the dinner meal only for a temporary period of time, but don't neglect to follow the next step. 2) Make up the difference in carbohydrate energy by substituting more color (more vegetables) at this same dinner meal. Double up on those veggies! 3) Eliminate fats "more often than not," meaning, NO added ping pong ball of fats or fried foods or cream sauces on four to five days out of the week. This is a more extreme step, but can save you quite a bit of unknown calories. Limiting added fats to only two or so days a week allows you to get in the healthy fats (the unsaturated fat choices) that you need for the essential fatty acids and fat soluble vitamins but reduces the possibility of getting too many extra calories from fats on a daily basis. 4) Maintain your water intake, and 5) Keep striving for four sessions of cardio activity each week, with two of the four sessions incorporating strength training as well. Most importantly, do *not* give up!

QUESTION #2: *I have been so stressed at work, and for some reason it makes me feel like eating all the time. My meal timing is off, and I just can't seem to get back on track. I found myself eating my third brownie yesterday even though I wasn't hungry, and now I feel so guilty! What's wrong with me?*

ANSWER: Stress is a very real situation in which we all find ourselves from time to time. So what exactly does stress do to your body, besides make your heartbeat faster, blood pressure rise, mood turn irritable and interfere with a good night's sleep? Stress actually uses or burns more energy (calories), especially the type of energy that supplies a chemical called serotonin. This chemical is produced by carbohydrates, so this helps explain why you tend to eat more when you are stressed and often want quick carbohydrates like sugars.

As stress burns energy, it simultaneously triggers the release of adrenaline and cortisol, two hormones called the "flight or fight" hormones-which help in emergencies-but may not be much help when you are at work, trying to meet a deadline, and have nowhere to run *or* no one to fight! The natural tendency is to eat carbohydrates, which trigger your brain to produce serotonin, a chemical that relaxes and calms you. This calming effect can be produced by a handful of whole wheat crackers, but often a handful of cookies are more appealing.

First of all, declare your desk, your computer, your television, loud music and any other distractions off limits until *after* you eat something. Try to plan ahead for these inevitable moments by keeping an "emergency snack pack" available. Avoid higher sugar, simple carbohydrate foods as much as possible, which can actually *increase* your appetite even more. Choose whole grains and a little lean protein such as a mozzarella cheese stick and whole-wheat crackers, or peanut butter and apple slices. Not convenient to have that kind of snack available? Prepare ahead by having your own trail mix of whole-wheat cereal squares mixed with slivered almonds and raisins handy, or have an energy bar made with protein and complex carbohydrates.

No matter what, slow down and give yourself a 10-minute break to fuel your brain with *good* fuel, relax those stress hormones and boost your energy. And if emotions sometimes take over and you dive into a plate of brownies, try to clear your head by sitting down, taking it slow, savoring every bite and adding a little protein-like a cold glass of milk-to diffuse that quick rush and fall. Mainly, get right back on track and don't let guilt cloud your way. Remember, it is what you do *more often than not* that guides your body's metabolism rate!

QUESTION #3: *I have really gotten off track, and blown it way too many times. I feel like giving up. What should I do?*

ANSWER: Don't let occasional splurges get you off track! Remember, "one lapse does NOT a relapse make"! Keep in mind the following tips as you continue taking small steps forward: 1) *Do not focus on calories-focus only on fuel groups!* Had a few doughnuts for breakfast, and wishing you hadn't? Don't skip lunch to make up the calories. Instead, try to round out what was missing at breakfast. Look for lean proteins, veggies, and low-fat dairy for lunch. That would be a great time to have a grilled chicken salad with lots of greens, vegetables and some grated cheese, with low-fat dressing on the side so you control the amount. Having a hard time getting those colors into your meals? Double up at one meal, like extra lettuce and bell pepper slices in your pita sandwich (You can ask for extra even at a fast food sandwich place!) Think balance, and think fuel groups, and just catch up on the missing pieces at the next meal. 2) *Do a quick review of what you ate at the last meal and/or snack.* Remembering what you have eaten most recently may help encourage you to eat less the next time around. Remember, "I CAN EAT AGAIN…just not right now!", and 3) *Never be fooled into skipping the next meal to punish yourself for a splurge.* Missing an entire meal to make up for too many calories at the previous will *always* backfire on you.

The key is balancing your fuel groups, trusting your hunger, and learning from your lapses. Failure is not possible. How can something be a failure when you can learn so much about yourself? The biggest splurge can result in more self awareness of the "why" behind your choice, which can result in greater confidence and motivation for the next time you find yourself in the same situation.

Eating better starts with just one meal--one day--one week at a time. Unhealthy patterns do not happen over night but over a long period of days that lead to weeks that lead to months that lead to years. Likewise, healthy patterns take time, so be patient. It's worth it!

QUESTION #4: *Why does the scale seem to fluctuate so much? I can gain 2 or 3 pounds overnight, even if I haven't done anything to justify it! What causes that?*

ANSWER: You have discovered how fickle the scales can be. They never really tell the whole story. Did you know that an overcast or stormy day can actually add several pounds to the scale? Low pressure keeps water in your tissues, and since our bodies are mostly water, an overcast day can make us "gain weight"…that is, fluid! Did you know (well, at least most women do!) that hormones can add 2 to 6 pounds over a three to seven day length of time? Anti-inflammatory drugs, like ibuprofen, or steroid type drugs for allergies may cause temporary fluid retention, resulting in temporary weight gain. Even not getting enough sleep may slow down your body's ability to burn carbohydrates, which makes more glucose available for fat storage, and increases the stress hormone cortisol, which stimulates your appetite for rich, high-fat foods. And did you realize that just three shakes of salt, or ½ teaspoon, can add 1 pound of body weight? One gram of sodium can hold onto 16 ounces of water, and that equals a pound. So that dinner at the local Japanese restaurant may explain why your clothes fit tighter the next day-salt!

So try not to obsess about the pounds on that scale. Remind yourself that your body's weight is a combination of water, muscle, bone, fat, and body tissues…so any change on that scale is *not* just a reflection of fat alone. About 65% of our body weight comes from water, so most quick body weight fluctuations are a result of water changes only. Don't get on the scale more often than once a week. Keep following the Rev It Up! principles, and enjoy how your body feels, the increasing self-confidence you are gaining, the changes you see in your strength and aerobic ability, the way your clothes fit, and the power that comes from taking charge of your wellness and health. Don't let a single number take that away from you.

QUESTION #5: *How do I tell if something is "whole grain"? What's the difference in whole-wheat or whole grain, anyway?*

ANSWER: Whole-wheat is always the same as whole grain, but not all whole grains are whole-wheat. Confused even more? That simply means that whole grain can mean whole-wheat OR whole grain corn or whole grain rice (brown rice), or any combination of the grains out there. So any bread that is listed as a multi-grain bread, like 7 grain, would be a great choice. And any bread listed as 100% whole-wheat or whole-wheat bread is a great choice. Don't be fooled by the label "wheat bread" alone, though, since that is really just brown-colored white bread. Regardless, even if white bread or white rice breaks down much more quickly than whole grain foods, if you eat these "white" foods with some kind of protein, the process slows down and does not produce a quick "rush" of carbohydrate calories. So when you can, choose whole grain, but when you cannot, you can still eat the lower fiber grain-just make sure you add protein to that meal or snack to help balance your body's response.

QUESTION #6: *I am heading to the beach with my family for summer break and am worried about what I am going to eat. I just love this seafood buffet at my favorite restaurant there. Do I have to avoid it completely?*

ANSWER: Summer vacation eating-how can you handle all of those temptations available? Try these suggestions: 1) Budget your fats. If you know you want to order fried shrimp, strip the fat from your breakfast and lunch meals so you have room for extra fats in the evening, 2) Balance a dessert by choosing a low-fat main course and lots of color (vegetables and/or fruits) as your side dishes instead of pastas, rice or potato. Plan to share it with someone else to save a few calories without missing out! 3) Beware of "drinking" all of your calories. A pina colada or strawberry daiquiri (7 ounces) can contain over 500 calories and over 17 grams of fat. Drinks that are mixed with cream, milk, fruit juice or soda can pack more calories, so remember to take that into account when ordering, and 4) Plan an after-meal activity, such as a beach volleyball game after breakfast, or skiing after lunch, or a sunset walk after dinner. This not only will burn calories but also help you limit heavier food choices at the meal knowing you are going to be active afterwards.

QUESTION #7: *My friend told me that I need to exercise every day, but I don't have time to go to the gym 7 days a week. How can I burn more calories outside of the gym?*

ANSWER: Aerobic exercise and strength training are very important for weight loss and maintenance. However, you can burn extra calories every single day by adding just a few small movements or changing a few simple behaviors. Try these: 1) Use "standing in line" at the grocery store or gas station as a chance to flex your abs or tighten your rear end (no one will know, honest!). It's like having your own "butts and guts" conditioning class on a mini scale! 2) Do calf raises while talking on the telephone. 3) If you have stairs at home, take them *each* time you do a load of laundry instead of accumulating all the loads into one before you make the trip. 4) Do crunches or push ups while watching TV-maybe not every time, but occasionally? 5) If you really want to make your family think you have lost it, do jumping jacks during commercials. Your younger kids will think this is a great new game (and your teenager already expects odd behavior from you anyway!), and 6) Do stretches in the shower, like neck rolls and shoulder shrugs. Remember, it's what you do more often than not that counts. Wellness is a lifestyle-not just an aerobics class. Enjoy your day, and get *moving*!

QUESTION #8: *I've been invited to a holiday party this weekend. Any tips on how to handle all those temptations?*

ANSWER: Here are a few health tips to take with you when you go: 1) Do not arrive at the big event hungry! Make sure you eat breakfast, lunch, and an afternoon snack as usual, because saving your day's calories for one big meal does not work! However, feel free to lighten up the fat content at those earlier meals. 2) Survey the entire table *before* you start filling your plate. Choose two or three items that are worth every bite, and skip the other higher-fat party choices like chips and dip that you can have anytime. 3) Enjo*y* your choices, but keep those portions small. You can have more items if you have smaller portions of each. 4) Wait about 20-30 minutes after eating before going back for seconds. Ask yourself, "Am I really physically hungry for more?", and 5) Drink a glass of water between every serving of alcohol or sweetened beverage. This will not only decrease calories but also slow the appetite-stimulating effect of alcohol and/or sugars.

QUESTION #9: *I hate to write in my journal. Do I have to?*

ANSWER: Journaling is the best way to visualize your progress. And it is one of the top three habits of people who have lost weight and kept it off over time. But it can be a hassle, especially when your lifestyle is fast paced and your schedule is full. Start simply by choosing small steps, like picking three days out of seven and journal those completely. Or if that is too much to assume, then at least journal the meal(s) that is most difficult for you. Dinner? Lunch? Afternoon snack? The journals are for *you*-to spend time with yourself (how often do we really do that?) and to get to know what triggers overeating for you, to understand when your biggest food challenges hit –and to see your progress. Don't forget that important point of journaling! How else are you going to be able to really see and applaud the changes that you are making unless they are written down?

QUESTION #10: *I don't really want to lose weight, I just want to learn to eat better and live a healthier lifestyle. Can I follow Rev It Up! anyway?*

ANSWER: Certainly! You will probably need to adjust your portion guidelines higher-but keeping an eye on your hunger and fullness will help you quickly discover if you are fueling for four hours, or over- or under-doing it! You learn by trial and error, and adjustments can be made, up or down, as needed for you. Rev It Up! is a healthy way of living for all bodies and ages and allows the flexibility you need to meet your energy goals, even if weight loss is not necessary.

QUESTION #11: *Is bottled water better for me than tap water?*

ANSWER: Not necessarily. Bottled water is everywhere, and sales of more than 2 billion a year certainly indicate it's here to stay. You may buy it just because it tastes better or you may be concerned about the safety of your own tap water. But as a general rule, you do not have to drink bottled water to stay safe.

By law, public water sources must be regularly monitored and tested for contamination. One of the more serious concerns has been the question of lead in public drinking water. You can have your tap water tested if you are worried, and a call to the Environmental Protection Agency Safe Drinking Water Hotline (1-800-426-4791) can direct your steps. But an easy way to decrease the amount of lead in your tap water is to "flush it out." Simply run the water through the faucet until it becomes as cold as possible. This helps for two reasons: First, it guarantees that water you end up drinking has not been exposed over a long period of time to pipes containing lead. Secondly, colder water is less susceptible to "grabbing and holding on" to the lead from the pipe itself.

Did you know that 25% of bottled waters are actually tap water that has been packaged to sell? A company is free to use water from a public source and bottle it in plastic containers for a profit. High-end brands, such as Perrier or Evian, are certainly not tap water, but your local or less-expensive versions may be. Regardless, most bottled water companies are members of the International Bottled Water Association, which ensures that they follow careful standards and are inspected yearly. One current concern to consider, especially if you have young children in your home, is that most bottled waters do not supply the right amount of fluoride to prevent cavities. However, bottled water companies are looking at this issue and several companies fortify their water with fluoride already.

So, bottled water or tap water? It's your choice. Consider your pocketbook, your home source of tap water, and your motivation to drink water in the first place. Find your favorite source, and commit to drink it daily.

QUESTION #12: *What about vitamins? Do I need to take a daily supplement?*

ANSWER: It depends on the individual. If you eat whole grains, lean meats, low-fat dairy, and lots of fruits and vegetables, the answer is "not really." But the reality is-you probably don't, at least not yet, until you complete the eight weeks of Rev It Up! Therefore, you may want to consider taking a multivitamin/mineral supplement that provides 100% of the RDA, or recommended daily allowances, of the nutrients you need for your age and gender. Do you need to spend a lot of money on specialized natural vitamins, or can you buy an over-the-counter version at your supermarket? The choice is yours, but the more expensive, natural vitamins are not necessary for most people. Regardless of the type, look for the USP label to ensure that it meets official standards for dietary supplements (www.usp-dsvp.org). In regards to specific minerals like calcium, do you need to take an additional supplement? Yes, if you do not consume three dairy servings every day. A daily multivitamin/mineral supplement does not provide over 10-15% of the recommended levels of calcium, usually. There is simply not enough room to include all that you need! An additional calcium supplement from a carbonate or citrate source is preferred, and usually comes in 500-600 mg tablets. An adult female should consume 1200 mg/day; therefore, one to two tablets in addition to your multivitamin supplement are recommended (depending on how much dairy you consume). Do make sure that your calcium supplement contains Vitamin D. Recent research indicates that Americans need more Vitamin D than originally thought to ensure optimal bone health.

QUESTION #13: *How do I choose the right energy bar for a snack? There are too many options, and I'm confused!*

ANSWER: Energy bars can be a convenient snack that meets the "two fuel group" requirement but not all bars are worth the effort or money.   Since a variety of products are available, ask the following questions:

1.   Does the product have a nutrition fact label? (If not, avoid it!)
2.   Does the product sound too good to be true? (It probably is!)
3.   What does the product claim to do? Does research back it up?

Once you have answered these questions, follow these guidelines to make the best choice for you:

1.   Choose a bar that is equal to a snack – not a meal! These foods are "engineered" and do not contain the same amount of fiber and nutrients found naturally in foods.
2.   Read the label. Look for an average of 200 calories, 10+ grams of protein, < 8 grams of added fats, primarily unsaturated, and preferably 3+ grams of fiber.
3.   Higher protein bars can fit in certain circumstances, but be aware that they are usually more expensive, often taste chalky and unpalatable, and require extra fluid intake.
4.   Avoid herbal additives if taking prescription medications because many can interact adversely.
5.   Read the labels carefully! DO NOT USE PRODUCTS CONTAINIING EPHEDRINE, MA HUANG, YOHIMBE AND/OR MATE.

QUESTION #14: *Are there any free Web sites that you recommend that provide nutrition or fitness information?*

ANSWER: Yes! The following list is not comprehensive, but provides you with a variety of Web sites for nutrition and fitness information. These are free to online users, but some may require registration.

1. www.eatright.org (the Web site for the American Dietetic Association)
2. www.fitday.com (an online tool for calculating calories consumed and burned every day)
3. www.sparkpeople.com (another online tool for calculating calories consumed every day)
4. www.myrecipes.com (the Web site for all Oxmoor House publications, such as Cooking Light, Health, and Southern Living magazines. Look for the Rev It Up! weight management tips coming in January 2010!)
5. www.healthierus.gov/dietaryguidelines (the Web site for the U.S. Department of Health and Human Services. New 2010 Dietary Guidelines coming soon)
6. www.webmd.com (an online tool that provides health information for the entire family)
7. www.healthydiningfinder.com (an online tool that highlights healthy menu items for fast food and sit-down restaurants that have been approved by registered dietitians)

Note: the inclusion of these Web site addresses does not constitute an endorsement of any one site. At the time of publication, all Web sites were operable.

Sample One-Day Menu Ideas Using Rev It Up! Guidelines

Example 1: Energy provided by grains, fruits and vegetables	Example 2: Energy provided by fruits and vegetables only
BREAKFAST: Whole grain English muffin Scrambled egg w/ 2% cheese (1 egg and 1 ppb cheese) Cantaloupe, 1 bb	**BREAKFAST:** Egg omelet w/ 2% cheese, tomato and green pepper (2 eggs and 1 ppb cheese) Cantaloupe, 1 bb 1% milk, 1 cup
SNACK: Nectarine, 1 bb	**SNACK:** Nectarine, 1 bb
LUNCH: Whole-wheat tortilla wrap, 1 bb Sliced turkey breast, palm size Lettuce shreds, diced tomato Fresh fruit cup, 1 bb 1% milk, 1 cup	**LUNCH:** Sliced turkey breast, palm size 2% cheese, 1 ppb Blend of lettuces, grape tomatoes, cucumbers Raspberry vinaigrette, 1 ppb 1% milk, 1 cup
MID-AFTERNOON SNACK: Lemon low-fat yogurt, 1 bb Frozen or fresh blueberries, 1 bb	**MID-AFTERNOON SNACK:** Apple slices, 1 bb Peanut butter, 1 ppb
DINNER: Grilled salmon, palm size Brown rice w/ mushrooms, 1 bb Broccoli, carrot mix, 1 bb Mixed greens salad Balsamic vinaigrette, 1 ppb	**DINNER:** Grilled salmon, palm size Grilled vegetables: zucchini, squash and carrot chunks Mixed greens salad Balsamic vinaigrette, 1 ppb
1 bb = 1 baseball	**1 ppb = 1 ping pong ball**

These two examples are based on weight-loss guidelines for an average female. Both days are approximately the same calorie level, but offer two alternatives for energy sources. Example 1 is designed using whole grains, fruits and vegetables, with animal, plant, and dairy proteins; Example 2 is designed using *only* fruits and vegetables, with animal, plant, and dairy proteins. Both provide energy and protein, but allow you the freedom to choose energy sources.

My Personal Rev It Up! Journey

Tammy Beasley, RD, CSSD, LD
Author and Creator, Rev It Up!

If you are reading this now, you have made a decision to commit, or are considering a commitment, to learn and live the Rev It Up! lifestyle. First of all, thank you for the trust you have placed in me and this program. I know that countless programs are available, and an endless stream of information bombards you daily from magazines, radio, and television. Because of this, I feel it is important to give you an opportunity to look inside the window into how Rev It Up! came to be in the first place. Where did the ideas come from? On what are the principles based? How is it different from all the other programs out there? Is it worth your time and financial commitment? Can you trust what you learn and are asked to practice? Will it make a difference in your life? Because of all of these questions, and more, I would like to share the story of my own personal Rev It Up! journey.

In 1984, I graduated from Auburn University with a degree in nutrition and foods, and headed to the University of Alabama in Birmingham to complete my dietetic internship. My decision to major in nutrition was not the first path I took when entering Auburn. Born in Huntsville, Alabama, the Rocket City and home of NASA and the Marshall Space Flight Center, an engineering path was encouraged and expected. I gave it a two year effort but I quickly discovered that even if my brain could make the grades, my heart was not in it. More importantly, the stress of those first years in combination with a compulsive, perfectionist personality led to my first experience with an eating disorder. My 5'6" frame dropped to 106 pounds, and it took a concerned family and a wise physician to make me recognize that the increasing stress I felt, decreasing grades I received, frequent illnesses I had, and overall anxiety I experienced were a result of poor nutrition. Realizing that my nutritional health had affected every part of my life, I was compelled to find out more about this field that combined science, psychology, and human behavior-a field that influenced every person, in every family, including my own. And I loved it!

The year in graduate school at UAB provided me a wide range of clinical experiences, where I saw firsthand how nutrition affects healing, wellness, and even psychological health. I was especially challenged by the nutrition support rotations, involving critically ill patients on total parenteral nutrition-where the nutritional medicine entering their veins could make a difference in life or death. Rotations in weight management, eating disorders, and even sports nutrition were not available outside of the occasional outpatient clinics. It didn't really matter to me, though. Surely my clinical experience and expertise should not be "wasted" on simple weight loss issues but used on more "important" causes, like renal disease or cancer treatment, right?! So I thought as I joined the UAB staff as a clinical dietitian for the gastrointestinal medicine unit.

It did not take long, however, before I realized that issues of weight management and how a person feels about body image infiltrated the care of almost every patient with whom I worked. And whether you could say I was in the right place at the wrong time, or the wrong place at the right time, after barely a year in practice, I was given the responsibility to create a weight-loss program for patients who would be undergoing the "gastric bubble procedure." The gastric bubble program included insertion of a balloon-type device in the stomach that would not allow as much food to be consumed and digested; therefore, these obese patients would be forced to eat less and as a result, lose weight. Of course, the weight loss would be permanent, if they simply followed the rules. As I worked with each client, I realized that my three or four visits and folder full of handouts hardly made a dent in changing life-long eating habits and mindsets.

These patients were in trouble, and I felt great responsibility to make a lasting difference, and great frustration when I saw few changes embraced. What was I doing wrong? What could I do differently, and what could the patient do differently? Why did the most motivated patient also struggle with consistent weight loss-even when following all the rules I gave him or her? The medical team found out that the gastric bubble did NOT work, and the procedure was no longer allowed. And I found out that weight loss was a lot more complicated and serious than I had perceived-even if all the knowledge was available.

My clinical interests began to change, and, yet again, I found myself in a situation where I was asked to direct another controversial weight loss program. This time, it was a fasting program, following on the heels of the popularity of the Optifast diet. UAB wanted to be on the cutting edge and was planning to offer a fasting program to the public, but I could not bring myself to commit to the idea that 400 calories, of liquids only, would produce anything other than quick weight loss and long-term problems with weight maintenance as well as health complications. So I studied, and researched, and created a new program that would solve the problem of quick weight regain-UAB would *double* the calories in its program and provide 800 instead! We would add behavioral modification sessions, and support from full time psychologists. Our program would make a difference, and I was proud to be on the cutting edge.

But guess what? Yet again, many patients had great success, if you look at success as weight loss only. Many patients attended every behavioral class, every nutrition class, and followed all the rules – but most of the patients failed to keep the majority of their weight off once the fasting portion ended. I will never forget how confused and discouraged and broken-hearted I felt when my favorite, most compliant patient called in tears, unable to prevent weight regain no matter what advice I gave and she followed. What had happened to these patients' metabolisms during these weeks and months? Had I contributed to a damaging cycle that would only worsen for them?

As I struggled with these questions, I was offering sports nutrition counseling after hours at a local fitness center through another hospital. Athletes would make an appointment to discuss how they could lower their body fat, eat for more energy, and improve performance in competitions. The atmosphere was quite opposite of what I saw in the hospital clinic. For the most part, these were health-oriented clients who only wanted the facts-none of that "touchy feeling" stuff. They were driven to perform, and wanted to know grams of carbohydrates and fats and proteins and how it affected their next race or workout. I enjoyed this arena, but was unaware of how it was affecting me personally. Sometimes an athlete would go overboard in his or her compulsiveness, and I began noticing some disordered eating behaviors over time. At the same time, I watched the obese clients from the clinic struggle with their own version of disordered eating. And I began pushing myself harder-since I had to be an example to others, I had to be one step ahead...one pound thinner...one minute faster...or I would lose credibility.

The more I pushed myself, the more panicked I would get and the more secret my eating behaviors became. Until I was into another eating disorder trap-this time, the compulsive overeating of fat-free ("good for you") foods, and the subsequent guilt from my lack of willpower, and the resulting drive to exercise even more and try to eat even less. It never worked more than a few days...I'd be back at square one. Able to encourage my clients to be kind to their bodies and take changes gradually, I was unable to give myself any comfort, grace, or acceptance.

Although I did not realize it at the time, my actions and words were a silent cry for help. My co-worker and friend, a psychologist by trade, confronted my behaviors-and I was finally able to see my behaviors for what they really were. The journey out of that circle was not easy, and involved taking a harder look inside at what was behind my behaviors and a softer look outside at what was realistic and healthy. I had been taught the fat grams, cholesterol content, fiber sources, calorie count for *every* food and drink. My brain was a walking calorie computer, ready to convert fat grams to percent calories with every bite. I had to learn to *shut the calorie calculator off*, for good, and learn to eat from hunger and stop eating when full. Learn to eat balanced, and include all foods in moderation. And what freedom it was!!! I will never forget eating pizza again after three years of missing out. It had never tasted quite so good, because it represented a freedom that I had not allowed myself for too long.

And the interesting thing is-as my mind became more balanced, my weight became steady and consistent, my eating became more balanced and calm, and my life became more full and rich. Self esteem struggles? Sure, I still have them sometimes, but I do not reach for another barbell or eat another cookie or rice cake, for that matter, to make it go away. The self-punishment behaviors do not automatically follow. In fact, they don't exist at all anymore! I have to work through my thoughts and emotions, and it's not always fun, but I find that I am back to more self acceptance within a few hours, or maybe a day or two, depending. Self-punishment by exercising and eating, or not, is long gone. And that "loss" is my greatest gain!

This three-year process of personal recovery concluded with meeting my husband-to-be, and marrying him within six months later. That marriage, however, meant a move to Miami, Florida, where for the next nine years, I lived in a world that literally breeds eating disorders and body image distortions. From the safety net of Alabama to the cross-cultural tangle of Miami, I had to grow up quickly. Professionally, I was not sure what direction I would take, and not being bilingual actually hindered me from receiving employment for the first year. However, a local hospital was interested in developing an outpatient nutrition counseling program, and I was hired to do just that. Within the first month, a hospital physician asked if I had ever counseled clients with eating disorders. This led to long discussions and the opportunity to begin working with an incredible professional team of psychologists, psychiatrists, and physicians specializing in this field.

At first I was concerned that my own personal history would be a hindrance, but I quickly discovered a great passion for this area of nutrition. My own experiences proved helpful and insightful and often opened a door for deeper trust between myself and my client. I pursued an additional certification as an eating disorder specialist in nutrition through the International Association of Eating Disorder Professionals (IAEDP), which I completed in 1993 and continue to maintain today. So my professional years in Miami concentrated on working with women and men, of all ages, who struggled with some type of disordered eating-the young grade school student, the high school athlete, the college undergraduate, the business professional, the at-home mom, and the list goes on.

Each client taught me something unique, and the medical team with which I worked provided tremendous support for personal and professional growth. I am so thankful for those years! However, after the birth of my two sons, my husband and I had the opportunity to move back home, to Alabama where my family lives and near the Tennessee state line, where his family lives. We took the chance, and I took a year off to help myself and my children adjust to what I now know as "reverse culture shock." I know I grew up physically here in Huntsville, but I grew up emotionally and professionally in Miami. It took some time to feel comfortable again in a city where the majority of people speak English-and Southern style at that!

After a year, I became a part time nutrition consultant for a local fitness center, and continued to see not only athletes but also clients with disordered eating. As time progressed, I heard myself continually teaching each client about his or her body, how it really works, and what it does to try to *help,* which often ends up only hurting. I heard myself encouraging behavior changes in the same way to each client, whether he was a competitive cyclist wanting to improve his time, she was a businesswoman trying to manage signs of early diabetes, or he or she was a young student struggling with body image. The athlete needed to learn how to listen to his own body's hunger and fullness cues and benefited from more attention given to the "why" instead of just the "what." The client with an eating disorder needed to know what foods would provide the most energy and when a meal or snack should be eaten and benefited from this practical knowledge. The inside look at "why" with an outside look at "what" and "when" proved to be powerful tools for change for *both* types of clients.

So, in December of 2000, I sat down and began writing a manual that I hoped would combine all I had learned in my professional and personal journey towards eating and living well. I wanted to translate onto paper the information that I shared in consultation after consultation, and thus, Rev It Up! was born! My initial class knew they were my "trial group" and had little more than a folder of handouts from which to work. But the privilege of watching lifestyle changes take place, and hope in their bodies restored where little was left, continued to motivate me to make Rev It Up! even more user-friendly, practical and whole. I began to offer the teaching tools I used to other registered dietitians, and to date, Rev It Up! has been taught in 25 states through the United States by over 55 registered dietitians. Each class, each person, has contributed in some way to this book as it reads today. Rev It Up! is a program that initiates one change at a time, creating a different way of thinking about the body and its relationship with food and exercise.   A program that encourages each participant to *own* the changes he or she creates and maintains. A program that offers a new way of living and a better way of feeling about yourself and your body.

Is Rev It Up! the only answer for America's struggle with weight, for *your* struggle with your own body? Of course not-many wonderful programs are available-but I believe, without a doubt, that it offers a simple way to break through the barriers that can prevent long term weight loss and a powerful, new way of thinking about yourself and your body's potential.   Again, thank you for your commitment to and trust in the program, and may your Rev It Up! journey lead you to a healthier lifestyle, a more confident mindset, and a life well-livcd!

References

Rev It Up! is the result of over 25 years of experience as a registered, licensed dietitian-experience that includes a variety of clinical rotations, five directorships of weight-management programs, three contracts as a sports nutrition consultant to a fitness facility or wellness center, over 15 years of specialization in the field of eating disorders, and, most importantly, hundreds and hundreds of individual nutrition consultations.   Specific references for each chapter of Rev It Up! would be impossible to list; however, the following includes the professional references that have been most influential on my practice over the years.

Clark, N. (1990, 1997). Nancy Clark's Sports Nutrition Guidebook (2nd edition). Champaign, IL: Human Kinetics.

Kleiner, S.M. (1998). Power Eating: Build Muscle, Gain Energy, Lose Fat. Champaign, IL: Human Kinetics.

McArdle, W.D., Katch, F.I., and Katch, V.L. (1991). Exercise Physiology: Energy, Nutrition and Human Performance. Malvern, PA: Lea & Febiger.

McKardle, W.D., Katch, F.I., and Katch, V.L. (1999) Sports and Exercise Nutrition. Baltimore, MD: Lippincott Williams & Wilkins.

Reiff, D.W. and Reiff, K.K. (1992). Eating Disorders: Nutrition Therapy in the Recovery Process. Gaithersburg, MD: Aspen Publishers, Inc.

Rodin, J. (1992). Body Traps. New York: William Morrow and Company, Inc.

Vredevelt, P., Newman, D., Beverly, H., and Minirth, F. (1992). The Thin Disguise: Overcoming and Understanding Anorexia and Bulimia. Nashville, TN: Thomas Nelson Publishers.

Zerbe, K.J. (1993). The Body Betrayed: A Deeper Understanding of Women, Eating Disorders, and Treatment. Carlsbad, CA: Gurze Books.

Tammy Beasley, RD, CSSD, LD
Rev It Up Fitness, LLC

BIOGRAPHY:
Consultant, speaker, adjunct professor, Spinning instructor, and registered dietitian, Tammy Beasley brings years of qualified experience to her work. She is a certified eating disorder specialist in nutrition through the International Association of Eating Disorders Professionals since 1993, and was the first Alabama dietitian certified in sports dietetics with the American Dietetic Association in 2006. She is an active member of the Dean's Advisory Board for the College of Human Sciences, Auburn University. She is the founder and creator of Rev It Up!, which originated in 2001 and has been or is currently offered in a class format in 25 states within the U.S.

Following her graduation with high honors from Auburn University and a dietetic internship with the University of Alabama in Birmingham (UAB), Tammy has been associated with some of the top health and wellness facilities in Miami, Florida, as well as Birmingham and Huntsville, Alabama. In 1995, she was selected Florida's Recognized Young Dietitian of the Year for her work with her professional associations (President of the Miami Dietetic Association) and the Miami community. After moving back home to Alabama in 1998, Tammy has served as President of the North

Alabama Dietetic Association and in various positions with the Alabama Dietetic Association, including media representative. Her work with the state culminated in her selection as Alabama's Most Outstanding Dietitian in 2007. When she is not consulting, writing, or speaking on nutrition, she can be found on the ball field with her husband cheering for their two sons, Adam and Luke!

Visit the Web site, www.revitupfitness.com, for more information on Tammy and the history of Rev It Up!